THE POLITICS OF SLAVERY

Laura Brace

EDINBURGH
University Press

Edinburgh University Press is one of the leading university presses in the UK. We publish academic books and journals in our selected subject areas across the humanities and social sciences, combining cutting-edge scholarship with high editorial and production values to produce academic works of lasting importance. For more information visit our website: edinburghuniversitypress.com

© Laura Brace, 2018

Edinburgh University Press Ltd
The Tun – Holyrood Road,
12(2f) Jackson's Entry,
Edinburgh EH8 8PJ

Typeset in 11/13 Palatino LT Std by
IDSUK (DataConnection) Ltd

A CIP record for this book is available from the British Library

ISBN 978 1 4744 0114 2 (hardback)
ISBN 978 1 4744 0115 9 (webready PDF)
ISBN 978 1 4744 0493 8 (epub)
ISBN 978 1 4744 5216 8 (paperback)

The right of Laura Brace to be identified as the author of this work has been asserted in accordance with the Copyright, Designs and Patents Act 1988, and the Copyright and Related Rights Regulations 2003 (SI No. 2498).

CONTENTS

ACKNOWLEDGMENTS

I am very grateful to the British Academy for the award of a small grant, 'Beyond Sale or Purchase?' which allowed me to carry out the research on the eighteenth-century sources on the antislavery campaigns and the proslavery responses in the St John's Library, Cambridge, the Bodleian Library, Oxford and the library at Canterbury Cathedral. Many thanks to the very helpful staff in all those places, and to the University of Leicester for a very welcome period of study leave that helped enormously with the writing of this book. I am also grateful to the British Academy for funding a Landmark Conference, 'Slaveries Old and New', in March 2014, jointly organised with Julia O'Connell Davidson, Mark Johnson and Zoe Trodd, and to the participants in that conference, particularly Tommy Lott, Nandita Sharma, Sam Okyere, Charlotte Sussman and Bridget Anderson, whose insights and scholarship inform much of the argument of this book. The ESRC funded a seminar series on 'The Politics of Victimhood' which proved a particularly fruitful forum for discussion of many of the ideas behind this book, and I am grateful to them and to my co-organisers, Julia O'Connell Davidson, Kelly Staples and Stephen Hopkins, and to participants including Svati Shah, Tony Burns, Sealing Cheng, Iman Hashim, Andrew Jefferson and Patrizia Testai. Jenny Daly and David Lonergan at Edinburgh have been very kind and patient editors.

As will be clear from reading this book, I owe a huge amount to Julia O'Connell Davidson and her work on modern slavery, and in particular her commitment to understanding the role of borders and the significance of the right to locomotion and mobility in the politics of slavery. It may not be so obvious from reading the book what a privilege it is to have her as an academic sister, but it really is. Many, many thanks to her for everything. I also thank Lucy Sargisson and Chris Pierson, and the other members of the 'Politics of Property' specialist group – John Salter, Colin Tyler, James Penner and Patrick Joseph Cockburn in particular – for allowing me to talk to them about the connections between property and slavery for years on end, and thank you to Anita Rupprecht for joining in the conversation. For intellectual support and encouragement (and excellent conference companionship) at various stages of this project, I would like to thank Moya Lloyd, Kim Hutchings, Raia Prokhovnik and Liz Frazer; very many thanks to Vicki Squire and Gary Browning for reading some draft chapters just at the right moment, and to Robbie Shilliam for some very helpful feedback.

For their friendship, kindness, solidarity and different kinds of help along the way, heartfelt thanks to Frances Brace, Renie Lewis, James Hamill, Lucy James, Inge Tong Wheeler, Jan Clark, Bob Clark, Emma Swanston, Suzanne Farrell, Roy Redhead, Paul and Monique Fryer, and, of course, Aunt Bette. My parents, Gordon and Anthea Brace, have held the faith in this book, and in me, for a long time and I am very grateful to them for holding on. Thanks to Matt Clark, as ever, for his forbearance, and most especially to Aether Blake, for being Aether, and for her alternative title: 'The Silent Sadness of Savage Slavery Revealed' by Laura Brace.

Chapter 1

SHINING A LIGHT ON SLAVERY?

DEFINING SLAVERY

The problem of defining slavery as an absolute condition or a fixed status has been at the heart of the politics of slavery. Liberals have often striven to draw bright lines between slavery as a wrong or a logical impossibility, and liberal autonomy as a good and a right. For socialists, the concept of slavery is more flexible and the borderlands between slavery, servitude and exploitation are more mobile and contested. The idea of slavery, for them both, carries what Robin Blackburn calls a 'mythic potency' that takes it beyond the facts and experience of history (Blackburn 1988, 269). This book is about that mythic potency, about the significance of the status of slavery as a lived experience and as an idea and a political concept. Its aim is to explore the injustice of slavery not just as the opposite of self-ownership and liberal autonomy, but also as the opposite of belonging and of free labour. Its particular focus is on chattel slavery, the possibility of defining a human being as an animate piece of property and then making that status hereditary. The chattel slave was unable to make a will, to bring formal criminal charges against others or to appear as a witness in most civil cases. A slave's evidence was acceptable in court only if it had been extracted by torture. People who had been enslaved could be bought, sold, traded, leased, mortgaged, presented as a gift, pledged for a debt, included in a dowry or seized in a bankruptcy. What does this mean for our political theories that take the autonomous individual as both their starting point and their goal? We have to ask, who are these chattel slaves, and what made them enslavable? What happened to their status as persons and as humans when they were enslaved? What about the people who enslaved them

1

and sought to convince themselves that it was possible (for others) to be both person and property?

Part of the answer to these questions lies in thinking about the definition of slavery, and what might be taken to be its constituent elements. The League of Nations definition began with 'the status or condition of a person over whom any or all of the powers attaching to the right of ownership are exercised' (Ste Croix 1988, 19). As Blackburn points out, this definition does not specify that the owner must exercise 'all' the powers of ownership over their slaves, but 'some' of the powers of ownership can be exercised over people such as employees, spouses or children, who are not defined as a slaves. It has to be 'the comprehensive extent of the property rights claimed by the slave owner' which distinguishes slavery from other forms of ownership and exploitation (Blackburn 1988, 274). Even so, this approach makes clear that slavery has significant continuities with other forms of exploitation and servitude, and we need to pay attention to the power relations, the legal structures and institutions, and the political and historical contexts within which the powers attaching to the right of ownership are exercised. It also suggests that the idea of ownership, the property aspect of slavery, might not be enough to distinguish slavery from all other forms of dependency and involuntary labour.

Orlando Patterson's seminal work on slavery, *Slavery and Social Death*, develops a conception of slavery as a 'relation of domination' rather than a category of legal thought (Patterson 1982, 335). His focus on slavery as a relation draws attention to the complexities of dependence, and to the personal and institutional dimensions of slavery as a system of parasitism. Patterson concludes that the slave 'was natally alienated and condemned as a socially dead person, his existence having no legitimacy whatever'. On this view, the slave becomes the ideal human tool, 'perfectly flexible, unattached, and deracinated', existing only through the master. As the slaveholder fed off the slave to gain the satisfactions of power and honour, the slave lost 'all claim to autonomous power, was degraded and reduced to a state of liminality' (Patterson 1982, 337). Patterson's account defines slavery as one of the most extreme forms of the relation of domination, and he draws a clear binary distinction between total power from the viewpoint of the master and total powerlessness from the viewpoint of the slave (Patterson 1982, 1). For Patterson, without the master the slave does not exist as an independent being, and instead becomes a dominated thing, an instrument for the master. Slavery, from this perspective, is not about the legal system or hard labour, but about this process of domination rooted in violence, force and powerlessness. Slavery, for Patterson, can be distinguished from other social relationships by its constituent elements of force, dishonour and permanence: 'slavery is the permanent, violent domination of natally alienated and generally dishonored persons' (Patterson 1982, 13).

This has become the key definition of slavery in academic discourse and the subject of intense political debate. It is woven into this book at all sorts of levels, but in particular into the discussion of Hegel's master–slave dialectic, the meanings of slavery in Aristotle and Locke, and the complexities of the relation between slavery, race and agency. As Vincent Brown argues, Patterson's definition 'distilled a transhistorical characterization of slavery', within which slaveholders annihilated people's social existence by first extracting them from meaningful relations of personal status, belonging and memory, and then 'incorporating these socially dead persons into the masters' world' (V. Brown 2009, 1233). This notion of social death at the core of Patterson's definition is, as Brown argues, an abstraction that is 'largely unproblematic as a matter of theory, or even law' (V. Brown 2009, 1236). It does, however, carry a danger of 'pathologizing slaves by allowing the condition of social death to stand for the experience of life in slavery' (V. Brown 2009, 1236). People subjected to social death are almost infinitely vulnerable to the will of others (D. B. Davis 1986, 15), and slaves come to symbolise extreme dependency with no claims or obligations to others.

Patterson's transhistorical characterisation of slavery is fundamentally about slavery as violence, a primal act of submission that comes out of a state of war, leaving the conqueror with the power of life or death over his vanquished foe. Should he choose to enslave rather than kill his victim, the slave is left living under a permanent death sentence, with his execution suspended but never unthinkable. This state of suspended animation, and the subjection to violence, is the core of Patterson's understanding of slavery as domination. Slaves lack legitimacy, they are excommunicated persons, because the 'slave is always conceived of as someone, or the descendant of someone, who should have died' (Patterson 1991b, 10). As Alexander Weheliye argues, Patterson's definition 'emphasizes mortality at the cost of sociality' (Weheliye 2014,

38). For many scholars, this conception of social death risks blotting out 'the lines of flight, freedom dreams, practices of liberation, possibilities of other worlds' of people coded as property and as totally powerless (Weheliye 2014, 2). James Sweet, for example, draws attention to the slivers and slender threads of belonging, shared language, culture and community that the African slaves used to build families out of nothing and to defy social death (Sweet 2013). The question here is how to respond to these 'miniscule [sic] movements' and 'glimmers of hope', how to give them substance and weight without denying the annihilation of the people who made and found them (Weheliye 2014, 12). This book aims to explore the relation of the slave to self-possession and to the category of the human through the canonical texts of Aristotle, Locke, Hegel, Kant, Wollstonecraft and Mill, and the slave narratives of Douglass, Prince and Jacobs. This illuminates the indebtedness of the ideas of freedom and the status of personhood to notions of property, possession and exchange, and confirms both freedom and slavery as founding narratives of the liberal subject (Hartman 1997).

Patterson's focus on social death, violence and dishonour, on the relation of domination between master and slave, means that he characterises slavery as the comprehensive loss of belonging for the slave. It is, for him, all about powerlessness. There is, for Patterson, nothing in the nature of slavery that requires the slave to be a worker, and 'in a great many slaveholding societies masters were not interested in what their slaves produced' (Patterson 1982, 11). Slaves could be used as workers, and their natal alienation made their exploitation particularly effective, but, for Patterson, 'this does not in any way mean that slave necessarily implies worker' (Patterson 1982, 99). This book takes a different approach, arguing that ideas about free and unfree labour as they developed in the abolition debates of the late eighteenth century were crucial in determining the status of personhood and of the liberal subject. In the debates over the immediate or gradual abolition of slavery, the questions of fitness for freedom and dehumanisation take centre stage. In the discussion of how to distinguish between servitude and slavery and whether the few could justifiably be enslaved for the good of the whole, the spaces between personhood, subpersonhood and humanity are opened up and made visible. There are many different ways to guarantee the unfreedom of marginalised and oppressed groups, and we need to pay attention to the connections and continuities between labour, morality and honour in thinking about the processes that transformed humanity into moral beings and left slaves on the outside. In thinking about slavery in social terms, rather than as a property relation, labour turns out to be a key vector in determining who counts as enslavable, worthless or abandoned, who can be subjected to savage, useless tortures, and who can achieve freedom as a unified moral self.

Labour is impossible to disentangle from the 'volatile rapport between race and the human' (Weheliye 2014, 8), and the connections between racialisation, labour and slavery are at the core of this book. The grounds for justifying slavery were constantly shifting, and the markers of dispossession, difference and inferiority were not always stable (Turley 2000, 29). Through the antislavery debates of the late eighteenth century, as the defenders of slavery set out their justifications for treating some persons as property by developing doctrines of black inferiority, the fluidity of race as a political concept becomes clear, and we can see how its 'meaning is affected by the set of historical, social and political institutions through which race is understood' (Sheth 2016, 94). As I have argued elsewhere, race formed an integral part of the social, political and ideological relations of power needed to underpin and sustain slavery (Brace 2004). This book explores some of the mechanics of this process by examining the colonists' positioning of the Native Americans as unable to cross the threshold into a polite and civil world, by looking at how race and slavery were woven together in the late eighteenth century in imperialism, in Kant and Hegel, and in Haiti, and by looking at their continuing complicated entanglements in the prison industrial complex and in discourses of trafficking. As Falguni Sheth argues, racial meanings change over time and across national borders, and the political question always has to be about which identities are visible and which identities matter (Sheth 2016).

One of the key identities that matters in the context of slavery is gendered subjectivity, and the chapters in this book on women's subjection and on the politics of trafficking explore the connections between unfree labour, empire and gender. The heroic and subordinate character of the slave, particularly the slave performing back-breaking work in the cotton fields, is often figured as a man, and this book explores the masculinity of ideas about violence, resistance and autonomy. It is more difficult to bring the figure of the female slave into narratives of modernity, self-possession and labour, and to consider how the story of transforming humanity into moral beings is gendered as well as racialised. Women's access to freedom, wages and marriage was formed and given meaning by the culture, politics and history in which it was embedded, and it is important to register how these meanings were different for the white women who endured civil and legal death and engulfment, and the black women who lived and worked within the plantation household as slaves. None of these women fit into the mould of the autonomous, enlightened individual and one of the key themes of this book is the importance of not taking autonomy and personhood for granted and starting our political theories and our understandings of freedom and emancipation from there. The chapters on gender discuss the disavowal of rape and sexual subjection, and the agency and power of women living under conditions of oppressive freedom. The spaces between personhood, subpersonhood and humanity emerge as loop-holes of retreat and assertions of the right to locomotion. The differ-ential meanings of slavery for men and for women are made visible by focusing on the 'collapsed geography' of the household and the power relations within it (Glymph 2008). Women were not understood to be able to live as independent beings in a free, industrious society. They could not find their way to freedom through the world or through the recognition of others, and instead lived lives in constant contact with each other within the 'unrestraint of home' (Mill [1859] 1997, 153). The struggle to find a cogent sense of self was, and is, different, when women are forced to remain within oppressive terms of existence both within the home, and when they find themselves on the move. Their mobility is rendered suspect in ways that are highly gendered, and deeply damag-ing to their self-possession because they carry risks of vagrancy, poverty and indecency both in the nineteenth and the twenty-first centuries. Migrant women's relations of power and powerlessness are imagined for them, and they are judged and blamed for their own predicaments. This brings us up against the limits of antislavery discourse, both in the past and in the present.

THE PASTS AND PRESENTS OF ANTISLAVERY DISCOURSE

'The relation between pasts, presents, and futures', David Scott (2004, 45) observes, 'is a relation constituted in narrative.' In trying to think about the pasts, presents and futures of slavery, this book rejects the idea of a clean break between past and present, old and new, and instead explores what of slavery survives in the institutions of race, gender and nation and some of the ways in which, as Paul Gilroy argues, slaveries provide a firm rebuke to the idea of history as progress (Gilroy 1993). The prevailing discourse of modern slavery tends to take the idea of rupture as its starting point, and it works hard to relegate racial chattel slavery to the past, to seal it off from the present and the future and to re-imagine the slavery of the present as different in kind. Kevin Bales, the key advocate of this approach, argues that this new form of slavery is a product of the global economy, driven by the pursuit of profit and the vulnerability of the slaves. New slavery is global, temporary and non-racial in the sense that ethnic differences are supposed to be secondary to economic considerations. There is a glut of slaves on the market, and so they are now defined as cheap and disposable rather than as long-term investments. 'Human beings', says Bales, 'have become disposable tools for doing business, the same as a box of ballpoint pens' (Jensen 2001). This is framed as a distinctively modern problem associated with globalisation. New slavery involves no legal ownership, high profits for the slaveholders, and a surplus of disposable slaves. 'Old' slavery is equated with the Southern US and the production of material goods (Quirk 2006). As Stephen Hopgood argues, there is 'underlying Bales's account, an under-theorised narrative of modernity, where bonded Indian labourers live in the "dark ages", where Mauritania is "almost medieval"' (Hopgood 1999) and there is little space for thinking about the more complicated antecedents for brutal exploitation and subordination. The danger, as Orlando Patterson points out, is that the definition of new slavery conflates slavery 'with forms of exploitation not considered slavery in most non-western societies or in any historically informed and conceptually rigorous use of the term' (Patterson 2012).

This book seeks to challenge the old/new split at the heart of the definition of modern slavery, and in particular the narratives of modernity and race that lend it much of its power. What happens if instead of relegating racial chattel slavery to the past we think instead about the afterlives and legacies of 'old' slavery that continue to haunt and inform the present? Such a focus brings us to a very different set of political concerns, and to a very different vision of the past and of human agency, culture and endeavour within which people bear very little resemblance to ballpoint pens. This book asks what happens when we make slavery the hub of our analysis of political thought and our narratives of modernity rather than treating it as an unfortunate and embarrassing lapse from which we should turn away. The shift in perspective changes what the project of political theory is saying about key concepts such as freedom, democracy, equality and citizenship by revealing the domination and violence that are 'un-seeable in prevailing theoretical frames' (Balfour 2016, 83–4). It also allows us to explore slavery as an idea and a political concept as well as an institution and a practice, and to understand its complex and contested relationship to social, economic and political relations, and to history. Slavery emerges as an integral part of colonialism, sovereignty and political thought and central to the meanings of class, gender and race. It remains part of the answer to the questions about which identities are visible, whose identity matters and who counts as human and as a person, as a subject and a citizen. Bringing slavery into history, into political thought and into the present troubles the narratives of progress and reminds us that change is not the same as emancipation, leaving us able to ask which problems and whose concerns are supposed to have been left to rest in the past (Balfour 2016, 81) and what is at stake in presumptions of political innocence and in claims to newness.

The discourse of the newness of new slavery is part of a story within which 'the *absence* of slavery comes to be viewed as natural or normal, rather than remarkable' (Quirk 2006, 585). Freedom appears as the innate human condition, an implicit longing within each individual and the inevitable outcome of liberal politics. This narrative makes it easy to lose sight of the distinction between freedom and unfreedom as an ongoing social struggle, within which 'free status may be nothing more than a trench', and the success of some in reaching this refuge 'may merely reinforce the boundary between them and those who remain in the line of fire' (Binder 1995, 2022–3). As Guyora Binder points out, no slave-holding class ever lost out in the process of disenslavement or manumission. The freeing of some individuals perpetuates the slavery of others, and '[e]ven sincerely motivated moral crusades to suppress slavery carry risks to freedom' (Binder 1995, 2075). This book is concerned with these risks to freedom which continue to trouble modern abolitionism, and with the impossibility of reclaiming an innocent modernity that can disentangle freedom from slavery.

For some, the brutal dislocation of slavery means that it cannot be given a history, instead the erasure of collective memory and the transgenerational haunting creates a 'nonhistory', a problem-space within which the past has not yet emerged as history. Writing about Haiti, Carole Sweeney argues that slavery rests on a core of unrepresentability, a central absence, within which traces of violence, rupture and dislocation are 'producing a present that is played out as repetition and recurrence, endlessly circling around a central lacuna of loss and dispossession' (Sweeney 2007, 54). As a result, many engagements with the pasts of slavery are about haunting stories, tales and memories 'that struggle to find a narrative' or a chronology (Sweeney 2007, 56). At the same time, recent economic history has begun to adopt a broader conception of the slave-economy, opening up the possibility of new narratives that can bring the slave trade and slavery in the New World 'properly back into British and European history' (C. Hall 2014, 25) in ways that problematise whiteness as an identity that carried privilege and power. The delineation of black men and women as property had, Hall argues, as 'its counterpoint the naming of whiteness as a different kind of property – the property of freedom – access to public and private privileges, the possibility of controlling critical aspects of one's own life rather than being the object of others' domination' (C. Hall 2014, 28). In bringing together the histories of both enslavers and enslaved, we can begin to unpick some of the ways in which the history of slavery has been assigned to black people as a kind of special property (Gilroy 1993). This is coupled with a set of parallel assumptions about political subjectivity that 'substitute an integrative ideal of whiteness for more transformative conceptions of freedom' (Balfour 2016, 81). Thinking through slavery and freedom together in the history of political thought and in narratives of modernity forces us to reconsider whose property the history of slavery is, and how it might be possible to forge more transformative conceptions of freedom. As Jared Sexton argues, following Grandin, the modern world owes its existence to slavery, and that is an 'impossible debt' (Sexton 2014, 11). The impossibility of that debt means that we find ourselves in the problem-space identified by Saidiya Hartman, between the no longer and the not yet. This book is an attempt to explore some of this space between old and new slaveries by thinking about the pasts, presents and futures of slavery as they are constituted in the ideas of Aristotle, Locke, Kant, Hegel, Wollstonecraft and Mill, asking how the past, present and future might emerge as history in political thought.

MODERN SLAVERY: KNOWING AND NOT-KNOWING

In 2000, Kevin Bales, founder of Free the Slaves, published and proceeded to publicise an estimate of 27 million slaves in the contemporary world (May 2013). In 2013, the Walk Free Foundation launched a report titled *The Global Slavery Index*, which enlarged this estimate to 29.8 million people, and their 2014 report puts the number at 35.8 million men, women and children. These numbers are largely arrived at by totting up estimates of people thought to fall into a series of other categories, such as bonded labour, forced labour, worst forms of child labour, early and forced marriage, and trafficking. These numbers are important for understanding the relationship between old and new slavery because they allow the new abolitionists to claim that there are more slaves in the world today than were shipped across the Atlantic as part of New World slavery. In terms of sheer, quantifiable, human suffering, 'the quantum of misery', they argue that new slavery wins out over old slavery. The rhetoric is all about how pervasive slavery is in its new globalised guise; it is an evil that is happening all around the world. As Theresa May put it in article for the *Telegraph* in 2013, it is 'hidden in plain sight. It is walking our streets, supplying shops and supermarkets, working in fields, factories or nail bars, trapped in brothels or cowering behind the curtains in an ordinary street' (May 2013). The key question, as Joel Quirk points out, has 'gradually become which practices and institutions are sufficiently similar to legal slavery that they deserve to be legitimately classified as such' (Quirk, 2006, 566). The UN Working Group on Slavery endorses this 'open-ended approach', deeming the forced exploitation of labour, serious hardship and serious deprivations of liberty to be legitimately classified as slavery. All of these categories taken as proxies for slavery present their own problems of definition, and none of them straightforwardly constitutes what people like Bales define as modern slavery. Instead, the focus is on the idea of a threshold, looking for practices that are as Quirk puts it 'sufficiently horrendous and/or analogous' to be classified as slavery (Quirk 2006, 578). The problem of the parameters of the concept remains, and that 'threshold' is constantly being renegotiated. Many of these are overlapping categories, and there is no coherent rationale that links these disparate practices together (Quirk 2006, 567). We can, as Quirk points out, 'quickly end up with a multifaceted continuum, where concepts such as trafficking, slavery, and servitude can be invoked interchangeably to highlight acute forms of suffering and exploitation' (Quirk 2006, 577). The new slavery discourse is caught up in what Quirk has termed 'classificatory conundrums' about where to draw the line between a slave and a non-slave, and about how to distinguish between literal and rhetorical claims of slavery (Quirk 2006, 598). How should we understand the entanglements between the literal and the rhetorical in the writings of Aristotle, Locke and Hegel on the subject of slavery and enslavability? What did they know about acute forms of suffering and exploitation, and how did that knowledge affect what they understood freedom to mean and their constructions of subjectivity?

This question of knowing and not-knowing structures our understanding of slavery both in the past and in the present, and calls on us to consider the place of wilful or motivated ignorance in relation to what we choose to remember about slavery and its place in our histories of freedom, enlightenment and empire and what we choose to label and fight against as instances of modern slavery. This is connected to what Charles Mills has called 'white ignorance', which can take the form of individuals blocking certain truths or of the social suppression of pertinent knowledge, and is connected to 'mainstream theorizing in political science that frames American sexism and racism as "anomalies"', the exception rather than the norm (Mills 2007, 17). As Mills argues in his discussion of Ralph Ellison's *Invisible Man*, this is about the refusal of white people to see the black experience, their 'systematic misperception' that means that they see, in the words of Ellison's protagonist, 'only my surroundings, themselves, or figments of their imagination', which captures very neatly a whole set of criticisms of modern slavery discourse (Mills 2007, 18).

The discourse of new slavery is all about uncovering, acknowledging and confronting the 'scourge' of modern slavery. This is presented as difficult to do because it is taken to be self-evident that, as Theresa May put it, it is 'scarcely credible that slavery can exist in our modern age' (May 2013). It is something that we are supposed to assume has been consigned to history books, belonging in a different century. Written into the new slavery rhetoric is the idea that slavery belongs to a benighted past. This is linked to a trope within new slavery rhetoric that assumes that 'we' know about slavery in the past, but not about the hidden evil in our nail bars. This is a concept of slavery that relies on a particular interpretation of the world and is oriented towards a certain understanding, and which plays on the idea of not-knowing, on the supposed ignorance of its audience and their inability to see and bear witness. In her TED talk, Lisa Kristine says, 'I felt so horrible and ashamed at my lack of knowledge. It burned a hole in my stomach' (Kristine 2012). To fill this hole, she describes her journey into modern day slavery, which is 'all around us, but we just don't see it'. For both May and Kristine, as self-styled new abolitionists, what they need to do is 'shine a light on slavery' (Kristine 2012). Theresa May introduced her Modern Slavery Bill by quoting from William Wilberforce: '[Y]ou may choose to look the other way but you can never again say that you did not know' (May 2013). What they see when they look around, when they shine their lights, are their own myths, themselves and figments of their imagination. The concept of new slavery is driving their perception of other people's exploitation and oppression and giving the abolitionists a conceptual apparatus that allows them to engage in the 'deliberate forgetting' of 'old' slavery while accusing others of, and retrospectively blaming themselves for, failing to see what is all around them. In drawing on Wilberforce and the history of abolitionism in this way, May was calling on 'feel-good history for whites' (Mills 2007, 30) at the same time as inviting them to feel bad and ashamed of their 'ignorance'.

This version of not-seeing is linked to presumptions of political innocence which are central to the new antislavery discourse, as they were to the original abolitionism of the eighteenth and nineteenth century. Abhorrence of slavery and an inherent love of liberty are constructed as defining characteristics of what it means to be British (in particular), and it is this that renders the idea of slaves on 'our' soil 'scarcely credible' (May 2013). In this, the new abolitionists are drawing on a much older story of Enlightenment and abolition which is also about nation, and about gender. For Benezet and Sharp in the eighteenth century, slavery was tainting the ideals and corrupting the character of the nation. As

Srividhya Swaminathan argues, the debates over the slave trade were central in helping to define the national character, setting Britons apart from other Europeans and creating a place for British colonial identity (Swaminathan 2009, 13). The debates created what Swaminathan calls a common morality, a national code of conduct that was applicable both at home and abroad. It is this delineation that a Conservative Home Secretary could still draw upon in the twenty-first century, a shared perception of cultural identity, the idea that the air in England is too pure for slaves, and of the superiority of English liberty and citizenship, a constellation of humanity, nationality and spirituality, with the value of liberty vaunted as its foremost characteristic. 'Let us', said Elizabeth Coltman in 1824, referring to the British, and to British women in particular, 'whose moral perceptions are unblended by interest or prejudice – whose charity is unwarped by partiality and hypocrisy' be the first to liberate our own slaves (Coltman 1824, 19). The Europe of the abolitionists in the eighteenth century and the 'West' of the abolitionists today, is a place of generosity and bravery, remarkable for its humanity and justice. New abolitionism feeds into what Anita Rupprecht has called 'a long dominant discourse of humanitarian triumph' (Rupprecht 2008, 266). While 'slaves' in India are understood by Bales to be 'trapped by tradition', in modern liberal democracies the chain of history has been broken by the legal abolition of slave trading and slavery in the nineteenth century. In this account, Europe entered history, and became the centre of the world, in the moment that it abolished slavery and moved out of the dark ages and into Enlightenment.

Bales, in Woods's view, is summarising the mainstream perspective of white civil society, which holds that slavery ended with abolition in 1865, and its vestiges were eradicated by the Civil Rights Act of 1964, so that any inequalities or iniquities that remain are to do with something other than racism, with 'the innate inadequacies of those left behind' (T. P. Woods 2013, 130). Bales's focus on the 'old slavery' of the Americas, Quirk argues, 'sanctions the popular notion that slavery was chiefly a European sin, which conclusively came to end in the nineteenth century' (Quirk 2006, 530). This ignores the persistence and prevalence of slavery, particularly in the nineteenth century, and the millions of slaves who remained in servitude in Africa, Asia and the Middle East after its formal legal abolition in Europe and the US. Antislavery always had a legislative goal: legal abolition was seen as decisive political action, and a clear sign of the British commitment to liberty.

In its twenty-first century incarnation, the abolitionist myth is more about the idea of a slavery that takes place elsewhere, in 'other' cultures, where the idea of slavery is suddenly no longer scarcely believable. Bales talks about how the slaves he has identified in Pakistan have an underdeveloped understanding of the world, are too honest to perceive they are being trapped, and cannot grasp the idea of choice (Bales 2000). Tryon Woods argues that modern slavery discourse presents modern slavery as a product of African culture, a mundane feature of contemporary Nigeria, for example, where it is described as 'woven into the fabric' of Nigerian national life. Woods quotes from David Puttnam in 2004, saying 'half of you feels sympathy, but the other half just wants to shake the people here and say look, this is a large, wealthy powerful country. Put the structures in place. Show some determination' (Little 2004). As Woods points out, this focus on the attitudes of the people in the Edo delta, their lack of determination, says nothing about how the state has been eviscerated by the multinational energy industry, and provides no political or economic context that would link colonisation to the present. Instead, in an instance of deliberate forgetting and systematic misperception, modern slavery discourse suggests that it is African cultural deficiencies that produce predatory economic processes which in turn cannot support civilised democracies. Modern day slavery, Woods concludes, 'reproduces a disabling historical amnesia' (T. P. Woods 2013, 126) that is underwritten by anti-blackness and by 'the specter of slavery that both haunts it and on which it parasitically feeds' (T. P. Woods 2013, 120). The ahistoricism of the new abolitionist approach obscures the 'ongoing calculus of racial slavery's afterlife' (T. P. Woods 2013, 122) just as it argues that it is shining a light on slavery.

It is possible to trace an abolitionist narrative that connects across from the eighteenth to the twenty-first century and is united around trying to identify the slave as the victim, the object of sympathy, and in the process takes the people identified as slaves and victims outside of history, and into a space where it is impossible to uncover the meanings and motivations of those involved. The disabling ahistoricism is to do with the insistence that it is possible to tell the difference between slavery and drudgery by using the market as the marker of freedom, by ignoring and disavowing race and racial inequality, and by objectifying the slave. It helps to spend time in the company of the eighteenth-century abolitionists and their opponents because they were tackling real slavery as an institution created and constrained by law, and because they too were selective in their worldview, and their approach has an afterlife – the afterlife of antislavery needs exploring in conjunction with the afterlife of slavery. The discourse of new slavery brings past and present into an uncomfortable relationship, and we need to consider carefully, as this book tries to do, how to bring the history of slavery back in.

Chapter 2

ARISTOTLE AND THE STRANGENESS OF SLAVES

Aristotle's theory of natural slavery, set out in the *Politics* and in the *Nicomachean Ethics* is a useful starting point for thinking about slavery in the history of political thought, and for introducing and developing some of the key themes of this book. The idea of conceiving of the slave as an animate tool raises a whole set of questions about the supposed subhumanity of the slave and how that status is understood in the history and politics of slavery. I am particularly interested in the 'incompleteness' of the slave, and the ways in which his or her soul was understood to be lacking in spirit, in the constituent elements required to build a free citizen. Aristotle is an important place to start because his arguments bring together political slavery and what Mary Nyquist calls psycho-ethical slavery, and because his explicitly political approach to slavery draws attention to the question of how we should theorise the relationship between slavery as metaphor and slavery as lived experience. Did his theory of natural slavery have anything to say about the lives of actually existing slaves in ancient Greece?

Nyquist discusses the differences between figurative, political slavery and chattel slavery, where political slavery is about the threat to the democratic polis and not about the condition of chattel slaves. Her analysis of the 'polyvalent metaphor of slavery' (Nyquist 2013, 5) draws attention to the 'entangled interrelations' (Nyquist 2013, 2) between political servitude and chattel slavery, and these entanglements are particularly gnarly in Aristotle's theory. Within the polis, political slavery is represented as the illegitimate domination of free, male citizens who expected to participate as equals in the political process, exercising their freedom as political agents, none of them ruling over others. Political slavery comes about when 'a leader fails to protect the citizenry's freedom, instead attempting to become its master' (Nyquist 2013, 22). As Nyquist points out, the injustice of this political enslavement lies 'in the attempt to enslave those who patently ought not to be enslaved' (Nyquist 2013, 23). Participants met in the political arena as equals, but they were masters within their own households. Aristotle's opposition to political slavery was not an attack on slavery as wrong in itself. Democratic citizens were the masters of slaves within their households, and the boundary between the household and the polis was crucial in guaranteeing the freedom of the citizen. Someone who failed to distinguish the polis from his own private household and presumed to treat citizens as if they were slaves became a tyrant by falling victim to his 'grandiose desire for power' and failing to maintain the boundary between public and private (Nyquist 2013, 38). Slavery was entangled in the structure of politics.

Nyquist argues that focusing on the structure of slavery within the household 'has the effect of naturalizing it' by bringing it into the same space as marital and parental relations, which are understood to be determined by nature (Nyquist 2013, 25), but at the same time to be social relations. The slave–master relationship within the household was ambiguous because the slave was classed as chattel and so 'ostensibly belongs to the same category as nonhuman animals and other possessions' (Nyquist 2013, 25). As long as the master's power was directed towards the fulfilment of purely private needs, despotic power was justified and it was accepted that the household master was not accountable to others for how he used his power. Free citizens were the masters of natural slaves. Nyquist identifies an opposition between those for whom slavery 'would represent a demeaning, traumatic loss and those for whom it was supposed to be natural' (Nyquist 2013, 26). Aristotle 'argues at one and the same time for the categorical *naturalness* of household slavery and the *unnaturalness* for Greeks of despotism in the political sphere, associating enslaved *barbaroi* with both' (Nyquist 2013, 49).

The big, behind-the-scenes question is about the where race fits in to these ancient conceptions of slavery. This is, of course, an anachronistic question, but the construction of the barbarism of non-Greeks, and the ways in which they were represented as fitted for slavery are fascinating and clearly have parallels with seventeenth-century narratives of the state of nature and with the eighteenth and nineteenth

centuries' apologies for slavery. This brings us to the vexed and difficult question of how to make comparisons and draw parallels between
ancient Greece and, for example, nineteenth-century America. In one
sense, of course, this is impossible to do, but the temptation is almost
irresistible when you read and engage with the arguments of George
Fitzhugh, or William Harper and his defence of slave-owning in 1838,
where he makes self-conscious use of the ancients' theory of natural
slavery and argues that slaveholders in Carolina should derive inspira-
tion and wisdom from the slavery model of Greece and Rome. Like
Aristotle, Harper sees the structure of slavery as resting on the categorical naturalness of household slavery and the unnaturalness of
attempting to enslave people who ought not to be enslaved. Harper
uses Aristotelian arguments about natural slavery to argue that 'society
must exclude from civil and political privileges those who are unfitted
to exercise them, by infirmity, unsuitableness of character, or defect
of discretion' (Harper 1838, 7). In his view, the civilised and cultivated
man had a right over 'the savage and ignorant': 'It is as much in the
order of nature, that men should enslave each other, as that other animals should prey upon each other' (Harper 1838, 11). Aristotle made
the same analogy between slavery and hunting. Harper's question
about slavery was one that had been answered by Aristotle: 'If there
are sordid, servile and laborious offices to be performed, is it not better
that there should be sordid, servile, and laborious beings to perform
them?' (Harper 1838, 33).

As Page DuBois argues, slavery appears in classical historiographical work as a closed and static system, and that stasis needs to be
challenged through the recognition that slavery is not monolithic,
but has its own histories and variations (DuBois 2008, 25). In Greek
slavery, the distinction between helotry, as the collective enslavement
of conquered peoples who remained in their communities, and chattel slavery, which brought slaves into individual households through
traumatic displacement, was central to the complex meanings of
slavery (DuBois 2008, 25). Then, there was a hierarchy among the
slaves. Some were trusted members of the household, others were
regarded as dangerous and hostile prisoners of war, and still others
worked down the silver mines or on grand public building projects.
There were slaves everywhere; public slaves worked in the police
force and picked up the bodies of the dead. State slaves were used

as the police force to restrain, arrest and detain citizens because '[a]n important part of what being a citizen meant was not being manhandled by other citizens' (Fisher 1993, 56). Public slaves also worked as managers of coin, weights and measures, as keepers of the archives and as clerks and assistants to the council. They were paid regular salaries and were able to accumulate some wealth. They are there in the archaeological record, in literary, historical and theoretical texts. Once we start to think about the ancient context, what does it mean to conceptualise slavery as a place of no return, an order of nature, especially in the context of manumission?

This means thinking about the meanings of the contested, in-between statuses of freedom and the mobile borders between humanity and personhood. This is particularly interesting in the context of ancient Greece and the processes of manumission. Rachel Zelnick-Abramowitz asks what it is to be a manumitted slave. That is a question that resonates throughout this book, but is posed most sharply in this chapter. The question of what it means to be a slave is linked to the question of what it means to stop being one. What lies on the other side of the slavery/freedom binary that ancient Greece and Rome did so much to construct and defend? (Zelnick-Abramowitz 2005). The interesting thing is how many common themes emerge here, and how blurry the line is between slavery and freedom even as it is being drawn. In Aristotle's theory of 'natural' slavery, we can already trace the elements of freedom, belonging and labour that intersect with each other to define what it means not to be a slave.

THE POLIS

The first and most important point to make is that Aristotle's conception of nature was 'thoroughly teleological' (Aristotle 1995, xi). The identity of the polis lay in its organisation and structure, and this organisation was the constitution. Human beings were polis-creating and polis-inhabiting animals, and the city or the polis existed for the good life. The positive moral purpose of the city was to enable citizens to live a life of virtue or excellence, to make possible a life of Aristotelian moral virtue. From the start, as R. F. Stalley points out in his introduction to the *Politics*, it is implicit in Aristotle's conception of the good life that not everyone can achieve it, and that the institution of slavery is essential in guaranteeing the possibility of a good life of virtue for some. When William Harper looked back to the great republics of antiquity, the lesson he took from them was that 'slavery is compatible with the freedom, stability and long duration of civil government, with denseness of population, great power, and the highest civilization' (Harper 1838, 45). The first natural form of association was the family, the next was the village and the final or perfect form of association was the polis, which 'while it comes into existence for the sake of mere life, . . . exists for the sake of the good life' (Aristotle 1995, 1252b7). Because in Aristotle's teleological theory the whole was necessarily prior to the part, the city existed by nature and was prior to the individual. For Aristotle, there was a natural impulse in all men towards an association of this sort because man is a political animal. He is, by nature, what Millett calls 'a polis-creature' (Millett 2007, 181), and the polis has priority in nature over the household and the individual. This inspiring vision of the city-state as the final or perfect form of association continues to define what many political theories mean by 'politics', and so what it means to be constructed as outside the scope of the political.

The polis as an inclusive system of social ethics underpinned by laws and unwritten rules was a shared, dynamic enterprise geared to the highest goal: of living a good life. The polis was 'a community of persons who associate because of their need to make a living, but who have as their goal the good life, i.e. a life of fulfilment exemplifying the characteristically human virtues' (Schofield 1999, 103). The exemplary humans who were members of the polis were assumed to be free and equal and, as Malcolm Schofield puts it, capable of determining their own strategies for living (Schofield 1999, 103). Freedom is rational self-direction. The free man could see for himself, through the exercise of his reason, the ends he ought to pursue for the sake of his own well-being (Walsh 1997, 499). This rational self-direction is connected to democratic freedom in particular ways through the shared capacity for deliberation. Such free men had the capacity to live as they wished, to share equally in public responsibility and office, and to be treated equally before the law. They were true citizens, not mere subjects, meaning that they were allowed to share in deliberation and decision, and that the good of the polis included their own good (Walsh 1997, 501). In a democratic polis, all the free inhabitants are 'full citizens, sharing in decision and office', and pursuing a common good that includes their own good. The flourishing of a properly ordered city is the highest good, and perfect freedom is to contribute to its flourishing, and to flourish within it (Walsh 1997, 503).

As Schofield argues, these egalitarian principles opened up the potential for hierarchy, and some people who were not slaves, such as farmers, manual workers and people engaged in trade, lived lives that were devoted to ignoble purposes, or left them no leisure for noble pursuits. Such men were only able to think in terms of wealth and freedom, rather than of virtue and excellence, and so it was clear that they should be excluded from citizenship (Schofield 1999, 106). The status of manual labour was demeaning in Ancient Greece. Greek cities developed as communities of farmers, and the ideal citizen was a soldier and an independent, nearly self-sufficient farmer. As Athens developed its craft and manufacturing, farming remained the most respectable basis for wealth. Working the land was regarded as more gentlemanly and masculine than manufacture, and as a better preparation for military action. These equal, democratic citizens were comfortable and materially secure, they listened to reason and they did not envy others (Patterson 1991b). The slave owner who was also a free citizen was capable of self-direction and of directing others, and the free citizen was also a slaveholder.

In Book 1 of the Politics, the basic unit of the polis is the household, which includes husband and wife, father and children and master and slave. Women, children, slaves and animals are all members of the polis 'constructed as a geographic, agricultural, social, religious, productive and reproductive community, though not as a political community' (Nyquist 2013, 49). In Book 3, the polis is less inclusive, and the basic unit of politics is the male citizen. The polis becomes a political community, whose end, the good life, excludes slaves and animals. Against this background, slavery appears as an institution of benefit to the master, and its 'individual, private character is suddenly thrown into relief' (Nyquist 2013, 49). The equality of political rule envisaged by Aristotle creates the polis as a community of those who are capable of virtue, where 'equality is secured only at the price of hierarchy: the subordination of those who perform the lower functions' (Schofield 1999, 112). Women and chattel slaves were relegated to the household, and placed 'below the threshold of political discourse' (Schofield 1999, 110). Women were incorporated into the *oikos* under the guardianship of their male kin. They were barred from legal proceedings and from making contracts to dispose of significant amounts of property, and they were not polis-creatures. Women and slaves were understood to be naturally subordinate beings in relation to free men, and free men were intended by nature to exercise permanent leadership over them. Women must obey because of men's innate inability to command, and because the good life of the polis concerns only free men 'whom women must serve as a functional contribution towards the males attaining perfection' (Femenias 1994, 170). Women played a vital role in transmitting citizenship rights and in contributing to the survival of the *oikos*. The polis depended on the presence of slaves and foreigners who were not members to sustain its own vision of itself as an inclusive system.

THE NATURE OF RULE AND THE NATURE OF THE SLAVE

Schofield argues that the dominant question throughout the *Politics* is about how many forms of rule there are, and Aristotle's answer is that there are several. His interest in slavery arises only in the context of 'his preoccupation with the different forms of rule' (Schofield 1999, 132). These different forms of rule are grounded in the nature of human beings, and slavery works at the limit, representing 'the extreme case in a range of cases in natural rule' (Schofield 1999, 132). Aristotle argued for a natural basis for the difference between slavery and political rule, and made a sharp distinction between rule over slaves and the rule of equals in the political process.

For Aristotle, there must necessarily be a pairing of those who cannot exist without one another. He was aiming for the union of the naturally ruling element with the element that was naturally ruled for the preservation of both: 'The element which is able, by virtue of its intelligence, to exercise forethought, is naturally a ruling and master element; the element which is able, by virtue of its bodily power, to do the physical work, is a ruled element, which is naturally in a state of slavery; and master and slave have accordingly a common interest' (Aristotle 1995, 1252a24). Masters and slaves had a different kind of knowledge. Slaves were instructed in the nature of their duties, and could learn to be skilled and proficient in cookery and domestic service, but the character of their knowledge remained servile. Masters of slaves must simply know how to command what the slave must know how to do. This knowledge, Aristotle points out, is not great or majestic, and many free men delegated the management of slaves to a steward, and spent the time they saved on politics or philosophy.

The question then arose of whether the slave had any 'goodness' or virtue beyond that of discharging his or her function as an instrument and performing his or her menial service. Did they possess goodness of a higher value, such as temperance, fortitude or justice, or did they have no virtue beyond the bodily services they provided? Either alternative presented difficulties for Aristotle's account, and for the theory of natural slavery. If they did possess such virtues, how were they different from free men? If they did not, how could they be characterised as human and as possessing reason? For Aristotle, the difference between those who were naturally ruled and those who naturally ruled was a difference in kind. The subject could only be properly ruled if he was temperate and just, and so those who were naturally slaves shared in goodness, but their goodness was of a different kind. Free men, women and slaves shared in moral goodness, 'but not in the same way – each sharing only to the extent required for the discharge of his or her function' (Aristotle 1995, 1260a4). The goodness of the slave was all about his relation to his master. Slaves were useful for the necessary purposes of life, and to discharge that function they needed just a little goodness: 'only so much, in fact, as will prevent them from falling short of their duties through intemperance or cowardice' (Aristotle 1995, 1260a33). Slaves lacked the *prohairesis* that enabled moral choice in advance of action (Millett 2007, 185). *Prohairetic* activity combined desire and intelligence and disclosed the character of the one who acted and allowed him to live a 'life based on choice' (Frank 2004, 96). Natural slaves could not engage in this kind of activity, and instead had to have their choices made for them by someone with foresight. The slave 'is a partner in his master's life' (Aristotle 1995, 1260a33), and once he was placed in that relation, he could mirror or approximate *prohairetic* activity (Frank 2004, 96).

It was better for masters that natural slaves existed because it made it possible for them to live better lives. It was an incidental benefit that being enslaved was good for natural slaves, making them 'capable of participating in and contributing to an intrinsically worthwhile life' (Heath 2008, 266). Dobbs argues that once we put the slave relationship into its proper teleological context, it becomes clear that it 'in no way involves the dehumanization of the slave' (Dobbs 1994, 87). For Aristotle, despotic rule exercised in accord with nature was not exploitative, and the slave was both 'property and partner of his master'. Through his relationship to the master, the slave shared in a distinctively human way of life and, according to Dobbs, 'property in a natural slave derives from the fact that all human beings *belong* in a life partaking in the distinctively human *telos*' (Dobbs 1994, 87). Dobbs argues that it was the master's responsibility to 'bring out such virtue as the slave can achieve' (Dobbs 1994, 87), and he should do so out of concern for the excellence of his property, not just in order to maximise output. The rightfulness of the master's dominion was 'conditioned upon the subordination of his own conduct to the natural order' (Dobbs 1994, 88). Dobbs reads a kind of 'humanisation' of the slave into the partnership that resurfaces in Harper's nineteenth-century defence of slavery when he talks about the 'virtues of slaves', which include fidelity, submission to authority and the disposition to be attached to superiors. The slave, he declared, had no need for heroic virtues or elegant accomplishments. It was for the master 'to compensate for this, by his own more assiduous cultivation, of the more generous virtues, and liberal attainments' (Harper 1838, 30). This kind of despotic rule was only justified as right by nature as long as 'the master's proprietorship in the slave derives from and duly respects the nature of the slave *qua* human being' (Dobbs 1994, 86).

Those who were fitted by nature to be slaves possessed only bodily powers and the faculty of understanding 'the directions given by another's reason'. The natural slave lacked *nous*, and 'has no insight into what is fundamental' (Dobbs 1994, 86). In Aristotle's schema, the soul ruled the body with the authority of a master, reason ruled the appetite with the authority of a statesman. The body should be ruled by the soul, the affective part of the soul should be ruled by the rational part, and in the same way, animals should be ruled by man and the female ruled by the male. For Plato, men and women all had the same virtues, exercised in different realms, and to be a ruler required the exercise of these same virtues. Anyone could (in principle for Plato) become a ruler, and anyone could be ruled. For Aristotle, virtue was different in different kinds of people, and ruling was different in different contexts, so that 'what it is to rule well cannot simply be a matter of science' (Deslauriers 2006, 59). The master was a master because he was a certain kind of person, who possessed *phronesis*, a 'practical intellectual virtue that informs moral character' (Deslauriers 2006, 61). The desires of a free man were informed by the dictates of his reason. The naturalness of slavery came from these differences in intellectual and moral virtues, the distribution of these 'psychic faculties' that rendered people capable of ruling well and with authority (Deslauriers 2006, 62). All men who differed from others as much as the body differs from the soul, or an animal from a man, 'all such are by nature slaves' (Aristotle 1995, 1254b16). For these people who were slaves by nature, it was better to be ruled by a master. For those whose function was bodily service, they produced their best when they supplied such service to their masters; 'Someone is thus a slave by nature if he is capable of becoming the property of another' (Aristotle 1995, 1254b16). This definition of what it means to be a slave by nature resonates through the centuries, putting the focus clearly on the deficiencies of the slave, gendering the slave as male, describing what it means to be 'slavish', not what it means to try to force someone else to become your property. The slave apprehended reason in another, but had none of his own. The deficiency of the natural slave was 'his failure to actualize the first-level capacity for *logos* he possesses' (Frank 2004, 96). The part and the whole, like the body and the soul, had an identical interest, and the slave was part of the master, 'in the sense of being a living but separate part of his body' (Aristotle 1995, 1255b4). Moira Walsh gives the example of her hand. It has no inherent purpose and cannot direct itself, but receives its purpose 'from me or my intellect, which commands it to move in a particular way' (Walsh 1997, 498).

THE SLAVE AS AN ANIMATE ARTICLE OF PROPERTY

Aristotle located the slave as property within the household. Property was part of the household, and the art of acquiring property was part of household management. The household had to be furnished with appropriate instruments if its function was to be fulfilled, and those instruments were partly inanimate and partly animate: 'Each article of property is thus an instrument of the purpose of life, property in general is a quantity of such instruments, the slave is an animate article of property' (Aristotle 1995, 1253b23). This is Aristotle's most famous formulation of what it means to be a slave, the slave as a living tool. The description sums up what is understood to be the 'problem' of slavery: the (im)possibility of reducing a human being to the status of an object. As Schofield argues, the 'ensouled tool' is not the name for a distinct species of animal, but a way of describing 'a perfectly recognisable sort of human being' (Schofield 1999, 128), just not the sort of exemplary and virtuous human being who can inhabit the polis. In belonging to someone else, slaves were, according to Vincent Rosivach, 'something less than fully human, and probably closer to animal than to free man' (Rosivach 1999, 146). Malcolm Bull argues that the slave's incomplete soul was not enslaved by the master's soul, but subject to it, so that the slave was still another soul. Aristotle constructed 'a justification of the enslavement of those whose humanity is somehow incomplete while retaining an awareness that slavery does not obliterate such humanity as they possess' (Bull 1998, 4). Someone who belonged to another person worked primarily for an external end, with no innate purpose or reason for being, but a 'being-for-other' remained a human being (Femenias 1994, 169).

Aristotle made a distinction between the slave as a slave and the slave as a man. He made some room for justice in every relation between humans who were capable of participating in law and agreement (Millett 2007, 186). Slaves needed to have a small amount of appropriate virtue, developed by their masters, and to be given reasons for their instructions. In Bull's analysis of the multiple self in slavery, this means that Aristotle captured something of the duality inherent in the condition of the slave. Fisher argues that the idea of friendship with a slave as a man 'brings out the fundamental contradiction very clearly' (Fisher 1993, 97), and is compounded by the 'single most glaring contradiction', the use of manumission as an incentive for all slaves. The slave was, potentially at least, fully human. The relationship between master and slave created a community of interest, a relationship of friendship between the master and slave 'when both of them naturally merit the position in which they stand' (Aristotle 1995, 1255b4). Zelnick-Abramowitz's analysis of friendship draws attention to the bonds of service and loyalty, and the wish to benefit the other. She argues that these relations of benefactors and beneficiaries could exist between equals and between unequals, and *philia* could exist in vertical and asymmetrical relationships. Slaves as human beings in relations with their masters depended on each other, and on social connections based on suspicion, fear, co-operation, expectations and obligations. Faithful and resourceful slaves expected the freedom they had been promised by their masters (Zelnick-Abramowitz 2005). In return for their promised manumission, slaves were encouraged to be loyal and diligent, and then often found themselves still bound by their debts and by the conditions of their manumission long after they were supposed to have gained their independence. Manumitted slaves remained 'essential, yet outsiders' (Zelnick-Abramowitz 2005, 60).

The slave as an animate tool was an instrument of action. Aristotle recognised different kinds of rationality, practical and technical. Natural slaves could not achieve *eudaimonia*, the best kind of human life, because it consisted in virtuous activity, beyond the scope of technical rationality. Natural slaves did not share in the practical, architectonic wisdom that provided overall guidance for life (Heath 2008, 247). They were incapable of *prohairesis* and *eudaimonia*, of virtuous action or deliberated choice, because they were characterised as not able to reason back from a goal to the action required to implement that goal. The slaves' deliberative capacity was permanently impaired. They lived without the guidance of a stable conception of the overall good (Heath 2008, 251). Aristotle's theory of chattel slavery within the private realm of the household made clear that slavery is about ownership: 'While the master is merely the master of the slave, and does not belong to him, the slave is not only the slave of his master; he also belongs entirely to him' (Aristotle 1995, 1254a8). It was a slave's nature to belong to another, and his nature was fulfilled only when he actually belonged to another person (Rosivach 1999, 146). As Zelnick-Abramowitz argues, it is crucial that we understand slavery as a complex set of social relations, and not just as a straightforward property relationship. At the same time, it is important that we take the property element seriously, and recognise that it is the asymmetry of property and ownership that Aristotle uses to construct his vision of natural slavery:

> Anybody who by his nature is not his own man, but another's, is by his nature a slave; anybody who, being a man, is an article of property is another's man; an article of property is an instrument intended for the purpose of action and separable from its possessor. (Aristotle 1995, 1254a13)

The slave, as DuBois argues, is 'a sort of uncanny object, standing at the blind spot of modernity where the place of the subject and that of object intersect' (DuBois 2008, 31).

The slave in this account is alive but socially dead, 'a personality without personhood' (Bull 1998, 17). The slave is at the same time both a tool and a human being, and Aristotle 'inscribed the social contradictions of slavery within the soul(s) of slaves' (Bull 1998, 17). This is a controversial and disputed reading of Aristotle which links him to Hegel and to W. E. B. DuBois, but it makes an interesting point about social death and about what Bull calls 'the duplicated selves formed through slavery' who do not fit the model of unified, authentic individuals (Bull 1998, 18). Aristotle's theory of natural slavery lays the ground for later theories based on the premise that selves that do not fit or are somehow incomplete will be excluded 'from consideration as moral subjects' (Bull 1998, 18). 'From Aristotle onwards, having a unified moral self has been seen as a privilege confined to a social elite' (Bull 1998, 20). Bull is making a further point about the relationship between interpersonal and intrapersonal models of slavery. In both Aristotle and Hegel, he argues, the master–slave dyad is an interpersonal relation constructed as an intrapersonal one. Freedom in Aristotle is the freedom of rational self-direction both within the polis and within the soul. Individual deficiency, for both slaves and women, entails political exclusion. Not having a unified moral self will involve not being a citizen, so that the privilege is confined to an explicitly political as well as social elite. The distinction between citizens and inhabitants turns out to make the number of beneficiaries of Aristotle's inspiring vision of the polis as an inclusive system much smaller than we might at first imagine, and opens up the question of the humanity of the slave, and of the process of dehumanisation.

SLAVERY AND LABOUR

The great majority of slaves in Athens were household slaves, in the sense that they were formally the property of an individual *oikos*. Large numbers of them worked in the fields, especially at harvest time, and the enlarged household in Athens included slave-craftsmen and artisans. Outside the confines of the household, there were hired-out slaves and those employed in the mines (Millett 2007, 203). They were all part of a differentiated and hierarchical system of slavery, with domestic slaves at one end of the continuum and slave miners at the other. As Millett and Nyquist point out, Aristotle's main concern was with the potentially close relationships and the complex psychological interactions of the household.

In his discussion of slavery in Roman history, Keith Bradley describes the dehumanising process of buying and selling slaves in the marketplace. Slaves stood on display on a raised platform, and potential buyers could insist that they jump up and down or undress. They were subject to intense scrutiny, and had to disclose any illness, wounds, scars or sores, deformities, pregnancy or menstrual difficulties. It seems, Bradley argues, a 'reasonable inference that the physical examination on the *castata* reduced the slave to the level of an object – an object that was generally mute, passive, and devoid of any human dignity' (Bradley 1992, 129). Bradley concludes that 'it was as though the slave were in fact an animal' (Bradley 1992, 129). Sales of oxen, cattle and mules, he points out, required similar disclosure of diseases and defects, and jurists made no distinction between animal and human. This chapter and the rest of the book will return to the 'as though', the 'as if' construction of conflating slaves and non-human animals, but Bradley's wider point about the brutality of slavery in the ancient world is important.

The wealth of the rich in Athens was traditionally based on small-scale, scattered landed estates, and there is debate over how much slave labour was employed in agriculture. Fisher's survey of the evidence in the sources concludes that 'all prosperous and rich Athenians owned some slaves, as domestics and status-symbols' and would have used them for agricultural work at peak periods (Fisher 1993, 41). He paints a fairly fluid picture of slave ownership, with some poorer households investing in slaves when they were prospering and selling them again when times got hard. Slaves seem to have cost about twice as much as a cow or an ox, though they were cheaper than a mule, and poor families would have required a sizeable loan to make the purchase. It may well have been worth it for them to employ a few all-purpose slaves much of the time, both for the labour provided and the status it gave them in terms of freedom and citizenship.

Large numbers of 'the most expendable' slaves were employed in the state-owned silver mines (Fisher 1993, 49) doing the most unpleasant, dangerous and unhealthy work. The less dangerous work at the surface was done by less expendable slaves who were bought or hired by the people who leased the land. Slaves were also used in manufacturing weapons, pots, statues, knives, lamps and clothes, and manufacture of such items was an important source of 'new wealth' (Fisher 1993, 50). It is interesting that slaves, even in ancient Greece, were associated with new as well as landed wealth. This seems to me to undermine some of the assumptions behind the old/new slavery split as it operates now. Slavery appears from the start as a flexible, adaptable form of labour and source of wealth. Occupations such as artisanal crafts, smithing or potting were considered to be demeaning, and living by buying and selling encouraged double-dealing and misrepresentation (Fisher 1993, 100). Manufacturing warped the spirit of the free Greek, rendering it slavish 'since the work was done inside, in the dark and crouching over, not outside in the open air with the upright posture of a free man' (Cartledge 1993, 173). It was shameful to be poor and compelled to perform such slavish labour. This brings us back to Harper's description of sordid, servile and laborious beings, fitted by nature for sordid, servile and hard work. Like a domesticated animal, the slave-by-nature helped his or her master by means of their body (Rosivach 1999, 147).

The identification of the slave with the body was central to what it meant to be enslaved in Athens, and it extended beyond their sale and their labour. The testimony of slaves in an Athenian court was admissible only if it had been extracted under physical torture. As Cartledge points out, this was because, by definition, only free men could tell the truth: 'Against the pristine purity of the self-controlled democratic citizen's body there was counterposed ideologically the aboriginal impurity of the un-self-controllable servile body – a body which was controllable, moreover, only by the master's whip' (Cartledge 1993, 175). Corporal punishment was a central and defining feature of what it meant to be a slave. Slaves were understood to lack the moral capacity to lie or to tell the truth without being compelled to do so, 'and so the truth must be sought from their bodies' (Rosivach 1999, 152). Giving evidence in court was a signal of free status, of having witnesses who were prepared to vouch for your story. Open access to the courts, as Fisher argues, was part of what it meant to be free, and so had to be denied to slaves (Fisher 1993, 60).

Slaves were often treated legally as the property of their masters and bought, sold, bequeathed or confiscated 'like land or beds', as

Fisher puts it (Fisher 1993, 62). They could not form sexual relation-ships without their masters' approval, their partners or children might be legally sold, and they were precluded by law from exercising in wrestling grounds or being the lovers of free-born boys. Slaves, Fisher concludes (with an implicit assumption that the slaves are male), 'had to accept that their bodies might be penetrated by free males, but they might not themselves penetrate the bodies of the free, male or female' (Fisher 1993, 62). At the same time, the law assumed that slaves were persons, and had some minimal honour that deserved to be protected. The death of a slave was treated legally as the kill-ing of an inferior person. If the slave were killed by someone other than the master, the master could prosecute the killer for homicide (Fisher 1993, 62). It is important to remember that the process of dehumanisation was never complete, even where slaves were most closely identified with property, limited to their bodies and described as animate tools. It was impossible for them not to be involved in entangled interrelations, not only of chattel and political slavery, but also of social and property relations.

NATURE AND SLAVERY

For Aristotle's structure of slavery to work, to function smoothly, nature needed to erect a physical, tangible difference between the bodies of freemen and the bodies of slaves: 'But nature, though she intends, does not always succeed in achieving a clear distinction between men born to be masters and men born to be slaves' (Aristotle 1995, 1254a13). Nature was able to distinguish slaves from non-slaves, but Frank argues that nature 'secures no absolute boundaries and offers no permanent foun-dations' (Frank 2004, 96) because nature continued to be guided and determined by activity. Natural beings could always be otherwise, and claims about their identities were claims about their activities, and our activities are changeable and in constant interaction with our circum-stances (Frank 2004, 98). The contrary of nature's intention often hap-pened, and so Aristotle argued that slavery by nature was a matter of the differences between souls, so that he could conclude that 'just as some are by nature free, so others are by nature slaves, and for these latter the condition of slavery is both beneficial and just' (Aristotle 1995, 1254b39). Aristotle made a distinction between natural slavery and conventional slavery, and rejected the idea that just slavery could be based on force. For Aristotle, it was a question of enslavability, of who naturally deserved to be in a condition of slavery. If slavery became about force rather than desert, then it would risk enslaving men of higher rank if they happened to be captured and sold. The possibility of slavery as a result of war contradicted the idea of natural slavery, and the categorical claim that 'there are some who are everywhere slaves, and others who are everywhere free' (Aristotle 1995, 1255a21). Those who were 'everywhere slaves' were barbarians. Aristotle pointed out that among barbarians, the female and the slave occupied the same position because there was no naturally ruling element among barbarians.

The assumption was that barbarian and slave were by nature one and the same. For Aristotle, barbarians were naturally slavish, and since most of the slaves in Athens were barbarians, Aristotle can be characterised as accepting that most slaves in his own society were natural slaves (Schofield 1999, 133). Athenian chattel slaves were *barbaroi*, either born outside Greece or born in Greece of forbears who were born outside Greece. Usually, they had names that marked them as *barbaroi*, ethnic labels that were used to denote a 'typical slave' (Rosivach 1999, 129). The Greeks' stereotypes of different peoples were a product of their interactions with them (E. Hall 1989, 108). As the *barbaroi* lived for longer amongst the Greeks, the dominant myths of slavery changed, and instead of being characterised as speaking different languages, they were coded as 'language-less', not speaking any intelligible language at all, but making the sound of twittering birds (Rosivach 1999, 153). Not speaking Greek became a sign of their intellectual deficiency, their inability to command themselves and their lack of interior *logos*. The natural slave was described as always having his neck bent and slanting, and as disproportionately small, ugly or tattooed. The archetypal slave was Aesop, a Thracian who was imagined as 'pot-bellied, weasel-armed, hunchbacked, a squalid, squinty, swarthy midget with crooked legs' (Millett 2007, 196). The Scythian hinterland was seen as remote, intractable, desolate and untamed (E. Hall 1989, 114), and its inhabitants were coded both as nomads, armed with powerful bows, and as unspoiled innocents living in a well-governed utopia. The barbarians were portrayed as impudent, rash and unsophisticated, relying on the 'outdated machismo' of their monarchs that was no match for the 'covert and cunning activities of the Greeks' (E. Hall 1989, 122–3). Many of the stereotypes surrounding the invention of the barbarians coalesced around their inability to restrain their passions. The failure to control his sexual desire was the standard trait of the barbarian male in Greek writers. He was a tyrant who let loose the savage appetites in his soul (E. Hall 1989, 125).

Edith Hall makes the important point that as well as being constructed as savage, violent and highly masculinised, at other times barbarians appear as excessively refined and effeminate, luxuriating in exotic clothing and sumptuous funerals. Their concern for comfort and their excessive displays of grief were part of the 'vocabularies of barbarism' (E. Hall 1989, 128) which emphasised the Greek 'appropriation of moderation' against different kinds of extremes (E. Hall 1989, 127) and the 'systematic feminization of Asia' as emotional and subservient (E. Hall 1989, 157). Hall argues that the Greeks' view of the barbarians was inherently contradictory, incorporating 'the idea not only of primitive chaos, but of a more virtuous era, when men were nearer to the gods' (E. Hall 1989, 149). The Greeks' idea of the past overlaps with their conception of 'the elsewhere', and they lived with and produced a barbarian world of their own that was the home both of savages and tyrants and of idealised, innocent peoples with a harmonious relation to heaven (E. Hall 1989, 149). In terms of thinking about the parallels between ancient Greek slavery and the slavery of the eighteenth and nineteenth centuries, this vision of 'the elsewhere' is strikingly similar to the ways in which Africa was imagined as an uncorrupted state of nature and as a space of savagery and degeneration. For both imperial Greece and colonial Europe and America, the people they enslaved came from a place of no return. Societies outside Europe are positioned in what Nyquist terms 'a privative age', a pre-political space (Nyquist 2013, 16), without ordered social relations, 'a state where slavery is at home' (Nyquist 2013, 17). For Aristotle, man achieved completion as an exemplary human as part of the city, as a citizen (S. D. Collins 2006, 172). He 'is worst of all when apart from law and justice'. In Aristotle, slaves 'and other creatures' were explicitly denied the ability to constitute a polis (Millett 2007, 182). Without the polis, men were rendered unscrupulous and savage. For Jill Frank, the distinction between Greeks and non-Greeks rested not on their immutable natures, but on Aristotle's observations of the behaviours of those foreigners. The proper determinant of slavery, as we have seen, was not foreignness, but worthiness or character and it was these internal characteristics and activities that could justify enslavement (Frank 2004, 101–2). Asians, because they lived in hot climates and under hereditary tyrannies, tended not to act on their own initiative. Living under tyrannies rendered them naturally slavish, and this brings us back to the entangled interrelations between chattel and political slavery that define non-Greeks as natural slaves.

Rachel Zelnick-Abramowitz's study of manumitted slaves in ancient Greece draws attention to the complex statuses in between freedom and slavery that unsettle the freedom/slavery boundary. Freed slaves found themselves subjected to a range of conditions, often including being obliged to remain with their ex-masters for a fixed period. On leaving slavery, they were not wholly free, but in a state of semi-slavery, 'a twilight zone between the completely free and the completely non-free' (Zelnick-Abramowitz 2005, 6). To understand this twilight zone, Zelnick-Abramowitz argues that we need to define slavery in social terms rather than as a property relationship. Manumission was a social transaction involving exchange and reciprocity, and social bonds that protracted dependence. Manumitted slaves did not become citizens, they were barred from taking part in the political process and from land ownership, and they were required to pay a poll tax that marked them as inferior to citizens and to metics and continued to bind them to their former masters. It is important to recognise here the complex social realities behind the binary of slavery and freedom. The metic was less free than the citizen; the foreigner was less free than the metic; the helot was regarded as less slavish than the chattel slave. Zelnick-Abramowitz extends Moses Finley's spectrum of statuses at the free end, insisting that 'freedom itself has different shades' (Zelnick-Abramowitz 2005, 38). Freedom and slavery are better conceived of as dependence and independence, as economic, moral, internal and external, rather than just as property relations.

CONCLUSION

Jill Frank draws attention to the complex relation between nature and politics in Aristotle's theory, and her arguments are important for constructing a historical and dynamic politics of slavery. In her view, Aristotle treats nature as a 'question for politics' (Frank 2004, 92). Human nature is, at least in part, constituted politically and nature and politics are both changeable. This has several important effects. First, it means that citizens are involved in constructing their own identities through making and doing, 'where doing is a kind of self-making' (Frank 2004, 94). Citizens are made citizens by the collective activity of sharing a constitution and making institutions. The polis is an active, dynamic space, full of individuals acting in concert. The fundamental difference between citizens and slaves is that slaves 'are the product of citizen activity alone' (Frank 2004, 95). What starts off looking like a defence of a static model of slavery as based on unchanging constituent elements turns out to be a theory that it is politics that produces the institutions that help make citizens and slaves. Human beings and the polity itself emerge 'as both natural and made' (Frank 2004, 99).

On this reading, human nature is vulnerable to and shaped by both politics and by self-determining activity (Frank 2004, 102). Aristotle's defence of natural slavery 'at the same time serves as a warning about the dangers slavery poses to politics' (Frank 2004, 102). In the end, according to Frank's interpretation of Aristotle, Greeks can become slaves if they act like slaves. Even the hierarchies of the polity and the household are insecure and reversible. Aristotle is offering not immutability, but perpetual 'boundary-setting and keeping' (Frank 2004, 102). This is an important corrective to a static conception of slavery as fixed by nature, and opens up for discussion what DuBois (2005, 109) calls 'the strangeness of slaves', their unsettled status at the boundary of subject of object, their instability as both property and partner. It shows us how problematic the idea of 'dehumanisation' can be when it gets divorced from these intensely political questions of boundary-setting and keeping. It takes us back to Aristotle's own emphasis on the participatory and deliberative character of politics and challenges us to think again about our capacity to see which means will lead to the given ends. In thinking about the spaces in between slavery and freedom, and in between the household and the polis, women, slaves and barbarians emerge from their privative state of nature into 'a complex, cross-institutional, cross-discursive' world of politics (Nyquist 2013, 27). At the same time, I am not convinced that the boundaries of this space are so porous that Greeks could become slaves if they acted like slaves, or that all the relations between master and slave were social rather than property relations. There is something about Aristotle, about the nature of political rule and the structure of the soul, and about the private world of the individual set against the public world of the citizen, that fixes that difference between those who are considered as full moral subjects and those who are lacking, duplicated and incomplete. In the next chapter, the focus is on Locke and his understanding of the space in between slavery and freedom, and in particular the borderland between the state of nature and civil society. The social relations of slavery in the seventeenth century continued to be intensely political, and deeply concerned with boundary-setting and keeping, even as the ground shifted over the nature of slavery and the intersections between subject and object.

Chapter 3

LOCKE AND HUTCHESON: INDIANS, VAGABONDS AND DRONES

'How could Locke's passionate advocacy of universal natural rights be squared with an institution that annihilated these rights altogether?' (Farr 1986, 263). Locke returns us to questions of slavery and war, and to the status of barbarians. I have written elsewhere about Locke's theory of property and its relationship to colonialism, and about the distinction he makes between drudgery and slavery. In this chapter, I consider Locke's vexed relationship to the idea and the politics of slavery in more detail. What is the significance of his personal connections to the slave trade and to the institution of slavery in Carolina? In accounting for the politics behind slavery, Locke helps us to explore some of the links between theory and practice, and between ideology and context. In studying these links, what emerges is an ambiguity and a complexity that is perhaps unexpected from a modern perspective within which slavery is regarded as a universal wrong and natural rights as underpinning our understanding of that wrongness. This chapter is not about resolving the contradictions that emerge, but about exploring what they mean for the politics of slavery. Neither is it my aim to condemn or to exonerate Locke as an individual, but rather to think about how his involvement in the slave trade fits with his wider theory and worldview and about how later reactions to and interpretations of his theory have shaped how we give slavery a history and how we think about it as a political relation.

LOCKE'S THEORY OF SLAVERY

In 1668, Locke was appointed secretary to the Lords Proprietors of Carolina and helped to write its Fundamental Constitutions, which granted every free man absolute power and authority over his 'Negro slaves', and at the same time made it lawful for slaves to choose their own congregations and guaranteed their freedom of conscience. Their baptism allowed for the existence of Christian slaves, who remained subject to the civil dominion of their masters. In 1671, Locke took out shares in the new Royal African Company and in 1672 he was part of the company of merchant adventurers trading in slaves with the Bahamas. In 1673, he became secretary to the Council of Trade and Foreign Plantations and served until 1674. The *Two Treatises* was finally published in 1689, and in 1696 he was appointed commissioner of the Board of Trade, dealing in particular with slavery in Virginia. Throughout his career, as James Farr argues, Locke had intimate knowledge of colonial life, slavery and the slave trade (Farr 1986, 269).

Chapter IV of the *Second Treatise*, 'On Slavery', tells us that a man cannot by compact, or his own consent, enslave himself to anyone. He cannot put himself under the arbitrary power of another because 'No body can give more Power than he has himself; and he that cannot take away his own Life, cannot give another power over it' (Locke [1689] 1991, §23). Slavery, according to Locke, is a forfeit. It is possible for an individual to forfeit his life by some act that deserves death, and his conqueror can then choose whether to put his captive to death or to delay his execution and instead 'make use of him to his own Service' (Locke [1689] 1991, §23). This is not an injury to the enslaved because 'whenever he finds the hardship of his Slavery out-weigh the value of his Life, 'tis in his Power, by resisting the Will of his Master, to draw on himself the Death he desires' (Locke [1689] 1991, §23). The only possible agency that the slave can exercise as the protagonist in his own life is to engineer his own death. The deferral of death is not about preservation, but is simply a part of the victor's right to kill: 'From the enslaved's perspective, it results in an infinitely prolonged social death accompanied by the ongoing threat of physical death' (Nyquist 2013, 346). For Locke, this is the perfect condition of slavery, which is the state of war continued between a lawful conqueror and a captive. Farr locates Locke's just-war theory of justified slavery in the tradition of natural law, and makes the link back to Grotius in particular. Grotius argued against Aristotle that no man is by nature the slave of another, but he proposed that men could become slaves 'by a human Fact', such as agreement, crime or conquest (Farr 2008, 502). Locke adapts Grotius's argument to limit the idea of slavery by rejecting the possibility of slavery by agreement, and by arguing that conquerors in a just war could not enslave whole populations or impose slavery on subsequent generations.

For Locke, slavery was not possible by agreement because no one can hand over to another 'that which he hath not in himself, a Power over his own Life' (Locke [1689] 1991, §24). Slavery was the ultimate consequence of coercive force, and never of consent. For Locke, slavery existed as a matter of fact when 'a conqueror subdues his enemies and forces them to exist under absolute bondage' (Farr 1986, 270). This means, as Farr points out, that slavery is not in all cases categorically unjust. The 'act that deserves death' was committed by a free, equal and rational being who violated the natural rights of other free men (Farr 1986, 271). In this, Locke was refuting Aristotle's claim that by nature some are free and others slaves. Enslavement had to be the result of unjust action and aggression, and only a just war could justify slavery (Farr 1986, 272). Locke was arguing for 'the (im)possibility of voluntarily electing degraded, unfree human status' (Nyquist 2013, 348). Freedom is something that can only be taken away by force, 'by coercive conversion into enslavement' (Nyquist 2013, 351). As Mary Nyquist argues, slavery and the state of war need to be understood as mutually constitutive. In the state of war, the aggressor uses force to subjugate and enslave the victim, and the criminalised captive is never shown to consent to enslavement.

The Lockean individual may legitimately destroy a man who makes war on him for the same reason that he may kill a wolf or a lion. It is reasonable that the liberal subject has the right to destroy anything that threatens him with destruction, and the would-be destroyers are not under the 'ties of the Common Law of Reason' but live according to the rules of force and violence, and so may be treated as 'Beasts of Prey, those dangerous and noxious Creatures, that will be sure to destroy him, whenever he falls into their Power' (Locke [1689] 1991, §16). The hostile aggressor, as Nyquist points out, appears even more threatening in the plural. In response to this aggressor, Locke constructed 'the Euro-colonial civil subject' in the singular, as an individual who cannot part with his freedom, but who can hold the power of life and death over his 'criminalized counterpart' (Nyquist 2013, 343–4), the thief who uses force when he has no right, who introduces a state of war 'and is *aggressor* in it' (Locke [1689] 1991, §18). The liberal subject cannot voluntarily transfer the power over his own life that he does not have, but at the same time he comes to hold 'despotical' power over the enslaved, substituting the threat of death as a means of extracting labour.

The victor, the liberal subject, is a slaveholder and Locke defends the slaveholders' legitimate power over their slaves. In the Fundamental Constitutions of Carolina, Locke assumed the existence of slavery and affirmed the slaveholders' power of life and death. The planter in the West Indies and the freeman of Carolina were understood to have the legislative power of life and death over their 'Negro slaves'. This 'despotical' power was a function of ownership and was operated in order to impose labour discipline. It could only obtain outside of civil society where it was 'as limitless as the state of war itself' (Nyquist 2013, 346). It was a legitimate form of power, unlike tyranny – the power of the conqueror over the conquered in an unjust war – but it was incompatible with civil society. Despotical power was a relation between individuals, a private power, exercised within the household but with its origins in the military power of the victor in warfare (Nyquist 2013, 333). In this sense, the institution of slavery was 'categorically not political' (Nyquist 2013, 332). The slave was not granted the possibility of legitimate political resistance because just-war slavery was not a political act but one that took place outside of civil society. Enslavement occurred in a state of war, separated off from civil society. As soon as there was a compact between the conqueror and the captive, and power and obedience were regulated by consent, the state of war and slavery ceased 'as long as the Compact endures' (Locke [1689] 1991, §24).

The slavery that just war could justify was limited, and Locke explicitly ruled out the seizure of wives and children, who were taken to be innocent victims: 'They made not the War, nor assisted in it' (Locke [1689] 1991, §183). The children, whatever may have happened to their fathers, were free. The conqueror had no right of dominion over the children. Their lives and their futures could not be forfeited. Land, too, had to be protected, and the destruction of a year or two's produce was the 'utmost spoil' that could be taken, leaving intact the perpetual inheritance of land 'where all is possessed, and none remains waste to be taken up by him, that is disseiz'd' (Locke [1689] 1991, §184). The conqueror had no right of dominion over those who joined him in the war, or over the posterity of his enemies (Locke [1689] 1991, §185). Farr argues that this means Locke ruled out hereditary slavery, or slavery as an institution, as unjust, and placed severe constraints on what counts as 'just slavery' (Farr 1986, 273). The African slave trade and chattel slavery in the seventeenth century lay far beyond these limits and was unjust because of the ways in which slaves were captured, the enslavement of women and children, and the inheritance of slavery as permanent bondage. For Farr, this means that Locke cannot have regarded Afro-American slavery as a justifiable institution, and he cannot have regarded the slave raids to capture black Africans as just wars (Farr 1986, 276). Farr's point is that 'Locke could have been explicit about tying new world slavery to just wars, had he wanted or intended' (Farr 2008, 505). Instead, his focus was on England and the Whig resistance to Stuart absolutism as 'the site in mind' (Farr 2008, 506), and from that site his restrictions on Grotius make sense. Farr concludes that Locke 'was making a case against "slavery" on *his* island, not *for* slavery in the new world' (Farr 2008, 507). Throughout the reception history of the *Second Treatise,* Farr argues, '*no one* thought Locke *succeeded* in justifying slavery in America' (Farr 2008, 515). This approach tends to de-politicise or at least de-racialise Locke's theory of just-war slavery, and as Nyquist argues, allows slavery to escape from being a political institution by placing it outside the boundaries of civil society.

LOCKE AND THE INDIANS

Farr then goes on to consider the question of Locke's racism, and points to Locke's silence and the lack of evidence of his 'assessment of black people' (Farr 1986, 277). Farr is intrigued by Locke's opinions of American Indians and his positive assessment of their natural reason and modes of government. He cannot be counted as a degeneracy theorist, and he says nothing about black Africans morally deserving their slavery (Farr 1986, 280). In assessing Locke's racism in 2008, Farr gives weight to the specifically racialised reference to 'Negro' slaves in the Carolina Constitution, but does not find in Locke a racist doctrine or theory that normatively justified slavery on the basis of race (Farr 2008, 510). Farr concludes, along with John Dunn, that Locke was guilty of immoral evasion and of living with a glaring contradiction that made him 'strangely indifferent' to the lives and liberties of the people made slaves in the new world (Farr 2008, 516). In order to understand what was going on, we have to read Locke's work in the context of the threat of royal absolutism, his rejection of sovereignty by conquest and his justification of political resistance. 'For this fight', says Farr, 'the shores of Africa and America were out of sight and

out of mind' (Farr 1986, 285). In saying nothing, he 'averted his eyes from
the glaring contradiction between his theories and Afro-American slavery' and invested alongside his patrons (Farr 1986, 281). This turning aside
is interesting. For some, it means that we too can sigh and move along,
leaving the question of transatlantic slavery to one side and focusing on
Locke's attack on absolutism in Britain. For others, it means that we need
to interrogate Locke's theory of slavery more creatively and fill in some of
the gaps ourselves. Both these approaches assume that we are being confronted with some kind of contradiction within the theory, a problem that
needs solving. In this chapter, I want to take a slightly different approach
by arguing that we need to understand Locke's theory in the context of
a process of racialisation, and the seventeenth century as a transitional
phase in the development of the social imaginary of slavery. We need
to pay attention to the interplay between the material conditions of the
actors and the cultural and ideological processes within which they operated (Garner 2007a). By focusing on the questions of enslavability, civil
society and humanness, Locke's 'strange indifference' to Afro-American
slavery emerges in a different light.

In Nyquist's analysis of Locke's account, non-Christians living outside Europe are habitually charged with the kind of monstrous crimes
that convert them into beasts of prey and noxious creatures. Africans,
she argues, are 'more or less expected to enter readily into Locke's state
of war, since in "hard" versions of the privative age they are basically
already there' (Nyquist 2013, 360). In her reading of Locke on America,
Nyquist argues that he shares the dominant early modern view that
the people already living there 'inhabit a precivil temporality or privative age' (Nyquist 2013, 336), a view that animalises and criminalises
the indigenous people and provides a rationale for taking their lives.
The process of racialisation, the opposition between the subject and the
slave, and the legitimacy of despotic power operating outside of civil
society, meant that first Native Americans and later Africans could be
'construed as subhuman, monstrous transgressors' (Nyquist 2013, 337).
This is part of what David Armitage has identified as a well-developed
'colonial reading' of Locke's political theory and of the *Second Treatise*
in particular (Armitage 2004). It rests on the argument put forward by
Martin Seliger that war between the planters and the natives was inevitable, and that the indigenous people's defence of their 'waste' land
turned them into aggressors and the Europeans into the 'just conquerors' (Seliger 1968, 115). Taken further into the African context, slave

raids count as just wars. On this reading, Locke's theory is taken as underpinning settler colonialism and the erasure of Indigenous territorial claims to land (Hoogeveen 2015, 122). On the whole, here and elsewhere (Brace 2004), I endorse this 'colonial reading', but in relation to slavery, we need to consider a more complicated and nuanced picture of these subhuman, monstrous transgressors.

It is important to remember that early modern English people 'did not think of the world in modern racialized terms' (Guasco 2007, 390). As Michael Guasco points out, their encounters with indigenous peoples in America were conditioned by questions of national identity, natural philosophy, and environment rather than by biological differences. William Uzgalis argues that Locke provides a non-racist account of the differences between peoples because the differences he saw between Englishmen and those in other lands were 'purely cultural' (Uzgalis 2002, 83, 87). In his *Letter Concerning Toleration*, Locke made clear that pagans could be strict observers of the rules of equity and the laws of nature, and argued that they should not be turned out of their lands and inheritance on the grounds of religion. Uzgalis argues that Locke's account of the reason required to exercise rights of life, health, liberty and property is less Eurocentric than others, such as Barbara Arneil and James Tully, claim. Native Americans in the state of nature were human, reasonable people 'in the full sense of that term' (Uzgalis 2002, 89), living according to the law of nature without violating the rights of others. Men became fully human when they conformed to natural law by thinking for themselves and acting on their reason. The wilderness in which they lived was like the sea, the last great commons, and Europeans could settle on the Indians' hunting grounds as long as they left enough and as good for the natives, but they were not entitled to appropriate agricultural land. Native American land that was tilled and cultivated, but not fenced counted as property for Locke (Uzgalis 2002, 91). Uzgalis interprets Locke as suggesting that there was 'enough room in America for both colonists and Native Americans' (Uzgalis 2002, 95).

Locke focused on reason as the measure of how the individual attains his status as a full moral being, and he drew a distinction between someone exercising unrestrained liberty and exercising a liberty constrained by moral judgement (Marden 2006, 93). Reason depended on ideas, and ideas depended on the environment, and this approach 'potentially placed a crippling limitation on the scope of reflection possible in underdeveloped societies' (D. Carey 2006, 70). The conditions of their existence meant that they risked missing out on a range of ideas of great importance. They were not dispossessed of their reason, but their lives left them 'so little Use of it, that one cannot but wonder how the Soul can be depressed into so low a Degree of Brutality' (D. Carey 2006, 89). Some categories of people had such major natural or cultural disabilities that they were incapable of self-control, and were figured as lacking in virtue and competence, and so in the moral worthiness that would entitle them to rights and designate them as human (Marden 2006). They failed to use their minds and expand their horizons, thinking only about the ordinary wants of the body: fishing, hunting, dancing and revenge. They lived 'mued up within their own contracted Territories' (D. Carey 2006, 89), their freedom restricted by the contingencies of life, and their use of reason unreliable. When Locke considered the 'primitive', he concluded that their notions were few and narrow, borrowed from the objects they had the most to do with, and their heads were filled with 'Love and Hunting' according to the fashion of their tribes. A 'wild Inhabitant of the Woods', he decided, would seldom mention general propositions or abstract maxims, or be capable of innate speculative principles (D. Carey 2006, 87). At the same time, and importantly unlike African slaves, they were active men, and apt to learn, according to Richard Ligon in 1647, but also craftier and subtler than 'the Negroes' (Guasco 2007, 403).

As Nancy Hirschmann argues about landless workers and women, Indians were positioned as less rational than landowners because the pragmatic realities of their lives created a disjuncture between their natural potential and what they could actually do with their reason (Hirschmann 2008). Even the most advanced minds among primitive peoples 'would lack an array of thoughts extending beyond their circle' (D. Carey 2006, 90) because they did not take part in conversation with thinking men, balancing rival positions in the search for truth. Like women and landless workers, their minds could not achieve the 'comprehensive enlargement' (D. Carey 2006, 91) required to underpin right reason, positive liberty and self-mastery. They were bracketed together with women, children and idiots, and their relationship to reason and so to liberty had to be understood as 'uncertain and incomplete' (Hirschmann 2008, 116). In Locke's essay on the *Conduct of Understanding*, Indians are not characterised as being born with worse understandings than the Europeans, and their exercise of reason remained possible, but to 'achieve sufficient moral sophistication one needed to enter a polite and civil world' (D. Carey 2006, 91). A more improved English man had the benefit of living in a superior society, and the diligence and industry to pursue higher conceptions of the divine. Unlike Aristotle's natural slaves with their deformed souls, there was nothing intrinsically slavish about the Amerindians, but their circumstances made them potentially enslavable, in ways that set them apart from Europeans.

Brad Hinshelwood argues that the context of Locke's theory'was not the coasts of Africa, but instead the forests of Carolina' (Hinshelwood 2013, 564), and in particular the Indian slave trade. For Hinshelwood, Locke should be read as developing a just-war theory that works hard to protect the property and freedom of those outside the conflict by placing clear limits on justifiable slavery. He did so in the context of the proprietors in Carolina trying to balance their interests with Indian rights (Hinshelwood 2013, 568). Early in the development of the colony, the Indians acted as trading partners and advisers, but where the colonists found themselves, or at least their servants and their crops, under attack, they sometimes took Indians prisoner and shipped them to the West Indies as slaves (Hinshelwood 2013, 569). For some colonists, this trade was a way of making a quick profit compared to the burden of trying to make money from the land. The settlers failed to develop a cash crop for the colony, and turned instead to this alternative source of income. During the 1670s, the settlers in Carolina were involved in conflict with the Coosa and fought wars with the Westo, and'began to speak of Indian slavery in just-war terms that resonate with Locke's theory of slavery' (Hinshelwood 2013, 569). The colonists, Hinshelwood argues, were careful to portray their slaves as captives taken in just wars, and their own actions as punishment.

According to Hinshelwood, Locke maintained an interest in Carolina, and its agricultural improvement in particular, during the late 1670s and the 1680s, while he was writing the *Second Treatise*. The textual evidence (from a change in his citation style that helps to date the composition of the chapters of the *Second Treatise*) suggests that Locke was working on his theory of slavery in 1682 at the same time as he was revising the Fundamental Constitutions after a 'devastating war spurred by the Indian slave trade that had seriously undermined his patron's interests in the colony' (Hinshelwood 2013, 574). Shaftesbury regarded war for trade as illegitimate, but a defensive war against Indians who destroyed crops was justified. In this context of wars in the colony, most of those who were enslaved were male warriors who were shipped to Barbados, so that hereditary Indian slavery'was not a concern for Locke and the Proprietors' (Hinshelwood 2013, 576). In other words, this form of enslavement met Locke's criteria for justified, limited slavery because women and children were largely unaffected, and the land and property rights of later generations and of those who did not take part were left intact. From his analysis of Locke's involvement in Carolina, Hinshelwood concludes that the conditions there 'provide an example of real-world practices that the theory could work to justify' (Hinshelwood 2013, 580). The Carolinian context allows us to understand why Locke attempts to legitimate slavery, and to see that he was supportive of at least some of the forms of slavery that were practised there (Hinshelwood 2013, 581). For Hinshelwood, this allows us to restore the colonies to our understanding of Locke's theory of slavery, 'while avoiding the interpretive problems that arise from linking the *Second Treatise* to African slavery' (Hinshelwood 2013, 582).

People in the seventeenth century did not regard the indigenous inhabitants of America as a separate race in the modern sense of the term, but that was not enough to make them 'safe' or to secure them against enslavement. The grounds for justifying slavery were like shifting sands, moving between essence and circumstance, and proving the instability of otherness. On Locke's account, where, in the beginning, all the world was America, America 'exists as kind of embryo'. The Indians gave the Europeans an insight into the development of civil societies: 'they show us our history' (D. Carey 2006, 95) rather than creating their own. The Indians were subjected to a narrative in which their current practices would be transformed into those of Europe. The salient differences between Amerindians and Europeans were not fixed and incommensurable but 'temporary and occasioned by historical situation' (D. Carey 2006, 95). The Indians found themselves in a temporal trap, unable to leave the state of nature, but still a part of the passage of history.

In the late seventeenth century, English government officials recognised that if the English wanted Indian land they would have to buy it, and treat the Indians as the owners of their land (Banner 2005, 10). Their claim to property could not come from conquest, and in the end much of the land acquired by the settlers came to them through purchase. The colonists in America found Indians who were farmers and owners of their land, but who moved on when their soils were depleted and they were allocated new fields by the village chief. In comparison to the cramped conditions of England, Indian farmers had more space and more room to move. In terms of property rights, the ideas of occupation, use and cultivation were highly contested. It was not that Locke's theory of property denied the Indian's claim to the deer that he killed, but there were doubts over whether indigenous activity extended to resources such as land (Ypi 2013, 164). If the American Indians were landowners, did they own their hunting grounds as well as their fields? What about the lands that lay fallow, waiting to be cultivated when the soil depleted? What about the waste land? Did the whole of North America belong to them?

The settlers were inconsistent in their claims, often starting by relying on narratives of honourable conquest and ending up relying on purchase or gift as the basis of exchange. By the early nineteenth century, settler Americans came to think of the Indians as nomadic hunters and they constructed them as only owning the land they cultivated and not their hunting grounds. Their mobility and their use of space meant that they were seen as not actually needing the land: 'land simply did not relate to their culturally specific ends in a way that was relevant to ground property claims' (Ypi 2013, 165). De Vattel argued that the Native Americans had no reason to complain if other more industrious and populated nations came to take possession of parts of their land because the 'people of those extensive tracts rather ranged through than inhabited them' (Ypi 2013, 165). Gradually, the property rights of the indigenous peoples were weakened as the colonists rethought the legal relationship between Indians and their land. The courts decided that their claim to occupy the land should not carry with it 'a permanent right to exclude needy settlers' (Ypi 2013, 166). The indigenous people had a duty to receive the colonists. Like their grasp of reason, their hold on their land was uncertain and incomplete. They had interests in the realm of right, but they were structurally incapable of making the right choices in the realm of virtue (Hirschmann 2008). The right of occupancy replaced the idea of Indians as landowners, and the government took over from the tribes as the fee simple owner of the land. The freedom of the Indians was a social relation, determined for them by others, and by their material conditions as well as by the cultural and ideological processes that were constructing the social category of whiteness to exclude them (Garner 2007b). Their relationship to the land was not fixed or static, but it was intimately connected to their access to civil society and to 'humanness' as a political category.

As Stuart Banner points out, the story of colonisation was about the power to establish legal conventions and rules to enforce land transactions (Banner 2005, 6). Colonialism involves 'both the subjugation of one people to another and the political and economic control of a dependent territory (or parts of it)' (Ypi 2013, 162). It grants certain prerogatives to colonists but denies them to natives, allowing one side to place constraints on acquisition and decide the extent, limits and enforcement of property rights (Ypi 2013, 167). For Ypi, the wrong of colonialism lies in the kind of political relation it exemplifies, and in particular the establishment of a form of association that 'fails to offer equal and reciprocal terms of interaction to all its members' (Ypi 2013, 178). The colonial injustice at stake then becomes not the wrongful taking of territory but 'the establishment of an objectionable form of political association' (Ypi 2013, 187). To understand the wrong, Ypi argues, we need to focus on the terms of political interaction between colonisers and colonised. We also need to recognise, as Nyquist argues, that through this process, indigenous people were placed outside politics and the possibility of resistance (Nyquist 2013, 367). In terms of slavery, this is about recognising that slavery is not a static institution. We need to think about it as a cultural construction that emerges out of 'negotiations between Europeans and indigenous peoples, rulers and ruled, and men and women' (Guasco 2007, 389). Michael Guasco argues that the case of Indian slavery also allows us to see that the early settlers in America justified and understood the enslavement of Indians in different ways from their simultaneous enslavement of African peoples (Guasco 2007, 390). Locke certainly fits this pattern in keeping the different slaveries distinct, and his approach highlights the dynamic histories and power relations that underpin slavery. In early Anglo-America, Indian slavery was 'a problem related to the construction of legitimate Anglo-American societies' (Guasco 2007, 390). This legitimacy question was simply not raised in the case of enslaving Africans for their labour, but the enslavement of Indians unsettled assumptions about who could be enslaved and for what ends, and about the enterprise of colonialism.

In part, what was at stake was differentiating British colonialism from Spanish cruelty and destruction. This involved opening up the possibility that 'Indians *could* be enslaved but, unlike Africans, only for reasons that might be applied to the English themselves or the inhabitants of other recognized nations' (Guasco 2007, 395). There were moments when indigenous people emerged as 'candidates for Christian instruction and inclusion in the Anglo-American community' (Guasco 2007, 398), usually on the basis of their status as trading partners and as allies against Spain. The possibility of justifiable enslavement was linked to the idea of just-war slavery as punishment (which, as Guasco says, was often understood as redemption), and to a whole set of stories about military origins and defeat, rather than about bodies naturally fitted for hard labour. Even where indigenous people were taken captive, such as the Pequot Indians in 1637, the English distinguished them from Africans. When they needed to bring the Pequots closer to enslaved Africans, they labelled them as cannibals and as 'negros'. As Guasco points out, this was not about ethnic confusion or conflation, but about aligning the Indian with 'the definitive slave in the broader Atlantic world' (Guasco 2007, 399). It was part of their punishment, of their social death and of their generalised dishonour to be rebranded as 'cannibal negros'. The plan was to train them up in the principles of religion and then ship them back to New England to convert their compatriots to Christianity. In this seventeenth-century context, slavery was treated as 'an agent of conversion' (Guasco 2007, 399), carrying within it the seeds of redemption. This was only possible in a world where the indigenous Americans had something in common with the Englishmen who enslaved them, and certainly shared reason and humanity with them. The enslavement of the Pequot, according to Roger Williams, should have normative limits: it should only be temporary, and it should include instruction in Christian morality. This kind of slavery within strict limits was 'their path to salvation' (Guasco 2007, 400). Guasco argues that this was part of a wider 'utopian conception of slavery' within which enslavement was used as part of the criminal justice system, as a means of punishing not only Indians but also English settlers, such as William Andrews who assaulted his master in Massachusetts in 1638 (Guasco 2007, 401). In other words, enslavability could be extended to the English poor.

ENSLAVING THE ENGLISH POOR

This possibility of enslaving the English poor opens up all sorts of questions about the construction of the social category of whiteness that was in transition in the seventeenth century. As Steve Garner makes clear, it took generations for 'free labour' to refer unequivocally to whites and 'unfree' labour to blacks. Not being white and being black were two different things in the seventeenth and eighteenth centuries, when the national and the racial coexisted, and Irish indentured labourers in the Caribbean, for example, found themselves subject to direct social control through a pass system and the withdrawal of the right to bear arms (Garner 2007b). The Irish's hold on their whiteness was tenuous, but unlike black, Mexican, Asian and Native American people, they were 'always salvageable for whiteness' (Garner 2007b, 126), and could potentially be incorporated into the dominant element of society. Their access to whiteness was mediated through their labour and their relationship to the market as whiteness became a kind of property. Slavery, indenture and the free market were influential in specifying and assigning whiteness and blackness, and these processes of racialisation were about differentiating Indians from 'Negroes', and both from Europeans. The eighteenth-century schemes for enslaving the English poor were about slavery as conversion and redemption, but also about the fragility of some people's grasp on their status as members of civil society (Locke [1697] 1997).

Locke was harsh in his analysis of the character of the poor, and attributed their growing numbers to the relaxation of discipline and the corruption of manners. As Hirschmann puts it, 'Locke believed that people were poor because they were lazy and corrupt' (Hirschmann 2002, 336). He regarded the poor as a burden on the public, due to their lack of industry and virtue, and his proposals to reform the poor laws centred on setting the poor to work and making them useful to the public. This involved distinguishing the deserving from the undeserving, those with moral worthiness from those without. The first step towards setting the poor on work 'ought to be a restraint on their debauchery' (Locke [1697] 1997, 184) by suppressing brandy shops and unnecessary alehouses. The impulse behind Locke's proposals for reforming the poor law was to ease part of 'the burden that lies upon the industrious for maintaining the poor' (Locke [1697] 1997, 184). His answer to poverty was work. Vagrants and 'begging drones' were characterised not only as idle, but also as fraudulent and dishonest, and as an inferior order of men (Hundert 1972, 6–7). They pretended that they could not get work, and lived 'unnecessarily upon other people's labour' (Locke [1697] 1997, 184). His proposals for amending the poor law included compulsory labour and punishment for the able-bodied, to correct them through discipline and close supervision. Unlawful male beggars living in a maritime county were to be taken to a seaport town, 'there to be kept at hard labour, til some of his majesty's ships . . . give an opportunity of putting them onboard, where they shall serve three years, under strict discipline' (Locke [1697] 1997, 186). He also recommended that the children of poor families should be put into 'working schools', a euphemism for working in wool-spinning factories, to allow both parents to work for wages and the children not to be a burden on the parish. They were to be paid not in wages, but in food, or more specifically bread and water, and warm gruel in the winter (Hirschmann 2002, 338). This diet fits with Locke's wider recommendations for children's upbringing and education, and, as Hirschmann points out, these strictures were about building health, mental discipline, reason and character, rather than about punishment (Hirschmann 2002, 339). Locke's scheme aimed to accustom the children to work, inculcating habits of sobriety and industriousness, and rooting out irrationality. Like the Native Americans, the English poor were not constitutionally irrational, they possessed the capacity for natural reason, but their 'poverty was evidence of a failure to *use* their God-given rationality' (Hirschmann 2002, 339). Drones who lived off the labour of others found that their reason deteriorated from lack of use, and they no longer reached the threshold of full personhood. Their failure to work was 'both an indication and further cause of their irrationality and idleness' (Hirschmann 2002, 342). True and proper relief of the poor consisted of finding work for them and taking care they did not live parasitically on the labour of others (Locke [1697] 1997, 189). The failure of the poor lay in their passivity, their lack of self-discipline and their failure to seek out property, even in their own person, where 'seeking property is not just the most fundamental of rights, it is the essence of human individuality' (Hirschmann 2002, 348).

It is important to bring Locke's scheme to force the poor to work together with his theory of slavery because it helps to explain something of his 'strange indifference' towards Afro-American slavery. In the *Essay on the Poor Law*, it is possible to see how labour is treated as the property not of the poor themselves, but of the industrious. People needed to be restrained from living off the labour of others and making themselves a burden on the public. The short step in Locke's thought is not from just wars to slave raiding expeditions, but from three years of forced labour to permanent bondage. The common denominator is the idea that some people are so incapable of using their rationality that they have to be forced to work. The contradictions in Locke's thought are not about his personal involvement in the slave trade or about his racism, but about emerging conceptions of civilisation, 'humanness' and civil society. His theory reconfigures the intersection between subject and object, and enters the complicated space in between slavery and freedom where the meanings of personhood and humanity were pulled apart.

In the early to mid-eighteenth century there were several projects to promote slavery in England. They fitted into the utopian conception of slavery as a tool for improvement and the public good, and as an effective and useful punishment for criminals. The reformers targeted 'vagabonds' and vagrants whom they characterised as drunk, cursing and blaspheming, and as incapable of productive work. There were proposals to employ them, to set them to work hedging and ditching. Reformers drew on the distinction between the deserving and the undeserving poor, fellow citizens and vagabonds, and focused on control over the labour of the underclass. They proposed a limited version of slavery for the English poor. Servants under such a scheme, Francis Hutcheson argued, would retain all the rights of mankind and be able to hold them against their masters, 'excepting only *that* to his labours, which he has transferred to his master' (Hutcheson 1755, 200). The masters would have no power of life and death over the slaves, and the servant remained subject to the law rather than to the arbitrary power of the master as an individual. They would have a right to obtain support and to defend themselves by violence against 'any savage useless tortures, any attempts of maiming them or prostituting them to the lusts of their masters, or forcing them in any worship against their consciences' (Hutcheson 1755, 201). These limits to violence distinguished this scheme from true slavery, and Hutcheson argued that this kind of slavery, used as punishment or to discharge a debt, had 'a just foundation' (Hutcheson 1755, 202). It was an effective way to promote general industry and to restrain idleness. Slavery was a proper punishment for people who ruined themselves and their families through intemperance and other vices, 'and made them a publick burden' (Hutcheson 1755, 202). Hutcheson suggested that there could be a trial period of seven years enslavement after which people could be set free if they were found to have acquired the habit of diligence. If not, 'they should be adjudged to slavery for life' as a useful punishment (Hutcheson 1755, 202). For both Locke and Hutcheson, slavery was legitimate as long as the enslaved had in some way forfeited their liberty and therefore the idleness of poor and masterless men, their refusal to seek property or to activate their property in the person, justified forcing their labour out of them. Rozbicki argues that this 'should make us sensible of the deep, taken-for-granted, elitist rather than universalist meaning of liberty used in the whole argument' (Rozbicki 2001, 38). For Rozbicki, this combination of natural rights and slavery should not be viewed as a contradiction or an inconsistency. We need, he says, to think about slavery and liberty not as ideas but as specific social relations. If we do so, he argues, we uncover a 'deeply hierarchical understanding of society' based on the master/servant dichotomy within which liberty 'continued to be largely understood as class privilege, applicable in full only to a group entitled to it by property, reason, and virtue' (Rozbicki 2001, 39).

This conception of servitude was about maintaining social order through subordination to the patriarchal authority of the elites, who sustained a notion of freedom that could contain inequalities that were regarded as just and justifiable (Rozbicki 2001, 39–40). Within this scheme of freedom and subordination, servants and slaves 'had no sovereignty over their rights, nor were these rights separate from their duties as a lower, labouring order' (Rozbicki 2001, 40). Vagabonds and 'begging drones', those who failed to seek property even in themselves, were regarded as almost a different order of beings, 'virtual outsiders' who were irrational and morally depraved. Beadles, Locke suggested, should be authorised to seize upon any stranger begging in the streets (Locke [1697] 1997, 197). Beggars needed to be saved from themselves through servitude and, if necessary, a system of state-sponsored slavery. The few were enslavable for the good of the whole. It was an approach that 'amplified class distinctions' and reinforced hierarchical social relations (Rozbicki 2001, 44) through an emphasis on punishment, work and moral reformation.

In the early eighteenth century, the distance between servitude and slavery was easily travelled. Rozbicki concludes from his analysis of early eighteenth-century proposals for slavery as poor relief that slavery within Britain was not necessarily regarded as socially and legally anomalous. This in turn means that Rozbicki assigns race a relatively small role in legal decisions about slavery during the eighteenth century. By understanding liberty as a social relation, he argues that we can see its contemporary meanings as involving 'a spectrum of freedoms, assigned in various manners and degrees to different ranks of society' (Rozbicki 2001, 47). It should come as no surprise to us that such a tradition was able to accommodate the enslavement of all kinds

of non-rights-bearing individuals deemed not to be morally com-
petent. In this context, slavery was 'an act of charity' to promote the
public good. It was possible to imagine a form of slavery that did not
violate individual rights or liberties, since no crime 'can change a rational creature into a piece of goods void of all right' (Hutcheson 1755,
202–3). Slavery could be legally and morally justified, even in England
and even within the natural right tradition, providing it was a response
to damage, debauchery or debt.

NEW WORLD SLAVERY

The connections between slavery, punishment and the state were
complex and by comparing the proposals to enslave the English poor
with the actual enslavement of black Africans in the Caribbean in the
seventeenth and early eighteenth centuries we can see to the end of
the 'spectrum of freedoms' and into a form of slavery that was understood to change a rational creature into a piece of goods. There is, of
course, a difference between being forced to labour for the state for
three or seven years and being subjected to permanent slavery. Some
of that difference is to do with the role of the state. The slaveholder's
power of life and death over his slaves was 'legally considered a del-
egation of state authority' (Paton 2001, 927). The 1664 slave code in
Jamaica gave the master legal authority to decide on the guilt and punishment of his slaves, even when the misdemeanour had been committed against somebody else. A free person would inform the owner
or the overseer who would then take responsibility for the punishment
or prosecution of the slave. Slaveholders who took their slaves to court
were probably hoping for punishments of mutilation, transportation
or the death penalty, which they could not impose themselves, and for
which they would be compensated (Paton 2001, 935). Planters could
hire state employees, the 'common Whipman', to flog their slaves on
their behalf. Slave courts operated sporadically throughout the year
in Jamaica and were presided over by local property holders, usually
major planters. Diana Paton argues that while the courts in England in
the eighteenth century were designed to dramatise 'the majesty and
essential justice of the law' and to demonstrate the idea of equality
before the law, the Jamaican court system was set up to tell 'a different story, one centered on the division of the population into free and
enslaved' (Paton 2001, 928). Paton's argument is that in Jamaica the

planters' control was fragile and needed constant support, so that their participation in slave trials as magistrates, freeholders and prosecutors was about affirming and legitimising 'their private power to punish', asserting their fairness and control (Paton 2001, 936). Like the citizens of ancient Greece, the planters in Jamaica needed to be able to show that they were not tyrants who had fallen victim to the grandiose desire for power and failed to maintain the boundaries between public and private. The procedures of the courts, and the social relations of punishment, operated differently in different contexts, and being the captive of a conqueror had different implications for enslaved Africans in Jamaica, Indians in America and for labourers in England. It would be difficult to deny that one of the registers of difference at work here was race, even in the seventeenth century.

Slave offences punished by the Jamaican courts were mainly property crime, often thefts of sheep, and other 'status offences' that could only be committed by slaves, such as the crime of running away. Planters prosecuted slaves who escaped for more than six months, and those who were said to be 'in rebellion' (Paton 2001, 930). The 1696 slave code specified that fugitive slaves who ran away for more than twelve months were to be declared rebellious and could be sentenced to transportation. The slave codes in the Caribbean were built on the principle that violence by slaves against white people was more serious than violence among slaves or between white or free people. In the Code of 1674, the relevant crime was assault on a *white* Christian' and in 1677 the offence became 'assault on a white *person*'. As Paton points out, the principle of whiteness is clearly salient. These laws, along with the punishment of runaways, extended the English legal principle that murder by a subordinate of the person who had legitimate authority over them was considered to be 'petit treason', 'a crime analogous to treason against the state' (Paton 2001, 931). The violence of subordinates was presented as a threat to the social order, and the punishments inflicted were a response 'not to murder per se, but to the murder in particular of a propertied, elite, white man' (Paton 2001, 931).

Punishments involved the public infliction of pain on the body, creating a spectacle of suffering, particularly through flogging, but also through permanent disfigurement and dismemberment, cutting off ears, slitting nostrils, amputating feet (Paton 2001, 937). African slaves in the Caribbean were subjected to the 'savage, useless tortures' Hutcheson promised to protect the enslaved British poor from enduring. In Jamaica, sentences of flogging ranged from 39 to 117 lashes, while in Britain the usual range was from two to twelve lashes (Paton 2001, 938). It is significant that flogging was understood as fundamentally degrading and dishonouring, an 'ignominious sentence' that was associated with enslavement (Paton 2001, 939). European convicts were much less likely to be permanently mutilated than slaves in New World slave societies. Attacks on bodily integrity and this spectacular suffering 'had come to signify by the eighteenth century that the convict was a traitor, a rebel against legitimate authority' (Paton 2001, 939). Almost any crime the slaves committed could be interpreted as treachery and resistance. At the same time, punishment produced 'an arbitrary, haphazard, and discriminatory justice, whose primary goal was to display and reinforce the absolute power of master over slave' (Da Costa 1994, 231), and slaves were construed as not only outside the boundaries of civil society, but even beyond the reach of natural law where punishment was limited to reparation and restraint. The schemes for enslaving the British poor were different in that they were about using slavery as punishment, rather than punishing slaves. The proposed projects were about shaming and dishonour for the convicts, reaffirming the boundaries of the moral community and of civil society, disgracing the individual and intimidating others. Their 'utopian' goals were about gaining assent to the power of the state, addressing the 'public burden' and improving the public stock. They were aimed at reassuring the industrious that their property was safe and protected by civil society and at reforming the idle and the listless. They could not be characterised as haphazard, or as arbitrary. The power exercised by the West Indian planter, on the other hand, was a different form of rule that was understood to be based on brutal domination rather than a social contract: 'The displays of the mutilated body parts of convicted slaves were less about gaining assent to the power of the state than they were about emphasizing the extent of that power' (Paton 2001, 944).

This makes the mid-seventeenth to the mid-eighteenth century a very particular moment in the development of the idea of race, and in the social relations of slavery. In thinking about the colonial context of Locke's writings, for example, it is important to assign race, or, better, racialisation, more than the small role it plays in Rozbicki's analysis. It helps us to understand, as Nyquist argues, what it meant for the Amerindians to be shut out of civil society and denied the possibility of political resistance. It also helps, I think, to explain the significance of the differentiation between Indians and African slaves in the colonial records, and of turning the enslaved Pequot into 'Negro cannibals'. At the same time, it is important to hear the warnings in the accounts of Farr and Uzgalis and not to turn to racism too quickly to explain Locke's theory or the basis of slavery. Instead, enslavability needs to be placed in the context of the division between the state of nature and civil society, in terms of both space and time, so that slavery and freedom emerge as social and historical relations that need to be understood within their cultural, economic and intellectual contexts. The indigenous peoples of America demonstrated an 'inability to overcome space' (Beckmann 2005, 86) which also left them suspended in time, showing us our history rather than creating their own. They were not yet treated or understood as a separate race, but they lived in 'strange places that are located *in* the world but not *in* history', as Hegel later described Africa (Purtschert 2010, 1044). As states of nature, America and Africa were not historical places, because the historical had to be marked as European (Purtschert 2010, 1046).

CONCLUSION

In seventeenth-century America, the indigenous peoples were not treated as though they were natural slaves or ensouled tools, but the just-war justification of slavery was exercised over them and criminals were condemned to slavery (Guasco 2007, 402). The idea that slavery could be a just punishment or means of redemption posed new dangers to liberal politics. This fits with Locke's approach to the slave trade within which slave raids did not count as just wars, women and children should not be taken captive, and hereditary slavery was positively unjust. Without an unjust act, there could be no just enslavement. This was a shift in the politics of slavery, away from Aristotelian notions of natural hierarchy. Within Locke's view of natural rights was the idea that all human beings had 'a capacity, and therefore a right, to attain the moral status attributed to "humanness"' (Marden 2006, 97). They could only be prevented from that attainment by individual failings or by cultural and environmental disadvantage, not by their inherited status or their natures. This slavery-within-limits was not about discounting the possibility of slavery altogether, nor about fixing slavery as an institution. The ground shifted as the Indians began to resist the colonists, and in particular once that resistance became violent, and as the plantation system came to dominate the Atlantic economy. By 1710, the promotional literature for migrants coming to Carolina declared that two 'Negro slaves' were required in order to live comfortably, and suggested to newcomers that they could start out as overseers until they could establish their own plantations (Hinshelwood 2013, 579). As Hinshelwood points out, the change reflected the shift to rice as the staple crop of the colony after the 1690s. As a consequence of the influx of West African slaves cultivating rice, enslaved Africans imported by Barbadians became the majority population in Carolina. This was a process that shifted the social relations of power in the colony and was accompanied by new, racialised meanings of whiteness and blackness. At the same time, the colonies became places to transport and reform vagabonds, beggars and criminals through servitude. In this context of swirling hierarchies and privileges, and shifting meanings of moral worth and punishment, the indigenous people's insecure grip on their freedom and their identity meant that they could find themselves enslaved. As Nyquist puts it, racialisation is 'a reflexive, relational process that generates heritable liberties along with heritable slavery, voluntary servitude along with slavery, juridical innocence alongside incapacity or criminality' (Nyquist 2013, 367). The result of this reflexive, relational process is that legitimate political resistance became 'a privilege that is tacitly racialized' (Nyquist 2013, 367), and the liberal subject was able to disavow any kinship with the enslaved, who were understood to be neither persons nor citizens, and so unable to ground political resistance.

Locke's approach to the justification of slavery and its colonial context draws attention to what Marden identifies as the problems of making 'certain positive human attributes the measure of eligibility for rights-bearing status' (Marden 2006, 86). Defining humanness through reason 'encompasses both a universal logic and one that is exclusionary' (Marden 2006, 87). In this natural-rights logic of slavery, what emerges is not just the 'strangeness of slaves' but the roots of Locke's 'strange indifference' towards them. Rationality defines human beings, but not all human beings properly exercise this capacity. Once this universal/exclusionary logic is recognised as being at the heart of the theory, it becomes clear that this is not a question of resolving contradictions or solving puzzling silences. In the eighteenth century, a commitment to equality did not entail a rejection of social hierarchy. The American revolutionaries attacked hereditary privilege, but accepted subordination based on capacity, disposition and virtue (Marden 2006, 89). Thinking about Locke and slavery should return us to the dangers slavery poses to politics, and remind us of the inseparability of slavery from perpetual boundary-setting and keeping. The assumption behind human-rights language in its American manifestation was that most people would fall short of the standard of 'humanness'. Rights meant moral worthiness and access to equality of opportunity. It was clear that unequal industry and virtues necessarily created unequal rights. Marden argues that 'in practice different people would enjoy different rights'. The right to realise human potential, by entering into a civilised moral world, was universal, but the actual enjoyment of civil rights depended on reaching that standard (Marden 2006, 90) and crossing the threshold that separated the state of nature from civil society.

Chapter 4

EMPIRES OF PROPERTY, PROPERTIES OF EMPIRE

The threshold between the state of nature and civil society was central to the boundary-setting and keeping of the imperial project, as the possibility that some were everywhere slaves and others were everywhere free became a question for empire and for global property relations. This chapter explores the relationship between property, slavery, morality and the law at the end of the eighteenth century, as we move from Locke to Haiti. As Stephanie Smallwood points out, there is a tendency to treat slavery and freedom as fixed, stable categories 'when, in fact, the fuzzy boundaries and unclear content of these categories was precisely what fuelled debate about "slavery" and "freedom" in the eighteenth century' (Smallwood 2004, 289). This more historicised and dynamic approach to the idea of slavery is about trying to understand how ideas about property, slavery, humanity and enlightenment were forged together, and the tensions and frictions between them. As Smallwood argues, this is in part about recognising how the rise of slavery in the Americas was dependent on the nature of freedom in Western Europe, as slavery was built on a foundation of market relations and freedom on 'understandings of property underwritten and authored by slavery' (Smallwood 2004, 297). Eighteenth-century conceptions of self-ownership, universal rights and the rise of revolutionary antislavery grew out of the epistemological relationship between global markets and freedom that was informed by ideas of slavery and empire. Smallwood's argument focuses on commodification as a political process and a discursive system that crowded out other systems of representation and became the fullest expression of slavery. In the process, freedom was reduced 'to the ability to whittle things (and people) down (from all that they might be) to their own-able characteristics' (Smallwood 2004, 297).

In his speech to the House of Lords on the second reading of the bill for the abolition of the slave trade in 1807, Sir Thomas Plumer spoke in support of the West Indian planters. He stressed the legality of the slave trade, its foundations in the Royal Africa Company in the seventeenth century and John Locke's involvement: 'What, my Lords! Are we to be told that these men did not understand plain principles of humanity and justice?' (Plumer 1807, 11). He was responding to the links made by antislavery discourse between humanity, justice and property, arguing that the ownership of others was itself corrupting, not just for the slaves but for the planters as well. For the abolitionists, the planters' ownership was corrupt and cankered, and so unrestrained and unimproving. Both the West Indian planters and the enslaved Black Africans were somehow unable to husband themselves and to improve their property. In 1823, when the slave trade had been abolished but slavery continued, James Cropper contrasted the stability of landed income with 'the unjust and uncertain tenure of property in the persons and lives of . . . fellow men' (Gladstone 1824, 7).

This chapter explores that unjust and uncertain tenure in the persons of others as it was debated, contested and affirmed in pamphlets, letters, sermons and speeches in the 1790s as the West Indian planters responded to the anti-slavery movement. The Legislature, they argued, had entered into an implied engagement with the planters to secure their property and to permit the continuance of the slave trade. Mr Baillie, speaking in the 1792 debate in the House of Commons, maintained that abolishing the African slave trade 'will be an absolute breach of the compact that ties the colonies to the mother country' (Debate 1792, 54), and would be met with universal resistance. The laws in existence had guaranteed the security of the lives and fortunes of British subjects living in the West Indies in the same way as those living in Great Britain, so that 'their property cannot be meddled with or diminished in any shape whatsoever, without full and ample compensation'. The end of the African slave trade would breach the property rights of the slave traders and owners and bring 'an end to every species of improvement in all our Islands' (Debate 1792, 54). These debates illuminate the 'consensual limits to enslavability' as liberty became the hegemonic ideal in north-western Europe (Drescher 2002, 12). In England, the concept of the free man, able to alienate his labour through contract and to seek his own property, was embedded in law, practice and culture. He owned a 'self-property' in his labour as an individual. He was protected from being downgraded to chattel status by living in the 'zone of freedom', so that he 'retained bundles of rights and mechanisms of protection and publicity that were not available to most African labourers' (Drescher 2002, 14). Even where the demands for labour were most intense, Seymour Drescher argues, 'metropolitan norms were never sufficiently altered to accommodate the permanent bondage of Europeans' (Drescher 2002, 14). Drescher argues that the zones of freedom and unfreedom coexisted separately until the later eighteenth century, when they began to impinge on one another as Black slaves moved from the periphery to Europe and 'generated continuous friction over the metropolitan status of colonists' claims to their property in persons' (Drescher 2002, 19). These tensions and frictions are the subject of this chapter.

PROPERTIES OF COLONIALISM

The zones of freedom and unfreedom that were being drawn up and contested in the eighteenth century rested not just on the self-property of European labourers and the chattel status of African labourers, but also on the rights to property, land and territory in the New World. The story of property and empire was a story of dispossession, of the power of the state, and of a 'waving line' of enslavability – as we saw in the chapter on Locke. In the eighteenth century, Kant's theory of property rights held that no one living outside the state could legally possess any land, so that rights of ownership in the state of nature could never be anything more than provisional until they were sanctioned by public law. This opened up the legal and moral space for the colonial powers to take over the lands of the native inhabitants and leave them without redress. Practical reason, in Kant's account, required people to obey the legitimate authority in power, irrespective of its origin or the ways in which its property was acquired. A subject could lodge a complaint, but not offer resistance. Spencer argues that this combination of factors meant that the colonial masters had the right, according to Kant, to encourage immigration and the settlement of colonists against the opposition of indigenous peoples. Only the colonists' legally sanctioned private ownership of land needed to be respected, and rebellion, even in defence of indigenous property, was always illegitimate. In effect, this meant that Kant placed no effective limits of the sovereign's use of violence, and the balance of power always leant towards state authority over minority nations (Spencer 2015). Indigenous peoples and minority nations were left without 'any real protection for their autonomy as peoples' (Spencer 2015, 386).

Spencer argues that Kant placed a duty on all people living in a stateless condition to leave the state of nature and enter into civic relations under the coercive apparatus of the state. It was the only way for individuals to establish security from each other. Kant expressed contempt for all those who tried to live outside the strictures of the state, either as savages or as pirates, who 'prefer the freedom of folly to the freedom of reason' (Spencer 2015, 376). By 1778 Kant was arguing that the American Indians were too weak for hard labour, too indifferent for industry, and incapable of any culture. This was an important shift in Enlightenment thinking about indigenous peoples that moved away from relating to them as active men and trading partners, and drew on Rousseau's account of humans as 'self-making (and self-enslaving) agents' (Muthu 2003, 13).

For the earlier writers on indigenous peoples, the Amerindians were depicted as living in communal societies without private property, hierarchies or inequalities. They were understood to be living natural, simple, equal and uncomplicated lives, influenced mainly by the climate and by nature itself. As Sankar Muthu argues, this was a 'nearly acultural understanding of New World peoples' which 'leaves the work of the creation and maintenance of these societies largely to fortune and nature' (Muthu 2003, 17). This conception of 'natural' peoples could then be used as a critical tool to expose the injustices of more 'artificial' societies and to think about Europe in terms of its own savagery and barbarity. Muthu argues that these accounts also entailed a 'temporal claim' within which the New World represented the earliest stage of human history, an 'infant world' in contrast to the decrepitude and moral bankruptcy of a European civilisation that was now in decline (Muthu 2003, 23). Influential early eighteenth-century accounts of Amerindian societies saw the people in them as living simpler lives than Europeans, structured by equality and independence, embodying values of innocence, tranquillity and communal existence, balanced somewhere between the primitive and the civilised in a 'relatively peaceful and content middle state' (Muthu 2003, 35). In this carefully calibrated state, they were accorded a degree of humanisation, but their mental capacities were judged to be at an elementary level because they were unable to 'go beyond the simple association of basic ideas' (Muthu 2003, 42). This meant that their ideas about property were judged to be underdeveloped since their wants were simple and easily met, and they were not driven by competition and greed.

For Diderot, problems arose when modern travellers and commercial agents 'arrive[d] in foreign lands animated principally by the spirit of conquest' (Muthu 2003, 85). Driven by tyranny, guilt, ambition and curiosity and then unmoored from their own cultural contexts, they became 'unleashed tigers' who had a catastrophic effect on the non-European peoples they encountered because they were no longer moderated by their own rules of conduct (Muthu 2003, 86, 92). They allowed the grandiose desire for power to take over. Any limits that had been placed on slavery by Locke's theory were lifted. In this new commercial and colonial context they became what Ottobah Cuguano called a 'bramble of ruffians, barbarians and slave-holders, grown up to a powerful luxuriance in wickedness' (Cuguano 1787, 24). Cuguano, who was kidnapped by slave-traders in what is now Ghana when he was thirteen, characterised the slave trade as based on 'brutish barbarity and unparalleled injustice', carried on in the colonies with insidious, cruel and oppressive avidity. The longer the trade continued, the slavers grew more abandoned, until 'nothing in history can equal the barbarity and cruelty of the tortures committed under various pretences in modern slavery' (Cuguano 1787, 3). Their actions were inimical to every idea of justice, equity, reason and humanity, and meant that they 'must eventually resign their own claim to any degree of sensibility and humanity' (Cuguano 1787, 3). Slave traders, away from home, had made themselves into 'robbers of men, the kidnappers, ensnarers and slave-holders, who take away the common rights and privileges of others to support and enrich themselves' (Cuguano 1787, 4). They acted against every precept and injunction of Divine Law and contrary to the golden rule of doing as they would be done by. They cast themselves off not only from their local contexts, but also from any limits to their property and from the universal bonds between men, the ties that were supposed to secure them against injury and violence. They were left, Cuguano argued, with no scruples for dealing with the human species, so that they became 'not only brutish, but wicked and base; and . . . their aspirations are insidious and false' (Cuguano 1787, 5).

Antislavery arguments from Christianity grew out of this idea that the slave traders had transgressed the moral law, and created for themselves an immoral conception of property as conquest, based on force and dispossession. Europeans had, according to Granville Sharp, attacked, destroyed, driven out, dispossessed and enslaved the poor ignorant heathen in many parts of the world, without being able to produce 'an *authentic written commandment from God* for such proceedings', and so had to be regarded as lawless robbers and oppressors who had reason to expect severe retribution from God for their tyranny and oppression (Sharp 1776, 13). Their accumulation of property was reinterpreted as a process of civilisation that hid from view the dispossession of whole groups of people who came to be labelled as barbarians. For Sharp and Cuguano, the process of civilisation for some actively created the 'barbarity' of others by taking away their property. 'Or can the slave-holders think', Cuguano asked, 'that the Universal Father and Sovereign of Mankind will be well pleased with them, for the total transgression of his law, in bowing down the necks of those to the yoke of their cruel bondage?' (Cuguano 1787, 23). Thomas Gisborne argued that through the slave trade Europe contributed to retaining vast regions of Africa 'in a state of barbarity and ignorance' (Gisborne 1792, 16). He attributed this barbarity to the Europeans' spirit of conquest, and their deliberate policies to destroy the security of African life 'by keeping every individual in momentary fear of being seized by a lurking enemy, or even by his own kindred, and hurried on board a slave-ship' (Gisborne 1792, 16). The colonists and slave traders fomented continual, bloody and unprovoked wars and encouraged the savage tyranny of the princes, perpetuating iniquitous laws and customs, and failing to diffuse the religion of Christ. They were, William Belsham argued, 'engrossed by one fatal passion, the rage of accumulating wealth' (Belsham 1790, 11). Diderot used the example of the English arriving in India as traders and staying on to become absolute rulers. He saw this as a process of losing principles, of the 'moral blindness' of the imperial project and its accompanying atrocities that made him 'freeze with horror' (Muthu 2003, 90). It was, as he saw it, this spirit of conquest and moral blindness that had led the imperial powers to develop African slavery, ever more dehumanising non-Europeans and creating the conditions for more barbaric cruelty, undermining the general will of humanity so that '[i]n order to repeople one part of the globe that you have laid waste, you corrupt and depopulate another' (Muthu 2003, 93).

Diderot's account of the catastrophic effects of empire on non-European peoples was relational and global, and he attributed the moral blindness and the spirit of conquest to Europeans' self-serving failure to recognise the right to property as universal, and instead to insist that America was a *terra nullius*, an uninhabited land, untrammelled by any legitimate property claims. As William Innes, 'a West-India merchant' and plantation owner, said about Africa, sounding remarkably like Hobbes as he stripped away any workable rules of conduct, laws, customs or collective practices that may have existed there: 'Without religion, without morality, without agriculture, manufactures, arts and sciences, it is impossible for the inhabitants of the Gold Coast to avoid those evils which involve slavery' (Innes 1792, 12–13). In such a situation, Innes argued, slavery became inevitable, and European slavery was to be preferred to the savage and despotic African version. Many of the Africans traded by Europeans had, claimed James Adair, been prisoners of war, 'who formerly having been sacrificed to personal or political resentment, have, since the intercourse with Europeans, been preserved as lucrative objects of commerce' (Adair 1790, 144). Commodification emerges from this account as a step towards freedom, part of a political process that made Africans fit for market exchange by whittling them down to their own-able characteristics and removing them from contexts of barbarity and ignorance (Smallwood 2004). Cuguano was careful to contest this slavers' vision of Africa and its social relations. Even if Africans were dispersed and unsociable, that could be no warrant for the Europeans to enslave them. The continent of Africa, he pointed out, was vast, and divided into kingdoms and principalities governed by their respective kings and princes who ruled over their free subjects. When the Africans sold one another, they were 'only ensnared and enlisted to be servants', Cuguano insisted. Echoing the limits that Locke placed on slavery, he pointed out that they did not sell their own wives and children – 'nothing can be more opposite to every thing they hold dear and valuable' (Cuguano 1787, 27). For Cuguano, the governments of Christian nations were supporting and countenancing unlawful traffic and piracy, and stepping outside the Lockean contexts for limited slavery:

This seems to be a fashionable way of getting riches, but very dishonourable; in doing this, the slave-holders are meaner and baser than the African slaves, for while they subject and reduce them to a degree with the brutes, they seduce themselves to a degree with devils. (Cuguano 1787, 21)

Their intention was not improvement or redemption, but to advance their own ease and profit.

COLONISTS' PROPERTY

Defenders of the slave trade interpreted their way of getting riches very differently, putting it into the context of economic and social advancement, and insisting that their intention was improvement. They saw the growing demand for sugar as integral to the progress of civilisation, spreading through Russia and the north of Europe as their artificial wants increased and they made 'rapid advancements towards refinement' (Anon 1792, 23). For the proslavery thinkers, Europe's crusades had given way to colonisation, and 'Wars are becoming more humanized, private property more sacred; and prisoners, that used to be condemned or enslaved, are now exchanged.' The principles and objects of government were better understood, 'rights better defined, property and wealth increasing, and better protected' (Anon 1789, 2) through this process of commodification. In this more positive account of the colonial encounter, Europe was positioned as having been slow and gradual in its improvements, and so Europeans should not expect too much from Africa 'in its present crude and enslaved state, without arts or civilization, and having a cultivation so limited'. Africa had much to learn to be prepared to receive the seeds of civilisation and emancipation (Anon 1789, 2).

This process of civilisation and refinement was not only about what went on elsewhere. It was also central to the empire at home, and to the colonial dynamic of histories of consumption and new forms of culture and consciousness (De Groot 2006, 171). The profits from the slave trade were woven into the fabric of British property relations, particularly for the elite, and the zone of freedom was a zone of habits shaped by what De Groot terms intimate and extended links with a growing number of colonies (De Groot 2006, 171). William Innes, for example, held a half share in the Albion, Nigg and Lancaster estates in British Guiana, and left legacies of around £200–300 each to a series of individuals in Scotland, and an annuity of £100 a year to two of his nieces (UCL 2017b). The West India merchants owned 'estates in progress' and had expended large sums of money on them 'upon the faith of Parliament', which had declared the wisdom and propriety of the trade, and invited foreigners and British subjects to 'embark their capital in it' (Plumer 1807, 13). Abolition would, they protested, arrest

the progress of improvement and destroy what had been done, causing private property to 'fall into decay' (Plumer 1807, 17). The knock-on
effect would be to damage Britain's trade by taking away an important
market for all kinds of manufactured goods, from shoes and stock-
ings to implements of husbandry, provisions and luxuries, 'every shilling of which centers [sic] in Great Britain', where the planters also
spent the surplus revenue of their estates and educated their children
(Debate 1792, 55). The trade to Africa, they concluded, should be
encouraged rather than abolished. Some agreed that the slave trade
was an evil, but not an evil of such magnitude 'as to justify the ruin of
our colonies, our trade, and our manufactures' (Anon 1792, 42). The
planters and merchants who were opposed to abolition regarded it as
a risky venture with uncertain outcomes that would involve them in
irretrievable ruin and bring only uncertain and unimportant advantages to the slaves. Instant and unqualified abolition was regarded as
a dangerous experiment in a world that was so powerfully shaped by
colonial production and domestic consumption, and so unprepared for
emancipation.

In 1823, after the abolition of the slave trade but before the abolition
of slavery in 1833, James Cropper argued for the introduction of unre-
stricted free trade, but this was read by John Gladstone as an attack on
the property rights of the West India planters whose title to their slaves
was 'as strong and valid as the law of the land can make it' (Gladstone
1824, 70). Any interference with or injury to their property by the public would require full compensation, because '[t]o admit the principle of
requiring any higher title than that which the law recognises, would be
to strike at the root of all property throughout the kingdom' (Gladstone
1824, 70). The law had to be binding on those that made it, 'and, to inval-
idate or alienate the rights or property of the Planters, for the purpose of
either real or presumed benevolence, would be to recognise a principle
of general spoliation' (Gladstone 1824, 100). In the question of compensation, the slave was no party to the arrangement because '*that is between
the proprietor and the Legislature only*' (Gladstone 1824, 70). The zone of
freedom was rooted in these property rights and agreements made at
the centre, in the laws of the state. Immediate abolition was represented
as an existential threat to the law and to property.

In Innes's vision of gradual emancipation, the piety and goodness
of the world 'would wear away Slavery' in the Caribbean by degrees,
as it had in Europe (Innes 1792, 30), replacing it with the indentured

servitude of 'native Cultivators' who would labour the ground and reduce the need to import slaves from Africa (Innes 1792, 29). This gradualist approach was designed to protect the property rights of the slave owner, to ensure 'that no violent loss or disaster would accrue to the Planter, who, on the system of Slavery, and the faith of repeated laws, embarked his capital, his industry, his hopes in this world' (Innes 1792, 30). In this defence of the West Indian planter, he appears not as a gambler or a speculator, but as an industrious investor with a legitimate stake in slavery as a system of commerce endorsed by the state. Rather than condemning their absenteeism, Innes defended the transnational identity and the mobility of the West Indians. The West India planters, merchants, sailors and others were citizens of both Britain and the Islands 'which . . . are as a summer-house to England, since so great a number of its inhabitants are in the habit of going and coming between them' (1792, 65). The planters were, in his view, 'as warm Friends, as any of the British Empire, to the highest degree of Liberty, consistent with Order and Good Government, and the widest range of Humanity – Humanity not to Africans only, but also to Europeans' (1792, 88). Most of the natives of the West Indies were sent to England to receive a liberal education 'and imbibe those sentiments of liberty and independence, which are every where to be met with in that happy country'. There was, Richard Nisbet argued, no reason to think that a few years residence in the West Indies 'will make them, totally, forget humanity, that first and noblest characteristic of English-men' (Nisbet 1773, 16).

There were some problems with this picture of the West Indian planters as people of skill and 'unceasing, but unavailing industry', contributing to sustaining a sinking empire (Adair 1790, 202). Their own habits of industry were brought into question by the issue of absenteeism. The principal proprietors were described by Sir Thomas Plumer as 'the most opulent persons who possess estates [and] do not themselves reside upon the spot' (Plumer, 1807, 22). The great majority of planters were not absentees, but those who owned the largest plantations often were. The likely number of absentee proprietors in the late eighteenth century was between 150 and 155, or between 3 and 6 per cent of the white population, but more than a third of them owned estates of over 2,500 acres, meaning that they held 24.4 per cent of the land (Burnard 2011). Adair identified one set of absentee slave owners as proprietors who came to the West Indies to waste their

fortunes and leave their estates to unprincipled men on such low salaries that they were tempted to embezzle. The inevitable consequence
was ruin, and 'hence it is that their estates sometimes fall into the hands
of strangers, even *taylors* and *hucksters*' (Adair 1790, 199). As Trevor
Burnard argues, absentee slave owners were demonised as socially
harmful, hampering development, leaching money out of the colony
and fostering slave rebellion. The absentees symbolised Jamaican failure 'to become a tropical version of British society', to be civilised as
well as rich. Absenteeism was taken to signal a lack of commitment to
the colonies and 'an indifference to improvement' (Burnard 2004, 192).
The positive benefits of absenteeism were ignored, and patriotism was
equated with settlement. West Indian planters struggled to give their
property the permanence that was attached to revenues that derived
from a landed estate in Europe (Draper 2010, 3). They were struggling
for the recognition of West Indians as true Englishmen, since English
identity was becoming inextricable from the claim to be a friend to
liberty and humanity. Absentee landowners were 'tied to the colonies
but not of them', members of British society, but seen as 'West Indian'
(Draper 2010, 17). Their Englishness was compromised, and needed to
be defended.

Slave ownership was transmitted through inheritance and marriage
settlement, and more indirectly through annuities and legacies, such as
those left by Innes to his nieces, spreading through the undergrowth of
landed property norms, not always tainted, but not always visible. The
absentee slave owner was 'an essentially liminal figure' (Draper 2010, 7),
suspended between the stability of landed property and the 'terribly fragile' foundations of mobile property (Pocock 1975, 441). They were fundamentally engaged in the 'circulation and exchange of substantive things as
insubstantial commodities' (McKeon 2005, 26) in the virtual market that
crossed the globe as well as in the very real slave markets. A small number
of elite white West Indian men had access to upper-class white wives as
'genealogical capital', but many other planters and their surrogates only
had access to black concubines (Green 2006, 16), making it harder for
them to keep their property within the extended family and ensure its
racial 'purity' (Green 2006, 40). The planters' hold on their landed property
was not enough to ground their own settled Englishness because the West
Indies were figured as a morally suspect, 'disturbing place', full of death,
violence and hybridity (Burnard 2011, 186). The planters, like the slaves,

were affected by the heat, making them licentious and slothful, addicted to vice and luxury. They were not invited into the 'space of gentlemanly conversation' that connected the pursuit of self-interest to the fundamental demand to act for the benefit of others and to promote the common good (Klein 1994, 36). It was difficult for them to come to terms with the unpredictability and riskiness of their colonial property, and to insist on the absolute power to punish, and at the same time to ground their British identity as solid, independent individuals who could engage in commerce and improve the world.

The property relations underpinning the zone of freedom did not always feel stable and secure. The slave owners argued that they were struggling with their debts to keep their heads above water, and the abolition of the slave trade would sink them into the 'abyss of ruin', dragging the British empire along with them (Adair 1790, 202). In Antigua and the other colonies, a considerable portion of the land was unfit for cultivating sugar cane. In Adair's narrative of excess and decline, the planter became comparatively wealthy 'by the fruits of his limited industry', but that meant that his merchant in England advanced him more money and he was 'seized with the rage of becoming a sugar planter' (Adair 1790, 214–15), building expensive sugar works and buying slaves as rapidly as possible. In this account, there is something excessive about the sugar planters' relationship to property, a desire to use money to exceed the bounds of their industry, a determination to become 'rich and independent with all possible expedition' so that they could return to England and educate their children there (Adair 1790, 215). Their attitude towards their estates and their slaves was stigmatised as archetypally aristocratic, 'over and against the emerging norms of bourgeois self-discipline and systematic, impersonal justice and punishment' (Draper 2010, 48). In pursuing the goal of wealth and independence, the planters bought too many adult men as slaves, and pushed them beyond their strength before they were 'seasoned'. The planter's haste to get rich meant that he was often ruined: 'many great and irremediable evils have arisen from the ambition of the planter to become a manufacturer of sugar' (Adair 1790, 216). Depictions of their wealth were undercut by 'undercurrents of decadence and corruption coded as luxury' (Burnard 2011, 192), and they were in turn coded as non-British by their lack of self-restraint, their 'rage' to monopolise rather than to improve. Their response was to try 'to constitute themselves as "proprietors", as owners of *land* rather than as owners of slaves' (Draper 2010, 80), and it was this strategy that was undermined by the constant references to their absenteeism and their fatal, passionate, overattachment to wealth. West India property never became the equivalent of metropolitan landed property; it 'offered neither the stability nor the social cachet of English land' (Draper 2010, 184). The West India planters were figured as lacking the qualities of rationality, industry and improvement that could sustain a just and certain tenure. They were shut out of the Lockean vision of rational improvement and limited slavery.

CONTESTING PROPERTY RIGHTS

The antislavery writers worked hard to unsettle the basis of the slave owners' property rights in their slaves by arguing that, even if their ownership was embodied in the law, they had no moral right to claim such a property. 'Purchase', Joseph Woods argued, 'transfers no title but that which the seller possessed, namely *power*. If indeed *power* always implies *right*, the Europeans may, with a safe conscience, oppress and destroy the negroes at pleasure' (J. Woods 1784, 16). If, however, as they claimed, the personal benefit of the slave was the primary object of the slave merchant, then 'those philanthropists who engage in this traffic, from such noble and generous motives, must consider the previous consent of the Slave as absolutely necessary to give validity to the purchase' (Belsham 1790, 10). Woods argued in 1784 that it was incumbent on the 'individuals concerned in this species of property to satisfy the demands of reason and conscience by relinquishing it' (J. Woods 1784, 23). He did not hold out much hope. Experience had taught that 'it is too deeply entangled with motives of interest and habits of power to be voluntarily abandoned' (J. Woods 1784, 23). The law needed to change to help the planters 'overcome the temptation to persevere in what is known to be wrong' (J. Woods 1784, 23).

The slave owners were taking advantage of another's wickedness, and seeking to profit from the crimes committed by others. If an individual had been unjustly reduced to a state of slavery by the contingencies of war, 'no subsequent purchase can convert the wrong into a right; as the receiver of stolen goods, knowing them to be so, is equally culpable with the thief' (J. Woods 1784, 29). In the same way as Locke argued that it was impossible to transfer the right of life and death to another person, these abolitionists insisted that no right existed to alienate from another his liberty, and every slave purchase was a contradiction to the original inherent rights of mankind. Their account of natural rights could not be made compatible with slavery. For Gisborne, it was a question of conscience, about the impossibility of ever knowing 'whether that liberty is justly forfeited' and so justly at the disposal of the seller (Gisborne 1792, 13). Most slaves, Gisborne went on to point out, were the victims of avarice, treachery and rapine, kidnapped by their own countrymen and relations, stolen by the emissaries of the Europeans, or 'captured in wars commenced at their [European] instigation for the purpose of obtaining slaves' (Gisborne 1792, 14). The African slave trade derived its support and its very existence from 'unbounded oppression and injustice' (Gisborne 1792, 15), and ought to be instantly and universally abandoned. It was the duty of the legislature to pass an immediate act of abolition to prevent individuals from acting as principals, abettors or accomplices in such a system of iniquity and oppression.

The burden of restoring their 'alienated rights' to the Africans should not rest solely on the planters' shoulders. Woods accepted that they had pursued this 'iniquitous traffick' under the patronage of Britain and the costs of its abolition should be borne 'by all who share in its advantages' (J. Woods 1784, 23–4). The advocates of immediate abolition contested the basis of slavery in legal property rights. Engagements between the legislature and the West Indian owners could not be binding 'since they could not have been performed without flagrant injustice to the Africans, the invasion of whose rights the British government never was, nor ever can be, authorised to promote' (Gisborne 1792, 19). It could not, Gisborne argued, be in the interests of the kingdom to be supported by 'depriving unoffending foreigners of their rights' (Gisborne 1792, 21). It was a momentous truth, he asserted, 'and a truth little regarded' that 'the rules of morality are as binding on nations as on individuals'. 'What would have been robberies and murders, if committed by a single highwayman, are they not still robberies and murders though the perpetrators have previously coalesced into a troop, a society, or a nation?' (Gisborne 1792, 21). Antislavery writers used their belief in the innate liberty of all men to argue that if slavery could not be allowed in England, how could it exist on British soil anywhere? (Swaminathan 2009, 88). In the aftermath of the American Revolution, 'the slave trade became the issue through which British writers could reclaim the concept of liberty from the American revolutionaries', and in that process of reclamation, they narrowed the location of their critique to the West

Indies (Swaminathan 2009, 94). In this antislavery discourse, designed
to contest the basis of the zone of freedom in property rights, the state
was obliged to promote Christian liberty, 'to create a national conscience, strongly dependent upon their definition of Christian morality' (Swaminathan 2009, 99). In Gisborne's account we can also see the
global reach of antislavery as it built a new understanding of the scope
of rights that had to account for the natural liberty of Africans and the
shared humanity of Africans and Europeans. They argued that rather
than increasing civilisation, the enslavement of their fellow creatures
was a stain on the national character of the British (Swaminathan 2009,
95). Antislavery writers made clear that 'the whole substance perhaps,
of the most wealthy *English* or *Scotch* slaveholders would not suffice
to pay *what is due, in strict justice*, to those that have *laboured in his service*, if the reward is to be proportioned to their sufferings' (Sharp 1776,
58). Quoting from James 5: 3, Sharp told the slaveholders that, despite
having been encouraged and protected by the government, their gold
and silver was cankered, and they would be punished for withholding
wages and defrauding labourers who were worthy of their hire.

The antislavery impulse was to repudiate planter societies as 'exem-
plars of profiteering run amok', their property tarnished by the unregu-
lated pursuit of private gain and by the colonists' refusal to consider
the public good (C. L. Brown 2006, 81). They had tainted not only West
Indian society, but also their own national inheritance and the stability of the British economy. Henry Brougham talked about the 'wages
of national guilt', and asked whether the defenders of the slave trade
were trying to vindicate a mercenary murder on the grounds that it
had been profitable (Brougham 1804, 32). It had been argued that the
African trade opened up a wide channel for the beneficial investment
of capital, and that abolition would be a serious blow to the commercial
resources of the country. Brougham responded that the profits of the
slave trade had proved to be extremely uncertain and speculative, with
the few succeeding at the expense of the numerous failures of others.
The slave trade, he concluded, was one of the 'gambling trades', with
uncertain profits and remote benefits (Brougham 1804, 34). In eradi-
cating the stain of the slave trade, 'a traffic founded in treachery and
blood', the state should not be afraid of disappointing the expectations
of men 'who had arranged their plans with the hopes of fattening upon
the plunder of the public character and virtue' (Brougham 1804, 51).
The objections to abolition from commercial policy amounted to the

claim that religion and morality were subservient to avarice and luxury, 'and that it is better thousands of poor unoffending people should be degraded and destroyed in the most abject slavery, than that the inhabitants of Europe should pay a higher price for their rum, rice, and sugar' (J. Woods 1784, 18–19). The right to property in the zone of freedom emerged from this discourse not as a birthright, but as something to be earned through 'a demonstrated capacity for just dealings with fellow subjects', and the reputation for oppressing Africans damaged metropolitan opinion of colonial rights (C. L. Brown 2006, 126).

IMMEDIATE VERSUS GRADUAL ABOLITION

The campaign against the slave trade enjoyed what Christopher Leslie Brown has called 'moral prestige', and it became an indicator of individual and collective merit, and the ground for a new kind of heroism based on spectacular feats of charity and displays of service to injured humanity. For all the campaigners, and especially the Evangelical reformers, it was a way 'to bring morals into politics' and open up the space for moral reform (C. L. Brown 2006, 437, 389). At the same time, this space was still governed by the 'waving line' and the mobile border between slavery and freedom, and the abolitionists themselves often reinforced the fuzziness of the boundary and the unclearness of the content of the categories of slavery and freedom. Abolition had the capacity to mean different things to diverse participants. Gisborne, like many other antislavery writers in the 1790s, was caught between his condemnation of the slave trade and his acceptance of certain forms of slavery. He thought that those who argued that slavery could not be reconciled with justice had gone too far. The possession, sale or transfer of a slave was not, for him, 'in every instance an act of usurpation' (Gisborne 1792, 11). Such an assertion would take you beyond sober argument, and beyond the arguments of Locke and Hutcheson, and risk undoing the principles of punishment and the transfer of rights between masters and servants:

> For if natural justice permits a man to be deprived, in certain cases, of his limbs or his life, can it universally forbid the exaction of his labour? And if one man is entitled to the service of another, does not justice allow him to give or sell that right, like any other of his rights, to a third person? (Gisborne 1792, 12)

There were dangers in the doctrine of universal property rights, in breaking down the distinction between the zones of freedom and unfreedom and shifting the consensual limits to enslavability. Gisborne was expressing his fear of the power of self-property in labour, and of the impingement of freedom into spheres of unfreedom.

William Innes argued for recognition of the complexities of holding a tenure in others, and against drawing a bright line between slavery and other conditions:

> ... but let not our Reformers attempt the total Abolition of Slavery until they have shewn that there is not, and that there ought not to be, a diversity of conditions; that there ought not to be, in the moral world, such a waving line, as that which, rising and falling with hill and dale, both beautifies and blesses the face of external nature. (Innes 1792, 10)

This 'waving line' made possible, even for Gisborne, the idea of honest purchase from the *'proper owner'* either in Africa or in the West Indies of a slave the buyer believed in his conscience to have been deservedly condemned to slavery (Gisborne 1792, p. 12). Such a transaction, in Gisborne's view, would not violate justice. If the slave owner continued to believe, in good conscience, that his slave deserved to be a slave he was not unjustly exacting the labour of the slave during the term for which he was condemned, even if that term was life. Once Gisborne had allowed that not every act of possession of sale or transfer was a usurpation, and that labour could be bonded for life, his argument began to accommodate permanent bondage. The slave owner could dispose of his slave to any person he had reason to think would treat him properly without acting unjustly. James Ramsay, an influential abolitionist, argued for the education and gradual emancipation of the slaves. He too was against the indiscriminate freeing of slaves. As an Anglican minister on St Kitts, he had taken slavery as he found it (as he put it), and made a point of making his slaves' lives comfortable and communicating the gospel to them. In a letter to James Tobin, he described how he treated his slaves well by feeding and clothing them properly and not forcing hard work or unseasonable hours on them. They had the opportunity for instruction, and some were 'deemed worthy of baptism' (Ramsay 1787, 22). When he left the island, those who 'were judged worthy of freedom' were manumitted, and the rest were sold to masters they chose themselves or to people noted for their humanity.'They were not', he assured his readers,'sold with sang froid; the necessary disposal of them gave me more uneasiness, than every other circumstance attending my removal [from the island]' (Ramsay 1787, 22). He was worried about slaves who were freed too abruptly. Someone who had been enslaved for a long time, he argued, needed fixed employment and to be part of a family'in order to demean himself properly, and be happy in his new state' (Ramsay 1787, 22). He gave an example: 'One woman, whom I hastily freed, [who] though otherwise sensible, having no check on her conduct, has, I am told, turned out worthless and abandoned' (Ramsay 1787, 23). 'I wish improvement and privilege to go hand in hand,'he concluded (Ramsay 1787, 22). His abolitionist views, in particular his eyewitness accounts of overwork and punishment, and his racially integrated religious services alienated him from his fellow members of the plantocracy, but his arguments about improvement and privilege brought him close to their proslavery accounts of what it meant to be'fit for freedom'. Slave owners saw themselves as holding enslaved people in check, stewarding their self-property for them. Throughout the slavery debates, and forward into the debates over incarceration and trafficking, there is this constant sense of the enslaved being unworthy of freedom, the risk of worthlessness and abandonment, as if the slaves could not root their property in the person properly, as if their own tenure in themselves was uncertain without it being grounded in labour, industriousness and a family.

In the dynamic debates of the 1790s, much of the argument was about how to end the slave trade and close the gap between Britain's vision of itself as a civilised, humane and Christian nation, valuing liberty above all else, and the practices of colonial slavery. Both sides needed to tackle this question, and the answer 'immediate abolition' was not predetermined, even for some of the antislavery activists. Innes, the West India planter, argued for'a gentle and progressive alteration', for slow and gradual progress through'limited slavery' (Innes 1792, 15), where slaves were invested with certain privileges and protected from arbitrary cruelty, towards emancipation. Gradual abolition would meet with little opposition: 'In order to perfect the Emancipation of Slaves, it is necessary, in the first place, that they be capable of being made good members of civil society' (Innes 1792, 19). The 'Negroes' needed preparing by enlightening their minds and improving their understandings before they could obtain their liberty (Anon 1792, 38). Freedom, in other words, was contingent on this kind of membership of civil society, and in particular on understanding the boundaries between liberty and licentiousness, between 'reasonable sway and despotic rule'. Those who failed to understand these crucial, civilising binaries were likely to abandon themselves to 'the most infernal intoxication and excess' (Innes 1792, 20–1). Their ownership of themselves was precarious and easily undermined not just by external arbitrary power but by their own internal dispositions and failures of reason and conscience.

Advancement towards civilisation and liberty needed to be gradual. Innes advised the abolitionists to go to the West Indies and the coast of Africa to implant principles of morality, to teach the 'Negroes' the content of liberty and their duties to God and man, 'and, in a word, to set their minds free before their bodies' (Innes 1792, 11). Otherwise, the abolitionists were pursuing a course of conduct 'calculated to rouze them to an Insurrection, and act all over again the horrors of St Domingo' (Innes 1792, 11). A general sympathy with the enslaved Africans and indignation at their wrongs 'cannot but feed the secret sparks of latent discontent and revenge, and threaten some sudden eruption' (Innes 1792, 41). The barbarity and ignorance of those on the west coast of Africa and the indolence and licentiousness of the slaves in the West Indies meant that they could not ground the obligations and the duties involved in being their own masters, in exercising rational freedom and seeking their own property. Their precarious tenure over themselves, their propensities both for conflict and for submission, meant that they had not fully understood the meaning of property and its foundations in reason and conscience. They needed to be set free gradually, minds before bodies. Their habits of industry, ingrained and developed as enslaved persons, would render them worthy of a freedom that did not call into question the distribution of good fortune and rouse them to revolutionary fervour, but would instead allow them to develop towards increased productivity and moral improvement. In Gisborne's antislavery account, freedom was a prize to be 'held up to the spirited Negro, to be gained by industry and good behaviour' (Gisborne 1792, 31). The hope that he would gain his freedom would encourage the restraint of vice, the display of virtue and, above all, his industry, until eventually his 'habits of industry will render him worthy of Freedom' (Gisborne 1792, 31). The politics of slavery had shifted their ground again to hold out the possibility of freedom as an achievement and a prize.

HAITI: THE FRAIL VESSEL OF UNQUALIFIED DEMOCRACY

It was the proslavery writers who pointed out the dangers of the doctrine of 'one blood' and equality, but their fears of the revolution in Haiti were shared by many radicals, and expressed in the 'subdued abolitionism' of the Radical Dissenters which meant that they were willing to tolerate mitigated slavery until religious and political liberty had been established (Page 2011, 764). For the proslavery John Collins the revolution in Haiti served as a particularly dire warning of what would happen if slaves who were not sufficiently improved to be worthy of freedom no longer felt themselves to be inferior. The French National Assembly's declaration that 'elevated those of mixed blood to the rank and immunities of citizens', sowed 'a germe [sic] of discord which has unfolded itself, and produced that harvest of disorder' in St Domingo. The slaves there 'imbrue their hands in blood, which philosophy had told them was no better than their own' (J. Collins 1792, 43–4). The experience of the French colonies after the Revolution showed the dangers of 'the frail vessel of unqualified Democracy, ready to be agitated, tossed, and overset by every popular gale' (J. Collins 1792, 45). Without enlightenment and rationality, freedom degenerated into licentiousness and became the greatest of evils, as had happened in St Domingo, where the insurrection had been excited 'by instilling into the negroes the novel doctrines of the rights of men, inimical to all society – Rights of savages is the more proper epithet' (Anon 1792, 15). The danger, the anonymous author of *Observations on Slavery* went on, was that by teaching people (or at least men) that their natural rights were equal, they would come to expect 'an equal right to the possession of the good of fortune' (Anon 1792, 15). From there, they would question their obligation to labour 'for the support of the rich' and ask whether the rich had 'a superior natural right to their wealth' (Anon 1792, 15), pulling apart not only the basis of corrupt West Indian slavery, but of 'reasonable' slavery and of commerce as well.

Haiti was the first state to guarantee liberty to all its inhabitants, and to challenge the assumption that in practice different people would enjoy different rights. Their act of rebellion was 'the decisive moment in which they secured their equal status in the human race'

(Kaplan 1998, 49) and realised the truth that to be fully human meant having the desire for freedom and autonomy. Their 'self-liberation' made clear, Buck-Morss argues, that the French Revolution was not simply a European phenomenon, 'but world-historical in its implications' (Buck-Morss 2009, 39). In 1794, the French state was forced to acknowledge the abolition of slavery in Saint-Domingue and then expand that abolition to all the French colonies (Buck-Morss 2009, 37). Saint-Domingue was ruled by free former slaves from 1794 to 1800 when they defeated the British military and drafted a constitution that incorporated racial equality. In 1804, after the struggle with Napoleon, Dessalines took the final step of declaring independence from France and establishing a new nation of black citizens. The slaves' action laid bare the social and economic foundations of the colony and of the world (Fick 1998, 1). This was more than a rebellion, it was 'the beginning of a historical struggle toward a stage of human emancipation, waged collectively by almost one hundred slaves in arms' (Fick 1998, 2). Slaves were making history, forcefully making their presence felt, claiming their right to human potential by seizing power and control over the politics of resistance rather than by waiting to have their civil rights bestowed on them.

For twelve years from 1791 onwards, the slaves struck out against their oppressors, organised into mobile slave bands, and carried out highly effective guerrilla warfare using captured French weapons, sword spikes, clubs and torches. Their force came from their strength in numbers and their destructive power. Carolyn Fick points to the devastation of 200 sugar, 1200 coffee and several dozen indigo plantations by slaves who destroyed machinery and burnt the crops so that production had to cease entirely (Fick 1998, 2). Their struggle took place against a complicated backdrop of revolutionary wars in Europe and the spread of global imperialism which brought the zones of freedom and unfreedom into direct conflict with each other. Haitian society was made up of white planters agitating for self-government and free trade, free people of African descent who aimed for legal and civil racial equality with whites, and the slaves who fought to achieve their own freedom (Fick 1998, 3; Geggus 2002). On the island, there were 500,000 slaves, 40,000 whites and 30,000 free people of colour. This was, as David Patrick Geggus points out, an unusually large free non-white population, and it included rich planters who had been educated in France as well as recently freed African slaves, but was mostly made up of artisans and smallholders and women who were petty traders and the mistresses of white men. The slave population was the largest in the Caribbean, and in 1785–90 'an average of more than 30,000 manacled Africans were imported each year' (Geggus 2002, 7), meaning that the slave society was highly segmented and shot through with differences in language and levels of assimilation. On the lowland sugar plantations about half the adults were Creoles, producing their own food and marketing the surplus, making a 'slave elite' of domestics, artisans and slave-drivers (Geggus 2002, 72). The rebel slaves and their leaders found themselves at the centre of a complex web of aims and aspirations, of shifting and opposing interests and of finely-grained differences in status and privilege. Their struggle, Carolyn Fick argues, was less about the principles of liberty and democracy and more one that was 'grounded in the daily material realities of plantation life and labour' (Fick 1998, 4). In 1791 their framework was about liberation from slavery and it gradually became clear that this would have to be liberation on their own terms, not accepting freedom as 'a fatal and venomous gift' when the whites chose to grant it (Fick 1998, 5).

Throughout the thirteen years of warfare, revolution, foreign occupation and popular insurrections, the slaves broke new ground and adjusted their strategies and alliances to adapt to the changing military situation (Fick 1998, 6). In some areas, when the plantations were abandoned the freed slaves appropriated land for their own use, expanding their cultivated plots, gathering wood and using draft animals to take their goods to market. Even after the proclamation to abolish slavery in 1793, the plantation system remained intact in Haiti. General emancipation was achieved by stages and emerged from the heart of slavery and the plantation regime. It was, Fick argues, an incremental and pragmatic process, at times focused on trying to change the form of slavery through cutting the number of working days or abolishing the whip, but the rebels gradually increased their demands as they emerged as 'the peasant base of what would eventually become the Haitian nation' (Fick 1998, 9). The French Commissioner Sonothax intended to convert the slaves into 'profit-sharing serfs who were to be tied to their estates and subject to compulsory but remunerated labor' (Geggus 2002, 15). They were not to be allowed to till their own soil or become smallholders within a subsistence economy. Saint-Domingue was still a French colony, and parts of it were controlled by the enemy powers of Spain and Britain. France needed the plantation system to meet the needs of a war economy, to generate revenues through the export of goods, and to provide a peasant army (Fick 1998, 10).

In this zone of unfreedom, the revolution was in part a battle over land ownership and improvement. They were searching for new ways of stabilising property through the state, of divorcing production from the fatal passion of gambling and re-instilling the morality of work. The slaves were still legally bound to the same plantations and masters, and they resisted through vagrancy and going on strike, while the women demanded equal pay and rights. In June 1793, for example, it was decreed that insurgents should be granted freedom in exchange for military service. Women were defined as non-combatants and so could not take this route to freedom. Instead, they were offered marriage to a free man as the basis of their emancipation in order to strengthen the ideal of the republican, patriarchal and patriotic family (Colwill 2009, 115). The leaders of the revolution in Haiti supplemented the plantation system of control with attempts to make the patriarchal family the centre of post-slavery society (Garrigus 2007, 148). The labour codes they established brought together the private morality of the family with public order and economic progress, disciplining both to be productive and 'civilised'. The family was supposed to act as a kind of school for workers, to turn ex-slaves away from their attachment to peasant farming and 'inculcate obligations to the plantation system' (Garrigus 2007, 146). The narratives of freedom and the logic of citizenship were both gendered (Colwill 2009, 115).

Years later, Toussaint Louverture was also driven by the need to prove that free labour could be as effective as slave labour, and that the economy could function to sustain an autonomous (if nominally French) state. He needed the revenue to maintain a strong government and a strong army, and these were generated by exporting cash crops grown under the large plantation system, maintained through a coercive work code and military supervision (Fick 1998, 11). The 1801 Constitution enshrined freedom from slavery, but stopped short of claiming sovereignty for the people and declaring independence. Article 3 stated that there could be no slaves in the territory, and servitude was forever abolished. 'Here', it went on, 'all men are born, live and die, free and French' (Fischer 2004, 229). Slavery was abolished in the territory of Saint-Domingue, and all men regardless of colour were declared eligible for all employments. The only distinction between people was to be based on virtue and talent, and the law was the same for all 'whether in punishment or protection' (Aristide 2008, 47). Catholicism was declared the state religion, marriage was sanctioned as both a civil and a religious institution, divorce was prohibited, and the plantation system was brought under the special protection of the state. Property was proclaimed to be sacred and inviolable, and each person had the 'free right to dispose of and to administer property that is recognised as belonging to him'. At the same time, Article 14 stated that the colony was 'essentially agricultural', and could not suffer 'the least disruption in the works of its cultivation' (Aristide 2008, 48). Each cultivator and each worker was entitled to a share of the revenues from cultivation, but 'every change in domicile on the part of the cultivator threatens the ruin of the crops' (Aristide 2008, 48), so the workers continued to be tied to the plantations.

Louverture's moral focus was on the necessity of work, and on the importance of cultivation. In the Constitution, he authorised the slave trade because the island needed people to cultivate it. They would be brought to Saint-Domingue as slaves, but freed when they landed (James 1980, 215). The people were no longer slaves, but they were bonded to their plantations with no option to change their estate or their occupation. They worked under 'slave-like conditions' for the colonists who had been allowed to return, for the mulatto elite in the south, or for the state, which leased the plantations back to black military officers and generals (Fick 1998, 11). This contributed to the creation of a black ruling class and 'complications were arising already' within a state where distinctions of rank were supposed to have no place (James 1980, 201). The plantation system was enforced by military district inspectors and the rural police who apprehended vagabonds and runaways. This was, as Fick argues, a reinforcement of the repressive plantation system (Fick 1998, 12), using the army to impose a forced labour regime. The state was attempting to prove that the end of slavery would not be a serious blow to commerce, and that without the fatal passion and inflamed ambition of the planters, the profits would not be leached out of the system and the plantations could form the basis of permanent property rights and a stable economy. Henri Christophe's monarchical constitution continued to guarantee the plantation economy and its exports through militarised agriculture, long hours of work, and forcing the elites not to be absentees. Thefts were punishable by death, workers needed passes to travel, and the military police were hired directly from Africa (Fischer 2004). It was an approach that increased exports of sugar and cotton, and proved in some ways to be remarkably efficient, but it created a yawning gap between the elites, who controlled both the plantations and the state, and the mass of agricultural labourers who 'now saw little hope of ever making their freedom and their lives meaningful by acquiring a parcel of land for themselves' (Fick 1998, 12). They were not granted the right to seek property for themselves. 'No doubt the poor sweated', C. L. R. James concludes of this period of 1801–2, 'and were backward so that the new ruling class might thrive', but they were better off than they had been, and cultivation was improving (James 1980, 201). At the same time, state and nation, Fick argues, following Trouillot, were split apart by their incompatible ideals of liberty, and by their different notions of the meaning of liberation and that of property. Independence, when it was finally declared by Dessalines in 1804, confirmed the end of slavery but also sanctioned the existence of the state 'and in that, the gap between leaders and masses became virtually unbreachable' (Fick 1998, 13).

The great shift that was brought about by the revolution in Haiti was the idea that the spirit of liberty could be universal, that it could, as Susan Buck-Morss argues, cross the line between slaves and freemen, the zone between freedom and unfreedom. The slaves achieved self-consciousness by proving that they were 'subjects who transform material nature' (Buck-Morss 2009, 54) and who were willing to risk death rather than remain enslaved. The revolution showed that the goal of liberation from slavery could not be the subjugation of the master, but had to be the elimination of slavery as an institution. Fischer characterises modernity itself as a 'heterogeneous, internally diverse, even contradictory phenomenon that constituted and revolutionised itself in the process of transculturation', so that what happened in the Caribbean in the Age of Revolution was a struggle over what it meant to be modern, what counted as progress and what was meant by liberty (Fischer 2004, 24), as we will explore in the next chapter on Hegel. The struggle over the meaning of property in a plantation economy shows how even the radical antislavery of the Haitian revolution was inflected by understandings of property and freedom underwritten and authored by slavery. Questions of modernity, progress and liberty were inseparable from what it meant to be enslaved, as universal freedom emerged as the opposite of slavery.

For C. L. R. James, the Caribbean was 'the paradigmatic instance of the colonial encounter' (Scott 2004, 126) because there were no non-modern foundations, no deeply embedded institutions for the colonial powers to struggle against or negotiate. Slavery had been preserved in the modern system and the 'plantation in the Caribbean was at the advanced front of modern capitalism' (S. Hall 1998, 23). For James, slavery needs to be seen as central to capitalist modernity, and he insists that we should not understand the Caribbean people as traditional Africans decimated by the middle passage and plantation slavery. Instead, he argues that nothing could be turned back, and the people of the Caribbean had been 'transformed into a kind of prototypical, modern people' who were 'violently inserted into the most advanced ideas of the time' (S. Hall 1998, 23). The rage of the sugar planters and the drive to exceed the bounds of their industry meant that when the enslaved people arrived, they entered directly into the large-scale agricultural plantation system. James characterises the sugar plantation as both civilising and demoralising, forcing the slaves to relate to each other and to their masters in distinctively new ways, informed by modern ideas about property, freedom, progress and time (Scott 2004, 128). The plantation was a modern regime, with slaves living and working together in gangs in the sugar factories, bringing them, James argues, closer to a modern proletariat than any other workers at the time (Scott 2004, 129). Their conditions were unjust, demeaning and brutal in distinctively modern ways, operating through modern disciplinary techniques, forms of subjectivity and rationality. Stuart Hall suggests that this was what excited James about the Haitian revolution, seeing 'the backwardness of slavery existing inside the forwardness of modernity' (S. Hall 1998, 23).

CONCLUSION

The complications of the debates over the abolition of the slave trade in the 1790s show us some of entanglements of the relationship between property, slavery, morality and the law. The unjust and uncertain tenure that owners held in their slaves in the zone of unfreedom undermined the stability of their landed property in the metropolitan centre, but also drew attention to the uncertain tenure that slaves held in themselves. The radical antislavery of the Haitian revolution was itself a contest over land and ownership, which at the same time as affirming the enslaved people as agents of change and subjects in their own right also drew attention to the fuzzy boundaries and unclear content of the categories of slavery and freedom. The zones of freedom and unfreedom were brought together in ways which showed the borders between them to be constantly in motion, continuously adjusted. The 'waving line' in the moral world between slavery and freedom created 'spaces of mobility and uncertainty' with many crossing points, breaking points and constant flows (Konrad 2015, 3). Within this 'vigorous exchange zone', we need to make sure that we do not fall into the trap of assuming that freedom developed as an immutable framework, and that the borderline between slavery and freedom was fixed by the abolition of the slave trade, or even by emancipation. Instead, we can use the concept of the 'system of borders in motion' to explore humans as liminal beings witnessing, confronting, negotiating and accommodating the zones of freedom and unfreedom, and the meanings of property, slavery and modernity (Konrad 2015) in many different contexts, in particular in forging ideas about the master–slave relationship and the meanings of free and unfree labour, but also in confronting the limits to the universality of freedom as the opposite of slavery.

Chapter 5

HUMANITY, HEGEL AND FREEDOM

This chapter takes us back to the waving line at the border between slavery and freedom, and to the emergence of universal freedom as the opposite of slavery as the slaves in Haiti materialised as subjects who could transform the world. Ideas about freedom in the late eighteenth and early nineteenth centuries developed in the contexts of slavery existing inside the forwardness of modernity, and of shifting relations of domination and subordination between Europeans and the rest of the world. This is a complicated space where the revolutionary events in Haiti swim in and out of focus, sometimes thinkable and sometimes unthinkable, and the slaves themselves appear as liminal beings in Hegel's master/slave dialectic (Hegel 1976) until Frederick Douglass brings them forcefully to life. As Paul Gilroy has shown, it is important to consider the relationship between master and slave as characteristically modern, and to explore the ways in which 'the universality and rationality of enlightened Europe and America were used to sustain and relocate rather than eradicate an order of racial difference inherited from the premodern era' (Gilroy 1993, 49). This association of modernity and slavery is, for Gilroy, a fundamental conceptual issue that deeply unsettles the idea of history as progress and shows us how plantation slavery 'provided the foundations for a distinctive network of economic, social, and political relations' (Gilroy 1993, 55). The conditions of this modern social life were understood to deform and dehumanise individuals, and in the process, the humanity of the human came to be understood as an achievement, rather than a species-specific characteristic (Scott 2004, 91). This entailed new understandings of freedom and history which, as David Scott argues, introduced new ways of thinking about the failings of social institutions and suggested that the sources of those failings could be historical and, therefore, changeable (Scott 2004, 92). In the revolutionary moment at the end of the eighteenth century, the clash of the zones of freedom and unfreedom created shifting and unstable ground for slavery and for modernity, and the new sense of humanity that was forged by Kant, Hegel and Douglass did not always light a clear path to freedom.

THE DOCTRINE OF BLACK INFERIORITY

The starting point for Enlightenment theories of rationality and universality that focused on the person is Kant's assertion that you cannot sell yourself into slavery because your person is your entitlement to set your own purposes, and slavery is an annihilation of legal personality, turning people into objects, rendering them incapable of undertaking obligations and taking away their rightful power to bind themselves (Ripstein 2009, 135). For Kant, wrongly convicted prisoners must choose execution over becoming slaves so that they do not become merely the tools of others. People who choose to become slaves alienate their freedom and conceive of themselves as things. In Kant's view, as human beings we cannot relinquish our capacity to consent because that would undermine our status as rights-bearers. We cannot will ourselves to stop being. People cannot consent to be enslaved because by giving up their personhood they would not be bound by the commitment they made as people. The contract to be a slave would be void because it would constitute a complete renunciation of rights, undermining our inherent dignity and incomparable worth. A man can never treat himself as a thing, and he cannot 'rob himself of his freedom, which would happen if he were willing to hand over the totality of his forces for the arbitrary, absolute, unpermitted use of another' (Kant [1920] 1997, 348). At its core, on this interpretation, enslavement is a matter of dishonour and the denial of autonomy (Altman 2011). As individuals, we have duties to ourselves that relate to 'the corresponding right of humanity in our own person'. Any transgression of these duties means that we 'make ourselves unworthy of the possession of our person that is entrusted to us, and become worthless, since the preservation of our worth consists solely in observing the rights of our humanity'. In losing our inner worth, we can 'at most be regarded as an instrument for others, whose chattel we have become' (Kant [1920] 1997, 350). It is, as Kant says in relation to begging, 'a man's obligation to exert himself to the utmost to remain a free and independent being in relation to others' (Kant [1920] 1997, 351). In this account of worth and humanity the significance of personhood is linked to the triumph of moral egalitarianism, and equality of moral status is taken as the norm and as the basis for legal and political equality. As Charles Mills argues, that means that who counts as a person becomes the central question (Mills 2002, 1997).

The core assumption in this analysis is that the opposite of slavery is the capacity for self-legislation. The slave becomes someone who lacks autonomy and rational freedom, whose person is the property of another person. The enslaved individual is somebody who cannot exercise sovereignty, virtue or free will and is subject to an owner's authority. Under this kind of definition, the risk is that slavery comes to be understood as a fixed status, one that attaches to servile minds, to people lacking in morally good dispositions or unable to exercise vigilant government over themselves. It feeds into a binary between slave-holder and slave that allows for the possibility that one can extinguish the other and reduce them to the status of an object or a commodity, entirely under their command. Those who choose to become slaves and alienate their freedom emerge from this narrative as lacking in dignity and honour, as worthless and degraded from rational freedom. This has particular implications for understanding slavery in terms of social death, but also for thinking about slavery in the context of the slaves' social subordination and capacity for resistance and violence. This then raises the question of what happens when this capacity for autonomy, self-legislation and freedom is not universal, but is instead racialised.

The debates over how to interpret Kant's thoughts on race reveal the impossibility of fixing race or social death as static conceptions of the world. Vivaldi Jean-Marie argues that Kant's exclusion of non-Europeans from his discourse constituted an indirect justification of the slave trade and of dehumanisation. It is not just that Kant himself failed to condemn the Atlantic slave trade, but that the paradigm of humanity in Kant and the wider Enlightenment is based on the underlying premise of European citizenship and masculinity, and freedom from forced labour. Only European men were fully equipped to be able to overcome self-incurred tutelage and deploy their rational, public freedom. The Haitian revolution then appears as a moment of reassessment, 'a defining process for both the European Enlightenment and the African Diaspora' (Jean-Marie 2013, 243) that was successful

'because it took place within the blind spot of the Enlightenment conceptual apparatus' (Jean-Marie 2013, 247). The ideal subject of enlightenment was the propertied European man, and Kant constructed a
racial hierarchy with European men at the apex, and black people at
the bottom. In Jean-Marie's assessment, Kant constructed one of the
most 'systematic accounts of race prior to the flood tide of racial thinking accompanying late nineteenth century imperialism' (Jean-Marie
2013, 244–5). He talked about Native Americans as lacking in culture
and the 'drive to activity' to make themselves work, and as having a
half-extinguished vital energy. Negroes, he added, were capable of
being trained to be slaves, but incapable of any other form of education
(Kleingeld 2007). The Negro could be disciplined and cultivated, but
never genuinely civilised. Drawing on proslavery tracts by James Tobin,
Kant constructed a racial hierarchy in which Native Americans were
too weak for hard labour and unfit for any culture (Bernasconi 2002,
148). Humanity as a whole could make progress even if many humans
could not, and some races did not contribute to or benefit from historical progress, but were left behind. Kant's thinking was central to a
European enlightenment that 'defined European humanity in contra-
distinction to the inhumanity of slaves in the European colonies' (Jean-
Marie 2013, 246). For Robert Bernasconi, the question is 'Why were so
many Enlightenment thinkers apparently unable to articulate the new
sense of humanity without at the same time drawing the boundaries
within humanity more rigidly and explicitly than before?' (Bernasconi
2002, 146). How can the endorsement of racial hierarchy fit within a
theory of universal human equality?

For Charles Mills, the answer is that Kant intended the categorical
imperative and the principle of right to apply to whites only, so that 'his
so-called universalism is in reality no more than white egalitarianism'
(Kleingeld 2007, 583). Mills argues for a symbiotic relation between liberalism and racism, where racism is the dominant tradition and liberal
egalitarianism is racially inflected from the start: 'race is not in contradiction to but in symbiosis with Kant's moral-political-teleological discourse'
(Mills 2014, 150). The idea of the person that emerges so triumphantly
from Kant's theory 'is linked with a subperson as figure and ground, sym-
biotically related' (Mills 2002, 6). In Mills's analysis, personhood needs
to be understood primarily as a status, and its attainment requires more
than simple humanity. Not all adult humans are persons by virtue of
being humans, and while, for Kant, all rational human beings are worthy

of respect, it is '*not* a priori that all humans are rational beings (in the requisite full sense)' (Mills 2002, 24). Kant, in other words, makes internal differentiations in the category of human beings, and partitions humanity by creating an intermediate status, and a much fuzzier categorisation between person and thing. This mobile border is full of contradictions, inconsistencies, paradoxes and ambiguities, but, for Mills, the process through which humans transformed themselves into moral beings was racialised from the start. Natural slaves must be subpersons in a theory that is based on autonomy, and that autonomy is taken to be already accomplished for those whose personhood was never in question, who were never close to the borderline with thinghood.

In the debates over slavery in the late eighteenth century, the process of partitioning and drawing internal distinctions within the category of human beings was highly contested, and the complications of 'universalizing and particularizing at the same time' are clear (Mills 2002, 28). Britons and others had, as Roxann Wheeler points out, 'multifaceted ways to adjudicate the boundaries of human similarity, and these changed over time' (Wheeler 2000, 240–1). In particular, it is possible to trace some of the processes of 'epidermalisation' coming out of multiple and coexisting definitions and meanings of complexion. Skin colour, as Wheeler points out, was not the only 'register of difference' for much of the eighteenth century (Wheeler 2000, 5). Differences of civic status, of Christianity, virtue and rank, persisted as visible distinctions in dress, manners and language. Human characteristics were understood to be formed over time by external forces working on the body. Cultural, educational and environmental change were understood to affect both appearance and behaviour. Wheeler identifies confusion in contemporary usage after the 1770s as 'color was shifting out of an elastic climate/humoral sensibility and onto a more rigid anatomical model' (Wheeler 2000, 26). New discoveries about anatomy and the nervous system connected the body to the mind in different ways, and created an anatomical body that was 'more solid than its porous counterpart, the humoral body' (Wheeler 2000, 27). Wheeler detects a gradual shift at the end of eighteenth century, so that human differences began to be understood as less superficial, less changeable and more of a reflection of inferiority than they had been before. At the same time, in the 1770s, minds as well as bodies came to be regarded as affected by climate, so that black Africans were understood to be incapable of strong exertions and relaxed in their mental powers. In the 1770s and 1780s, there was a growing sense that bodily, intellectual and cultural differences might be connected and racialised to justify political and economic subordination. In this time of flux at the end of the eighteenth century, slavery was not inextricably linked to skin colour, but was primarily understood as a political and economic condition, caught up in ideas and debates about civil society, property ownership, education, Christianity, improvement and commerce. 'Over the century, Europeans' self-perception broadly shifted from defining themselves in relation to each other, Muslims and the naked, pagan savage to distinguishing themselves from black Africans' (Wheeler 2000, 48). Gradually, the colour of the skin became 'a surface indicator of the presence of deeper physico-biological causal mechanisms' (Mills 2002, 23). In Kant's view, humans had the capacity to adapt to different environments, and the racially significant adaptations were the ones which 'once triggered by different environments, [were] unfailingly heritable'. There was, for Kant, some inner structure that explained racial characteristics, rather than their being the temporary effects of interaction with the environment, and skin colour is the most significant of these hereditable traits (Allais 2016, 13). In Kant's account of germs and seeds as the source of differentiation and hierarchy between the races, 'it is the mechanisms of the body that are responsible' for the deficient culture of the inferior races, and he insists that they permanently fix the character of the races (Mills 2014, 132).

In 1792, the author of *Observations on Slavery* asserted that much ingenuity of argument had been used to prove the idea that Negroes and whites had sprung from one common stock, but that nothing convincing had been offered to make the case. Agreeing with Kant, he argued that such a 'degeneracy' could not have been the result of external causes, and while he admitted that the effects of climate on the complexion of the skin were very considerable, the difference between the Negro and the white remained remarkably striking (Anon 1792, 33). The form of the whole head, he went on, and particularly the face, 'is in the negroe very peculiar; totally unlike the rest of the human species, but which gives to the negroes an amazing general likeness'. The short black hair 'or rather wool, of the negro' was another striking difference (Anon 1792, 34). Having set out these physical differences, the author turned to the question of mental faculties. Still with a focus on the environment, he pointed out that every circumstance had tended to depress the powers of black Africans and prevented their abilities from

coming into action. Their spirit, he said, had been worn down by tyrannical governments and by indolence, which was the constant effect of
a hot climate. However, he went on, all other nations had at one time
or another surmounted these obstacles, pressing forward to the degree
of perfection of which they were capable. 'Negroes', by contrast, 'have
always submitted to their chains' (Anon 1792, 35). They had lost their
capacity for self-legislation and with it their inherent dignity. The implications of such loss were clear. 'Does not all this argue for some natural
inferiority of mental endowments?' he asked, and if so, 'where is the
hardship of destining them to servile employments, provided we treat
them with kindness and attention' (Anon 1792, 36).

Those who were opposed to the African slave trade needed to counter the idea that bodily, intellectual and cultural differences could be
racialised by arguing against the proposition that slaves had submitted to their chains, and against the existence of natural inferiority in
mental endowments. For its detractors, the African slave trade was a
flagrant violation of the most sacred and fundamental laws of justice
and humanity. First, its advocates were falsely alleging that the Negroes
were an inferior and subordinate race of men. William Belsham borrowed 'from the language of Shylock' to contest this argument, asking
whether a Negro has not eyes, hands, organs, affections and passions.
Are they not fed with the same food, hurt with the same weapons and
subject to the same diseases? (Belsham 1790, 6). His emphasis was
on the theory of shared origins within which the diversity amongst
humankind was 'technically insignificant' (Wheeler 2000, 15), and on
the fundamentally important ways in which all human beings are the
same. In a similar vein, John Beatson declared that the idea that there
are distinct races of men 'can never be admitted even for a moment, by
those who believe in Divine revelation' (Beatson 1789, 11). Humans, he
insisted, derive their origin from the same source, 'partake of the same
common nature', are equally possessed of immortal souls and endued
with the same faculties for pleasure and pain (Beatson 1789, 12). Differences between them are explained by climate, habits of life, diet, education and other accidental circumstances, and not by any unfailingly
hereditable internal characteristics. He condemned the use of the term
'Negro' as degrading, an 'invidious appellation' designed to cut the link
of brotherhood, 'and have it thought that the blood of such men is not
congenial with your own, but that they are marked for slavery' (Beatson

1789, 26). He went on to assert the personhood and moral equality of the black Africans by asking his readers to consider their fungibility with Europeans (at least in theory) once it was clear that accidental circumstances and injustice could have worked the other way:

> But, supposing that some opprobrious appellation were fixed on us, taken from our colour or exterior appearance, and for this reason we were treated as an inferior species in the rank of beings, and, like the beasts we use, were on that account doomed to be the mere instruments of severe labour, having no will of our own, and wholly under the lawless discretion of a stranger: Should we not feel an essential injury was done to us? Should we not be conscious that our just and native rights were violently encroached on? (Beatson 1789, 26)

William Dickson argued that from his observations he had never seen any mark of inferiority in the Negroes, or any mark of superiority in the whites. There was, he insisted, no connection between intellect and colour: 'A man may *associate* his idea of blackness with his idea of the devil, or with his idea of *stupidity*, or with any other of his ideas that he thinks proper; but he ought not to reason from any such arbitrary associations' (Dickson 1789, 62). There was, for Dickson, no connection between the colour of the human skin and the faculties of the human mind. Apologists for slavery who inferred natural inferiority from the colour and features of the Africans were making vulgar arguments and basic errors. The climate, he conceded, had an effect on human hair, for example, 'But what, I pray, has the hair of the head to do with the intellect?' He was scathing about French apologists for slavery who, he claimed, insisted that creatures who were all over black and had flat noses ought not to be pitied: 'Admirable reasoning! Just as if a man should say, A poor, old woman is full of wrinkles and, therefore, ought to be burnt as a witch' (Dickson 1789, 82). As Lucy Allais argues, racism that involves Kantian disrespect entails rational incoherence, and 'the racist will hold views in tension with other views to which they are rationally committed' (Allais 2016, 24). For Dickson, no conclusion could be drawn from the external or internal peculiarities of the bodies of black Africans. Long observation and comparison with whites should mean that 'a man may be satisfied that the one is as rational and intelligent, *ceteris paribus*, as the other' (Dickson 1789, 72).

William Belsham's account of the slaves' social subordination like-wise called on the proponents of the slave trade to explain what proof they had of the intellectual inferiority of the Africans, and then argued that their putative inferiority should give them an additional claim to indulgence and protection, rather than result in their exploitation. Power did not imply the right of oppression (Belsham 1790, 8) and freedom was intrinsically a matter of social relations. Dickson, too, was clear that it was European pride, avarice and tyranny that had kept the Africans in 'a state so brutish as to give sanction to a doubt, whether the slave and his haughty lord partake of the same common nature!!' (Dickson 1789, 59). At the same time, and despite their pro-testations, the antislavery writers struggled with the idea of Africans' intellectual inferiority. There was, they could see in every nation, 'a very considerable disparity between man and man, in the degree, and the exertion, of the intellectual faculties' (J. Woods 1784, 13) and they needed to find an explanation for these deficiencies that did not lie in permanent, hereditable characteristics. 'But the inferiority which is attributed to the whole race of negroes probably arises from that depression of mind which accompanies the state of slavery, and from the discouragement thrown in the way of every liberal inquiry, rather than from any original, intellectual defect' (J. Woods 1784, 13). The Africans 'in their low state of civilization' could not be expected to have arrived at any great attainment in the arts. Woods used the examples of the letters of Ignatius Sancho and the poems of Phyllis Wheatley to show that 'they are neither deficient in the feelings of humanity, nor the powers of understanding' (J. Woods 1784, 14). He reported to his readers that Africans were well acquainted with the planets, inge-nious in the mechanical arts, and had the capacity for the administra-tion of civil government. Having made these claims for the intellect of Africans, he then went on to say that, even granted the inferiority contended for by the slave traders, 'they cannot be denied to be *men*' (J. Woods 1784, 15). The probable means of removing their ignorance, he concluded, would be patient and gentle instruction, 'administered gradually as their unenlightened minds are capable of receiving it' (J. Woods 1784, 15). There was, he said, no proof that the Negroes would not be equally tractable with the whites under mild and gener-ous treatment. When 'put to a trade which happens to coincide with the bent of their genius', they became 'as good, and, sometimes, better artificers than white men' (Dickson 1789, 72).

The debates between proslavery and antislavery thinkers encapsu-
lated both the new sense of humanity and the impulse to draw new
boundaries within humanity. In their discussions of hair, epidermalisation and intellect, they were tackling questions of debasement and inferiority, and delineating the fuzzy space between person, subperson and
thing. They were also considering what it meant to become worthless,
to lose all inner worth and to be regarded as an instrument for others.
Dickson argued that the decisive proof that Negroes were, and were
recognised as, 'rational moral agents' was there in the slave codes and
the laws regulating slaves because 'laws are enacted to govern rational,
moral, accountable beings *only*'. If we suppose that slaves are not moral
agents, how can the 'the pretended superior race' inflict exemplary punishments on them, and give them more severe punishments than whites
for the same crimes? This was not something it would make any sense
to do to brutes (Dickson 1789, 77). The passions of the Africans proved
to Dickson that they were not created to be slaves, and 'Those who complain of the passionate vindictive tempers of the Africans cannot surely
be aware that they are demonstrating the utter repugnancy of slavery to
their nature' (Dickson 1789, 79–80). In focusing on their resistance, as
well as their rationality and morality, Dickson rejected the social death
of slavery and the subpersonhood of African slaves. He drew attention
to the contradictions of treating persons as property, and insisted that all
adult humans were persons. At the same time, even for him, the transformation of humans into moral beings was complicated by questions
of debasement and inferiority. He suggested that the people who were
currently enslaved could not bear any sudden alteration in their condition. They needed to be made sensible of their value and dignity as men
and to be converted to Christianity before they were converted to freedom. Sudden emancipation of the slaves would be too dangerous, 'little
short of disbanding legions of ignorant, lawless beings to destroy the
property and the lives of a small number of settled inhabitants'. Perhaps,
he concluded, 'the present generation of adult slaves ... must be left to
die in their chains, which are riveted into and have irretrievably debased
every power of their souls' (Dickson 1789, 92).

The link between the significance of personhood and moral egalitarianism was not always easily drawn in the context of slavery and abolition, and the question of who got counted in the moral community and
the status of slaves as rights-bearers was complicated and fraught even

for the abolitionists. The threshold for full autonomy was undecided and unstable, and the antislavery struggles to come to terms with the debasement and the low state of civilisation of the Africans they wanted to free show us that the border between person and subperson was another space of contradiction and inconsistency, for Kant and for Hegel. Hegel's discussion of the process of transforming humanity into moral beings through the master–slave dialectic returns to the question of making ourselves unworthy of the possession of our person, and of what it means to be brought into subordination. In Hegel's account, this process could only be understood intersubjectively as ideas about humanity and personhood develop through time and history, and in the context of our standing in relation to others.

HEGEL AND THE MASTER/SLAVE DIALECTIC

Hegel's parable of the relationship between lordship and bondage was written in Jena in 1805–6 and published in 1807 (Hegel 1976), by which time, Susan Buck-Morss argues, slavery had become the 'root metaphor of Western political philosophy, connoting everything that was evil about power relations' (Buck-Morss 2009, 21). The focus on slavery as the exercise of absolute, arbitrary power over individuals who owned a property in their person that could not be taken away from them created a political view of slavery as the opposite of freedom. During the eighteenth century, slavery came to be understood as the ultimate form of arbitrary power and as the most grievous loss of freedom we can experience as human beings. While the question of who counted as a rational, moral being was contested, at the same time a powerful binary emerged between slavery and independence as freedom came to be understood as non-domination, as not being subject to the arbitrary will of another, and in particular not living under the threat of force or violence. In this account, the question of 'who counts' gets pushed out of view by a theory based on autonomy that is taken as already accomplished (Mills 2002). The slaveholders became the epitome of arbitrary power, lacking in self-control and rationality, and imposing a regime of terror on their slaves. In this republican and political analysis of slavery, the basis of their power lay in violence, in the attempt to impose their rule by force. As Buck-Morss points out, the understanding of freedom as the universal Enlightenment value 'began to take root' just as the economic practice of slavery was increasing and intensifying, so that by the mid-eighteenth century it 'came to underwrite the entire economic system of the West, paradoxically facilitating the global spread of the very Enlightenment ideals that were in such fundamental contradiction to it' (Buck-Morss 2009, 21). As William Fox declared in 1791, 'We, in an enlightened age, have greatly surpassed in brutality and injustice, the most ignorant and barbarous ages: and while we are pretending to the finest feelings, are exercising unprecedented cruelty' (Fox 1791).

As we have seen in our discussion of Locke and his involvement in the slave trade, this paradox was in part about the structures of knowing and not-knowing that underpinned eighteenth-century society and made it possible for thinkers to make moral evasions and live with glaring contradictions in order to maintain a 'strange indifference' to the lives and liberties of the people being enslaved in the New World. The slave-driven colonial economy, as Buck-Morss points out, continued to operate behind the scenes and behind men's backs as they formulated their theories of freedom as a natural state and an inalienable right (Buck-Morss 2009, 22). Again, rather than treating this as a paradox, we need to look at slavery and liberty as specific social relations, and explore the mobile borders of humanity to see what it meant to reach the standard of humanness and cross the boundary into civil society. These social relations were being transformed by sugar production, and it was becoming increasingly difficult to treat slavery as a relation within the household with its origins in military force. Slavery was moving definitively onto the public, global stage. Sugar production demanded what Buck-Morss calls a 'seemingly infinite supply of slaves', and within France by the mid-eighteenth century twenty per cent of the bourgeoisie were dependent on slave-based commercial activity (Buck-Morss 2009, 29). The understandings of humanity that emerged in the early nineteenth century were underwritten by the economics of racial slavery, and this symbiotic relation of sugar to progress generated its own contradictions and affected perceptions of the shape of freedom and its edges.

In the face of these economic realities, political philosophers continued to write as if their concerns with the meaning of freedom and the significance of independence and autonomy could float free of the real world of slavery and exploitation. Rousseau declared all men equal, and regarded private property as central to the development of inequality, but never discussed French slavery for economic profit. For Neil Roberts, Rousseau presaged the 'pitfalls of enlightenment' as he aligned freedom and slavery as an 'inextricable couplet' (Roberts 2015, 196). As Buck-Morss argues, a complicated set of disciplinary boundaries between intellectual history and philosophy allowed the 'embarrassing facts' to disappear quietly under the radar (Buck-Morss 2009, 34). They come back into view in the context of colonial revolutions, and in particular in the face of revolutionary upheaval in Saint-Domingue where the slaves 'took the struggle for liberty into their own hands' (Buck-Morss 2009, 36) under the banner of 'liberty or death'. Haiti was the Latin American country most frequently mentioned in German newspapers at the start of the nineteenth century. We need to remember the existence of a European reading public and the 'countless newspapers' that circulated in a situation of 'cosmopolitan and open communication' (Buck-Morss 2009, 44), within which *Minerva* had a circulation of around 6,000 copies by 1809 and was read by King Wilhelm III of Prussia, Goethe, Schiller and Hegel. Wordsworth's sonnet about Toussaint Louverture was published in the *Morning Post*, a fashionable daily newspaper with a circulation of about 3,000 copies a day (Sack 1993, 16). The events in Saint-Domingue did not take place in silent isolation, or on a small island at the edge of the world. Enlightenment critiques of colonial slavery emerged in relation to problems of colonial governance, fugitive slaves, high mortality rates and the violence of masters. Thinkers like the *philosophes* in France adapted their arguments to economic, political and social realities and reflected on real examples of resistance (Dubois 2006). People in the eighteenth century knew what was happening in the world around them and sought to find their way to freedom through that knowledge. Buck-Morss concludes that Hegel knew 'about real slaves revolting successfully against real masters, and he elaborated his dialectic of lordship and bondage deliberately within the contemporary context' (Buck-Morss 2009, 50).

Hegel's focus on intersubjectivity, on what it means to be the master or the slave, means that the emphasis shifts away from Lockean questions about self-ownership, reason and consent towards a more developmental approach to morality in the contexts of empires and revolution. Freedom is intrinsically a matter of social relations, and indeed 'resides *only* within one's relations with others' (Talisse 2016, 63). As Stefan Bird-Pollan points out, Hegel takes a developmental approach to morality, and the demands of reason reveal themselves gradually through the process of human history as humans transform themselves into moral beings. As part of the same process, 'the conception of the individual as the bearer of intrinsic value is something which develops historically' (Bird-Pollan 2012, 240). This intrinsic value cannot be deduced from first principles. Instead, people have to learn to recognise each other as people and treat them as ends in themselves. This process of recognition, of coming to see other people as humans and as ends in themselves, constitutes our history and our civilisation, and the process of civilisation makes our potential for freedom actual. Bird-Pollan draws attention to how we have to develop our ideas about freedom – 'who is autonomous and who is not is a "fact" about the world which cultures as well as each subject must learn' (Bird-Pollan 2012, 242). People find their way to freedom through the world around them, by navigating the mobile borders of humanity, the significance of personhood and its relation to moral egalitarianism.

For Hegel, intersubjectivity was achieved through the struggle between two individual wills, who come together as two determined but separate entities, each expecting to bend the other to its will. Selfhood has to be understood as a process which involves struggle, and the relations between different consciousnesses are always conflictual. Up until now, the world has proved to be malleable, and each has been able to mould it to his or her purposes. They approach one another expecting to use the other in the same way, as a means to their own end. This means that they seek to destroy the other, 'to convert it into something that is useful to it' (Bird-Pollan 2012, 244). Inevitably, the other fights back in an attempt to maintain its own absolute dominance over its surroundings and so its own conception of freedom. The result is a struggle to the death. The other becomes a threat to the subject just by being there, 'by appearing', as Bird-Pollan puts it, 'in (for the first time) intersubjective space' (Bird-Pollan 2012, 244).

Both individuals find themselves at sea in this intersubjective space, not yet aware that they are participating in a social system and encountering another person with intrinsic value. In the confusion of this arena, each combatant is determined to vanquish the other, and is prepared to die for the 'principle of having the world yield before it unconditionally' (Bird-Pollan 2012, 244). At the end of the struggle, the victor keeps the right to treat nature as a means to his own end, and so maintains an instrumental relation to the world, and does not become intersubjective.

The loser submits to the will of the stronger, and his self-consciousness is replaced by motives that come from the outside, from the master. He is no longer entitled to decide what purposes he will pursue or to constrain the conduct of others. This means that the outcome of the struggle will always be a hollow victory. It is self-defeating just to overcome and cancel out the other consciousness, to try to dominate it in the same way as you would a thing, or to incorporate it into yourself. The emerging self-consciousness, the one that has the potential to have intrinsic value, demands an independent other to overcome, but without making the other cease to exist (G. Lloyd 1984).

For Bird-Pollan, the essential problem is that the master cannot truly enslave the slave because to do so, he would have to control not only the slave's actions, but also his motivations. For that to work, the master would have to become the slave's self-consciousness, and that would mean he had to be the slave. As we have seen in Aristotle's analysis, this is the internal contradiction, the 'problem' of slavery, that 'the slave cannot at once be completely under the control of the master and also serve the master's needs (as an independent being)' (Bird-Pollan 2012, 246). The emergence of self-consciousness comes from being aware of the possibility of death, of being destroyed oneself, rather than always able to control the world and its things. Genevieve Lloyd argues that this link between self-consciousness and death makes us aware not of things, but of our own desire, and our awareness of our own desire makes us realise that the object of desire is independent of us. The object is an other, and its otherness must be overcome for us to sustain our certainty, our 'grasp of self as there in the world' (G. Lloyd 1984, 88). There is a possibility that both sides survive the life and death struggle, but one is left in a state of subjection to the other. One or other of the self-consciousnesses is objectified and has no right to purposiveness. This does not mean that one entity becomes an object, but that, as Sartre put it, 'between the Other-as-object and Me-as-subject there is no common measure' (Hutchings 2003, 62).

This outcome reflects the argument that slavery originates in an act of war, the moment when one person is forced to submit to another in order to survive, and in so doing chooses life over liberty, and dishonour over death. In the just-war accounts of slavery that we have encountered so far, this interaction is understood to result in the ultimate defeat for the slave, after which they become a living tool or a beast living outside the bounds of human society. The struggle produces unequal and one-sided recognition, or the acknowledgement of domination and subjection. The slave becomes a servile consciousness in which the master cannot recognise himself, or see himself reflected back. As Kimberly Hutchings says, 'The participants in the life and death struggle are presented initially as heroic figures, but Hegel is clear that what they seek to prove turns to dust' (Hutchings 2003, 75). The master fails to find an external object in which his own, free independent consciousness can be mirrored, and instead finds himself faced with a reflection that is 'distorted by the subjection which has been the condition of its attainment' (G. Lloyd 1984, 90). The life and death struggle demonstrates the inadequacy of any account of self-consciousness that tries to show that it can exist independently of other people. The developmental, historical, dialectical process of coming to be the bearer of intrinsic value can only take place in the context of other people, in intersubjective space.

For Hegel, this has very particular effects on both the master and the slave, and his theory of the process of recognition and the development of individuals of intrinsic value means that he does not regard the moment of enslavement as the end of the story, or as the extinguishing of personhood. To understand our self as there in the world, we need to inhabit intersubjective space, and this can only be achieved through recognition. The master's relation to the world and to non-conscious things is now mediated through the slave's labour on them. The slave can make his master's wishes come true (Bird-Pollan 2012, 248), but the master does not have to make any effort for himself and is deprived of the chance to labour on things to externalise the self (G. Lloyd 1984, 90). The victory of the master gets him the servile consciousness of the slave, while the slave gets the free consciousness of the master because the slave, through his labour, is 'able to transform his immediate relationship to the world into self-conscious awareness of it' (G. Lloyd 1984, 91). For the slave, work is desire held in check, fleetingness staved off. Bird-Pollan explains it like this: 'By going up against the permanence of nature, the slave experiences himself as likewise permanent, that is, he experiences the world as resisting him. But what he creates despite this resistance is the authentic expression of his agency' (Bird-Pollan 2012, 248). The product of his labour bears the mark of his self-consciousness and his creativity, and of his awareness that he is separate from the world and can impose his will on it. For Bird-Pollan, the point is that the slave can understand the work he does for his master as his own work, and as part of his identity. Unlike the master, he is able to externalise himself through his work and to reflect on his awareness of himself and the world. In doing so, he comes to realise that doing as the master demands and making his wishes come true is a temporary identity (Bird-Pollan 2012, 248), and also one that has to be understood intersubjectively. The slave can see that freedom resides only within relations with others, and, through his work, he can begin to understand the distinction between autonomy and independence. In this account, the slave does not lose all his inner worth, and is not regarded as at most an instrument for others.

For Bird-Pollan, the end result is the realisation that the will of the other has an important place in the decision-making capacity of the subject: 'The point of Hegel's parable is to show that we *always* have a choice and that the choice is always *ours*' (Bird-Pollan 2012, 46). It is the slave who attains this self-consciousness in the life and death struggle because, through his enslavement, 'the slave realizes that identities are changeable and that identities come from the world itself' (Bird-Pollan 2012, 249). This understanding contains the seeds of hope for change and for justice and recognition, so that, as Bird-Pollan argues, the slaves' incentives for action expand, and they are able to endorse desires that come from outside their immediate urge to dominate things, and so their reasons become intersubjective (Bird-Pollan 2012, 249). By serving the master and granting his wishes, the slave recognises that he is acting both for the master and at the same time for himself by trying to ensure his survival. His agency emerges at the margins of the master's power (Bird-Pollan 2012, 250) and at the edges of our perception. Having confronted the fear of death, the slave is now aware of life 'as something not exhausted by the immediate and particular vanishing moments of experience' (G. Lloyd 1984, 91). At the margins of the master's power the slave enters into intersubjective space, and through his labour can stave off the fleetingness of life and acquire an element of permanence. For the slave as self-conscious being, and not as an instrument for others, survival involves being able to defer gratification and to divert energy into transforming the world. Work, awareness of death and fear of the lord combine to effect a self-transformation, and slaves can begin to work their way to freedom (Hutchings 2003, 75). On the other hand, the position of the master is untenable because he refuses to recognise that he is dependent either on life or on the slave, and so shows himself to be incapable of learning. Without an intimation of mortality or the necessity for labour, the master never goes up against the permanence of the world or experiences its resistance. He never really finds the edges of his power, and without the process of learning, he cannot understand who has autonomy and who does not, and so is unable to grasp fundamentally important facts about the world. The master finds that all his desires are satisfied by the slave, and he does not learn to be constrained by the world around him. He lacks both the experience of suffering and the possibility of hope, and so, Bird-Pollan argues, 'history leaves him behind' (Bird-Pollan 2012, 251).

The slave, on the other hand, by his social death and through living in fear 'becomes acutely conscious of both life and freedom' (Patterson 1982, 98). We are back at Patterson's observation that the slave is 'always conceived of as someone, or the descendant of someone, who should have died' (Patterson 1991b, 10). His physical life was spared in return for his social death and his permanent subjection to the will of another. In Patterson's analysis, the idea of freedom is born in the reality of the slave's (and only the slave's) condition because for the master the struggle remains all about control, and 'the perverse pleasures of absolute freedom over persons' (Patterson 1991a, 164). For the slave, freedom requires the consciousness that real life can only begin with the negation of his social death. Patterson argues that the deracinated, degraded and dishonoured slave was motivated to serve his master by the hope of escape and the promise of freedom. This allows the slave to see that freedom is continuously active, creative and forged through relations with others: 'The slave, in his social death, is already once transformed. The life he strives to regain cannot be the life he lost' (Patterson 1982, 98). Through the history and experience of his own social death, the slave develops a new, transformed conception of himself as an individual, and a different relationship to history which cannot leave him behind. The social death of enslavement thus makes possible 'a transition to richer forms of consciousness' (G. Lloyd 1984, 89).

Patterson puts the concept of recognition at the heart of his analysis of slavery. The inherent dishonour of slavery is, for him, connected to its origins in defeat and capture and its continuing basis in violence. His definition of slavery as the permanent, violent domination of natally alienated and generally dishonoured persons means that slavery has to be about individuals' relations to each other and their habitation of intersubjective space (Brace 2004, 165). Patterson argues that in this space the master experienced a strong sense of honour, balanced by the slave's experience of his loss. The slave had chosen to live rather than to die unvanquished, and this defeat, in the context of always having a choice and that choice always being ours, renders the slave fundamentally dishonoured by this primal act of submission. There is, for Patterson, a 'raw, human sense of debasement inherent in having no being except as an expression of another's being'. In Patterson's account, the degradation and debasement of the slave nurtures the master's sense of honour and lightens his soul (Patterson 1982, 78). The intersubjective space he imagines between master and slave is structured by honour and dishonour, by force and dependence, by power and powerlessness. He rejects the argument that the slave stands between the master and the world, and the idea that the master's victory and the recognition he receives for it are hollow and self-defeating. For Patterson, there was no 'existential impasse' for the master because he could and did achieve recognition not from the slave but from other free persons, including other masters. In Patterson's account the intersubjective space that matters is not occupied by just one master and one slave, but by groups of people, so that the individual master benefits from sharing in the collective honour of masters and the generalised dishonour of slaves.

While the master in Patterson's vision does not get caught in the existential impasse, this does not ensure his total victory or the absolute destruction of the slave. Instead, for Patterson, what emerges from the struggle is the central importance of self-worth to the slave as 'a person afire with the knowledge of and the need for dignity and honor' (Patterson 1982, 100). The slave does not internalise the degradation to which he is subjected, but is transformed by his social death. Out of the slave's weariness of degradation and social death comes 'a passionate zeal for dignity and freedom' (Patterson 1982, 101) which then has to be recognised by others. Hegel's core argument is that true recognition is always reciprocal recognition (Burns 2006). The struggle between lord and bondsman produces one-sided and self-defeating recognition that cannot ground an ethical consensus or underpin the shared values of civil society. In slave societies that rest on the power of the masters, deformed recognition generates a false consensus which is an indication of the masters' hegemony rather than of genuine collective honour. In Hegel's parable of the lord and bondsman, the wrong of slavery lies not just with the slavers and conquerors, but with the slaves and the conquered themselves (Burns 2006, 98). As we have seen in Bird-Pollan's argument, we always, as masters or slaves, have a choice, and the choice is ours. There is always conflict in determining social identity.

The struggle between lord and bondsman is in part about what it means to be human, to count as an individual of intrinsic value and of inner worth. The struggle itself involves working out how to be there in the world and how to negotiate what it means to live in intersubjective space with other subjects. It raises the difficult question of how to distinguish between subject and object in order for us to discover the self as a 'thinking subject' and establish the person as a 'unit of freedom'. As Tony Burns points out, man as a rational self-consciousness is a free being, ethically entitled to freedom (Burns 2006, 91). As a rational being, the individual is something determinate, able to make the claim 'I occupy this space' and actualise himself or herself by becoming someone definite. Only these concrete, definite individuals can be free, so that freedom in Hegel's view is inseparable from a determinate social identity given to us by the social institutions of the society in which we happen to live, our civic standing. Such a social identity is an expression of freedom and of belonging, the basis for civil rights which 'rouse in their possessors ... the feeling of oneself as counting in civil society as a person with rights' (Burns 2006, 94). This sense of definition and of counting is only possible though the recognition of other people. Self-consciousness only exists in being recognised through the interplay of the particular and the universal, personhood and humanity. As Burns explains, I can be sure that I exist as a definite being of intrinsic value because I can see that there are things about myself that are particular and to do with my determinate social identity, and other features of myself that I share with other selves: 'For Hegel it is only possible for me to value the differences that exist between myself and another human being because in at least some fundamentally important respects we are the same' (Burns 2006, 94). In this sense, the struggle between lord and bondsman can be read as an intervention on the debate about the boundaries of humanity, universalising and particularising at the same time.

In her analysis of Hegel's *Philosophy of Right*, Buck-Morss points to the significance of the slave's self-liberation and the idea that freedom of the will is integral to the human personality and what it means to count as an intrinsically valuable being. In his discussion of property rights, Hegel excludes the possibility of owning other people and makes clear that slaves need to become free not only in thought, but also in the world (Buck-Morss 2009, 61). Buck-Morss, Davis, Patterson and Gilroy all read into the dialectic the association between modernity and slavery, and Buck-Morss insists on a Hegelian understanding of 'a dialectical relationship between facts and ethics, history, and ideas' (Buck-Morss 2010, 177). Fischer agrees with Buck-Morss that 'Hegel knew', but she suggests that we need to ask further questions about his evasiveness and how we can infer 'what it might be that he knows' (Fischer 2004, 32). He knew, she says, and at the same time behaved as if he did not know. He fell silent at the end of the master–slave dialectic, and retreated 'into silence and obscurity at the very moment when revolutionary slaves might have appeared on the scene' (Fischer 2004, 32). His moment of clarity was a 'mere flicker of insight', right on the edges of his perception (Fischer 2010, 168). Fischer contests Buck-Morss's argument about the possibility of recovering a human history and a universal conception of freedom from this flickering silence. Instead, she says, we need to understand more fully what it is that has been erased and suppressed 'before any of the canonical formulations of modernity came into being' (2004, 33). Fischer's point is that Hegel's silence is ambivalent, and about fear, fascination and disavowal, so that he cannot tell a straightforward story of liberation and emancipation. It is not enough to recast the relationship between Haiti and the master–slave dialectic as a story of humanity that takes personhood and autonomy as already accomplished. The evasions, repetitions, inconsistencies and disavowals were a crucial part of how personhood came to be understood as a status, an attainment that required more than simple humanity. If we allow these evasions and inconsistencies to slip out of view, or try to gloss over them, then we will not see how difficult the abolitionists found it to resist the fragmentation of humanity, even within their own universalist frameworks. The danger then is that we will flatten and oversimplify what gets remembered and how, and take the unified moral self for granted as the basis for our political thinking about the pasts of slavery. From such a standpoint, we will fail to recognise the violence and repression that underpins equating modernity with humanity.

In his lectures on the *Philosophy of History* in 1822, Hegel cut Africa adrift from history and endorsed the gradual rather than the immediate abolition of slavery. Slavery, he argued, was an injustice, and freedom was the essence of humanity, but 'for this man must be matured'. The gradual abolition of slavery was therefore to be preferred to its sudden removal (Buck-Morss 2009, 68). Buck-Morss traces a process of becoming more bigoted and less enlightened through Hegel's writings on Africa. Hegel's philosophy of history, as we have seen, was steeped in cultural racism and Eurocentrism, but Buck-Morss perceives her project as rescuing a fragment of the possibility of universal freedom, a 'moment of clarity' in Hegel that needs not to be discarded, but 'redeemed and reconstituted on a different basis' (Buck-Morss 2009, 75). For Fischer, it is more about the discontinuities, gaps and silences, so that rather than assuming a continuous history, such moments fit into a more complicated set of 'conflicting emancipatory projects' that constitute what she classifies as a 'disavowed modernity' (Fischer 2004, 37). Saint-Domingue is better understood not as a singular revolutionary event, but as 'multiple revolutionary moments' in a history full of fits and starts and repetitions (Fischer 2004, 133).

FREDERICK DOUGLASS AND THE WORK OF RESISTANCE

In this version of history, full of starts and repetitions, we can explore the mobile border between personhood and humanity, and the complications of the process of humans transforming themselves into moral beings as it played out in nineteenth-century American slavery, and in particular in the life and works of Frederick Douglass. The fundamental similarity between humans is undone by the annihilation of the self in slavery, by the slave's social subordination and lack of self-mastery. At the same time, something about the human being's entitlement to be his or her own master, and the duty not to treat oneself as a thing, resists this annihilation. Leonard Cassuto makes the point that the masters did not succeed in turning the slaves into beasts or objects, but 'could only approximate doing so'. The slaves, he argues, retained their human connection, becoming not things but 'people who are being uneasily forced into the category of "thing"' (Cassuto 1996, 230). In Hegel's model, 'human objectification is a dynamic and unstable process that does not objectify the slave for long' (Cassuto 1996, 232).

Frederick Douglass offers an autobiographical version of the story of the struggle for recognition (Kohn 2005, 498), starting from the premise that slave owners would not have punished disobedience so severely if they had not thought of their slaves as people. As Dickson had argued in 1789, their cruelty was an acknowledgement of slaves as moral, intellectual and responsible beings with the potential to set their own purposes and undertake their own obligations. The slaveholders' 'effort to objectify require[d] constant vigilance', and only partially succeeded (Cassuto 1996, 231). Its limits were made clear by Douglass's story of intersubjectivity, resistance and violence and his struggle to count as a human being of intrinsic value. His written autobiography can be read as a 'quest for being', a fugitive slave narrative that tells his nineteenth-century readers about his transformation 'from labouring chattel into literate abolitionist' (Cassuto 1996, 237).

The story of Douglass's self-emancipation was centrally about this literacy, and he was taught to read by his mistress until she was forbidden by her husband. A slave, the master insisted, should know nothing but to obey his master; learning would make him unmanageable and unfit to be a slave. 'From that moment', said Douglass, 'I understood the pathway from slavery to freedom' (Douglass [1845] 2015). Margaret Kohn interprets this as the 'Kantian moment' in Douglass's account, when Enlightenment ideals of reason and persuasion brought about improvement in the conjunction of literacy, education and reason, and Douglass perceived what independence would mean (Kohn 2005, 498). Douglass went on to say that what the master most dreaded, the slave most desired. It was a Hegelian moment of self-consciousness and of intersubjectivity, of realisation that his identity was changeable and of how to begin to work his way to freedom. It was also a painful moment as freedom appeared as an ever-present torment to Douglass, meaning that he regretted his own existence and wished himself dead, 'and but for the hope of being free, I have no doubt that I should have killed myself, or done something for which I should have been killed' (Douglass [1845] 2015). Literacy allowed Douglass to see that he had been objectified in the eyes of others, but not to perceive himself as socially dead. Through being able to read, he retained a strong sense of himself as a human being. Once he learnt to read, 'he assert[ed] his human identity' (Cassuto 1996, 238).

But the key to Douglass's Hegelian life and death struggle is usually understood to be the confrontation with Mr Covey, which Douglass himself described as a turning point. Douglass went to live with Mr Covey in 1833 when his master 'resolved to put me out, as he said, to be broken' and sent him for a year to Edward Covey, a man with a reputation for breaking young slaves (a reputation that, as Douglass points out, was immensely valuable to Covey in getting his land cultivated). Douglass had been with Covey for a week when he was given a severe whipping 'cutting my back, causing the blood to run, and raising ridges on my flesh as large as my little finger' (Douglass [1845] 2015).

Later, Douglass was sent to the woods to fetch firewood with a team of unbroken oxen who took fright and ran out of control, upsetting and shattering the cart and entangling themselves in a tree. Once Douglass had got the situation back under control, the oxen bolted again and crushed him against a gatepost. In response, Covey had Douglass whipped every week for six months and worked him fully up to the point of endurance. For Douglass, this period represented 'the bitterest dregs of slavery':

> broken in body, soul and spirit. My natural elasticity was crushed, my intellect languished, the disposition to read departed, the cheerful spark that lingered about my eye died; the dark night of slavery closed in upon me; and behold the man transformed into a brute! (Douglass [1845] 2015)

In Douglass's narrative, this was the process that made him a slave.

In his final confrontation with Covey, Douglass had been working in the stable, throwing hay down from the loft when Mr Covey came and tried to tie him up. At this moment, Douglass resolved to fight. He seized Covey hard around the throat: 'My resistance was so entirely unexpected that Covey seemed all taken aback' (Douglass [1845] 2015). Douglass held on and continued to fight back for nearly two hours. The outcome was not entirely clear, but Douglass 'considered him as getting entirely the worst end of the bargain; for he had drawn no blood from me, but I had from him'. Gerard Aching argues that Covey did not lose the fight, but Douglass was never punished for his rebellion (Aching 2012, 914), and was not whipped again in the six months he stayed with Covey. Douglass described this battle with Covey as the turning point in his career as a slave: 'It rekindled the few expiring embers of freedom, and revived within me a sense of my own manhood' (Douglass [1845] 2015). It brought Douglass self-confidence and determination and 'the gratification afforded by the triumph was a full compensation for whatever else might follow, even death itself' (Douglass [1845] 2015). Douglass described his deep satisfaction at using force to combat slavery, and talked about it as 'a glorious resurrection, from the tomb of slavery, to the heaven of freedom' (Douglass [1845] 2015). The fight itself seemed to 'facilitate a psychological liberation, which is as powerful as physical freedom' (Kohn 2005, 500). The confrontation was not just about self-defence or avoiding injury or death, but about his courage and manhood. From that moment, Douglass resolved that 'however long I might remain a slave in form, the day had passed forever when I could be a slave in fact' (Douglass [1845] 2015). The balance of power in the violent encounter had shifted, changing the stakes of masculinity and honour, and the white man who succeeded in whipping Douglass must now also succeed in killing him if he wished to defeat him. There was no further public whipping because Mr Covey's reputation and income depended on his ability to 'break' slaves (Aching 2012, 914). He needed Douglass's labour on the farm and could not afford to indemnify Mr Thomas for the loss of his property, and so Covey was dependent on Douglass 'whereas Douglass, who had faced death, was, in a sense, independent of these "particularistic" concerns' (Kohn 2005, 505).

For Paul Gilroy, this section of Douglass's narrative should be read as an alternative to Hegel, 'a supplement if not exactly a trans-coding of his account of the struggle between lord and bondsman' (Gilroy 1993, 60). He argues that the violent encounter between Douglass and Covey is a reworking and an inversion of Hegel's dialectic. The slave emerges with a self-consciousness that exists for itself, and his master represents a consciousness that is repressed within itself. Douglass transforms Hegel's metanarrative of power 'into a metanarrative of emancipation' (Gilroy 1993, 60). Gilroy sees Douglass and Covey as locked together in a Hegelian impasse, each able to contain the strength of the other without vanquishing him (Gilroy 1993, 62). Mutual respect came out of their struggle, and Douglass emerged with the essential dignity of humanity at the moment when he reached the point of not being afraid to die (Gilroy 1993, 63). Physical resistance was crucial to his sense of honour, dignity and humanity and, as Kohn argues, the significance that Douglass attaches to his fight with Covey 'suggests that power rather than knowledge may be the key to personhood' (Kohn 2005, 503).

Douglass inverted Hegel's narrative by preferring death over life, choosing death above 'the continuing condition of inhumanity on which plantation slavery depends' (Gilroy 1993, 63) and, by doing so, distinguishing himself from the oxen who ran away, and resisting his 'brutification' (Kohn 2005, 504). Douglass's agency emerges from his counter-violence, his physical resistance which is, as Gilroy argues, 'an interesting though distinctly masculinist resolution of slavery's inner oppositions' (Gilroy 1993, 64). It is, as Cassuto points out, violence not reading that sets Douglass free. It was his conscious resistance that created and defined him as a person. The fight with Covey provides an 'external affirmation of his reality' and 'the confirmation of a sort of equality in physical force validates his internal conception of himself' (Kohn 2005, 504). Kohn, though, supplements this masculinist resolution with an emphasis on Douglass's experience of dread and fear before the fight, his time alone in the woods, when he confronted his fear of the master, which as Hegel argued, is the beginning of wisdom (Hegel 1976). In the end, she contends, Douglass resisted Covey 'because he became conscious of the contradictions between his own idea of freedom and its incomplete realization in the world' (Kohn 2005, 512). Cassuto contends that 'Hegel's version of work needs to be redefined in terms of conscious, pointed resistance against the master's control' (Cassuto 1996, 241). In other words, it is not his work, his labour as a slave, that allows Douglass to externalise himself and reflect on his own awareness of himself. In Douglass's account, his work for Covey made him feel like a brute in his own eyes, while his resistance brought him back to manhood.

Aching is troubled by Gilroy's interpretation of Douglass and Hegel, and its implication that the master–slave dialectic ends with a life and death struggle that liberates the slave. Instead, he argues, we need to recognise Douglass's continuing struggle with his bondage, the combination of hope and fear, his actions in teaching fellow slaves to read in secret, the ways in which he and his fellow slaves 'were linked and interlinked with each other' (Douglass [1845] 2015) and bound together by cords of affection and loyalty, and by what it meant to run away when 'it was a doubtful liberty at most, and almost certain death if we failed' (Douglass [1845] 2015). Slave narratives focus not just on autonomy and freedom, but also on slave communities as oases of support and protection in the search for freedom (Drake 1997, 97). Kimberly Drake points out that in Douglass's later narrative, *My Bondage*, he shifts away from achieving individual masculine self-definition through physical power, and places much more emphasis on his reliance on others, including his fellow slave Caroline who is restored to the scene of the struggle and refuses to help Covey to subdue Douglass.

For Aching, the life and death struggle of the master–slave dialectic 'describes moments of compromised freedom' (Aching 2012, 916) and helps us to see enslaved subjects as people who assimilate and grapple internally with coercion, using a range of psychic strategies to survive slavery (Aching 2012, 917). This fits with Cassuto's argument that work cannot perform the same function for Douglass as it does for Hegel because of the explicit racial ideology of American slavery. 'Unlike Hegel's bondsman', Cassuto argues, 'the American slave was held captive by a doctrine of black inferiority that encompassed his entire existence' (Cassuto 1996, 241). The racial element of racial slavery meant that a slave was a slave regardless of his work. Forced labour in this context does not awaken self-consciousness 'because American slaveholders divorce slave inferiority from labor and tie it to race' (Cassuto 1996, 249). The master–slave dialectic is then about the objectification at the heart of slavery, and the fugitive slave narratives are work, 'the work of writing resistance' (Cassuto 1996, 243). Douglass's account reveals the depths of denial required in order to objectify a person, and it forces its reading audience to confront the intersubjective reality of the process of objectifying someone, 'not just that the grotesque others are human, but also that we humans are the ones who made them out as different in the first place' (Cassuto 1996, 251). The doctrines of black inferiority were not fixed or stable.

CONCLUSION

The process of transforming humanity into moral beings, and of distinguishing between humanity and the status of personhood, was never straightforward but full of disruptions, ruptures, contradictions and repetitions. The mobility of the border between person and thing, and the intermediate statuses of Hegel's bondsman and the fugitive slave were inseparable from the development of ideas about epidermalisation, colour and inferiority. Slavery was part of the forwardness of modernity, of stories that we think of as about progress, freedom and humanity. The drawing of boundaries within humanity, the sense of partitions that became permanent, was contested, and the line between human beings, subpersons and rational, moral agents was not easily drawn. The '*threshold level* taken to be a minimal prerequisite for meriting equal treatment' (Mills 2014, 129) was difficult to assign, and finding its edges was an impossible task, despite Kant's insistence on its solidity. The symbiosis of race and the moral-political discourse of Kant and Hegel and the inextricable coupling of freedom and slavery worked together to undermine the possibility of taking autonomy for granted in the first place and to disrupt the 'happy ever after' story of modern slavery that wants to hold the historical past so firmly in

place (Buck-Morss 2010, 175). The process of transforming humanity into moral beings and fixing personhood as a status was linked to
labour and to gender as registers of difference as well as to race. Slave
inferiority was not, as Cassuto contends, simply divorced from labour
and attached to race, and Mills's category of subpersons was never
decided on the basis of the race alone, as we have seen in the abolitionists' struggle with the ideas of debasement and civilisation. In the
next chapters, we turn to thinking about labour and gender, and the
roles they played in transforming humanity into moral beings and in
defining the meanings of slavery and modernity.

Chapter 6

UNPARALLELED DRUDGERY AND THE
DEPRIVATION OF FREEDOM

The transformation of humans into moral beings in the context of modern slavery was a process that fundamentally involved labour. The abolitionists and the apologists for slavery both tended to assume that slave and wage labour were two separate systems, although they drew the line between them in different places. This chapter returns to the themes of humanity, race and empire and explores how they were caught up with the emerging binary between slavery and free labour. It brings us back to the debates between antislavery writers and those who came to the defence of slavery in the late eighteenth century, before the slave trade was abolished. The arguments between them help to illuminate the ways in which constructions of race and labour were inextricable from one another, and how thinking about slavery as a labour system is inseparable from understanding freedom as a contested concept, forged out of experience and struggle. Part of that struggle was about trying to find and define the limits of enslavability, and its location in a constellation of concepts of self-possession, labour power, race and property. As Emma Christopher puts it, these issues were central to the 'prolonged fight over who would be eligible for freedom' (Christopher 2006, 6). This chapter explores how that notion of 'freedom' came to be associated with the West, with capitalism and with 'the contractual relation between worker and employer as the *natural* and ordained condition of production' (Pleasants 2008, 206).

As we have seen, this was a struggle and a conflict that took place within modernity. As O'Connell Davidson argues, it is important to recognise that transatlantic plantation slavery was and is 'modern slavery'. Plantation agriculture 'resembled factories in the field and, with its carefully structured gang labour, anticipated in many ways the assembly lines and agribusiness of the future' (D. B. Davis 2006, 6). Slave

115

economies were at the core of industrialisation and commercialisation, contributing to British economic growth and the development of manufacturing and 'causally entwined with the emergence and consolidation of capitalism as the dominant worldwide social, economic and political system' (Pleasants 2008, 205). Slave work, as James Walvin puts it, was the hinge on which the modernising world turned (Walvin 1996, 48). Slavery and other forms of unfree labour were a necessary element of capitalist societies from the start. In the past few decades there has been a shift in economic history's thinking about the mode of production and a challenge to the idea that the commodification of labour power and the commodification of labourers can be thought of as two separate systems. Matthew Axtell, for example, argues that instead we need to think about a unitary structure of exploitation with slavery at its core (Axtell 2015, 280). Walter Johnson (2016) names this 'slave racial capitalism' and positions it as a historic form of neoliberalism. This combination of slavery and capitalism categorises people by race, fixes non-white people in their place, assigns them particular tasks, and then uses racism to mystify the social inequalities it has created (Axtell 2015). By returning to the debates over slave labour in the late eighteenth and early nineteenth centuries, we can go back to that distinction between the commodification of labour power and the commodification of labourers to see what significance it carried at the time, and use it to explore the meanings of freedom that emerged from the intensification of slave racial capitalism. Orlando Patterson declared that there was nothing in the nature of slavery that required the slave to be a worker (Patterson 1982, 99), but this chapter argues, as I have done elsewhere (Brace 2004), that labour is inextricable from freedom and from belonging.

The previous chapters on Hegel, Haiti and empire have allowed us to reflect on the meanings of blackness and of belonging in the late eighteenth century, and we shall return to those questions here through the debates between antislavery campaigners and the defenders of slavery over the status of bound labour. We need to remember the blurriness of some of the lines of distinction, the 'boundary trouble' (O'Connell Davidson 2005) with which so many of the thinkers and authors considered in this book were wrestling. This chapter takes up Peter Peckard's idea of the process of 'unhumanising' in the context of the debates around free and unfree labour and explores how the line of distinction between servants and slaves was being redrawn. It takes us back to questions of inferiority and debasement, and to the

internal fracturing of humanity just as it was being defined as universal. Labour as a moral and political category was caught up with ideas
about autonomy, morality and honour that were deeply contested, and
the mobile borders between free and unfree labour, labour and capital, persons and property were inseparable from questions about who
belonged, and who was eligible to be incorporated into civil society.

WRETCHEDNESS AND SLAVERY

When James Henry Thornwell visited Britain from the southern United
States in 1841, it strengthened his critique of the blatant hypocrisy of
Europeans and Northerners who criticised the slave system while the
waged working class died from starvation and lack of shelter. In his letters home he described the narrow, crowded, damp, dark, filthy streets
of Liverpool, full of paupers and beggars and 'families poorer than the
poorest I ever saw in America' (Wilson 2016, 125). The British working
classes, he pointed out, paid nearly all they could earn by hard labour
for rent. He concluded, 'This is *wretchedness*, this is poverty indeed'
(Wilson 2016, 125). Within his worldview, slavery was part of the social
fabric, and such wretchedness was avoided in the Deep South because
the Southern slaveholders upheld the civil interests of mankind, supporting representative, republican government against the despotism
of the masses. Slavery was an integral part of the preservation of property rights and of the social order, so that Thornwell felt confident in
declaring 'We cherish the institution not from avarice, but from principle' (Wilson 2016, 131–2). This principle was one of responsibility and
hierarchy. The Southern elite had a responsibility to look after the 'poor
of our land', to clothe and feed those who laboured for them. God
would punish those masters who did not treat their slaves well and
failed to recognise that they were bound by justice and mercy to care
for their souls. Slaves, Thornwell insisted, were a solemn trust, and
'while we have a right to use and direct their labor, we are bound to
feed, clothe, and protect them' (Wilson 2016, 134).

It is interesting that Thornwell's description of the condition of the
working class finds its echo in Engels's famous account of the misery
and insecurity of the East End of London which he called 'an ever
spreading pool of stagnant misery and desolation, of starvation when
out of work, and degradation, physical and moral, when in work'. Individuals were starving, and 'what security has the working-man that it

may not be his turn tomorrow?' No one ensured him of employment or made certain that he would have the means of living:

> He knows that every breeze that blows, every whim of his employer, every bad turn of trade may hurl him back into the fierce whirlpool from which he has temporarily saved himself, and in which it is hard and often impossible to keep his head above water. (Engels 1892, 80–1)

Engels's work is full of descriptions of filth, squalor and discomfort, of houses that are dirty and miserable, of the 'uninhabitableness' of the industrial towns, showing 'in how little space a human being can move'. Engels made the parallel with slavery:

> In the industrial epoch alone has it become possible that the worker scarcely freed from feudal servitude, could be used as mere material, a mere chattel; that he must let himself be crowded into a dwelling too bad for every other, which he for his hard-earned wages buys the right to let go utterly to ruin. This manufacture has achieved, which, without these workers, this poverty, this slavery could not have lived. (Engels 1892, 80–1)

This radical position tended to be hostile to official abolitionism, in particular because of its association with political economy and evangelicalism and the limits to its demands for reform (Epstein 2006, 263). Their focus on 'the *name* and *form* of slavery' had nothing to do with what the radicals regarded as the substance of slavery, which for them was about labour, and in particular working for twelve to fourteen hours a day for inadequate wages. In their view, the abolitionists were simply proposing to emancipate one set of slaves at the expense of another. Rather than tackling domestic slavery by reducing working hours, they 'proposed to aggravate it, by adding to its burdens, under pretence of removing slavery abroad'. The people of England

> would doubtless give liberty to the negro, but they never proposed doing so at the expense of mortgaging their industry to the planter to the amount of £20,000,000 of money. They would, in short, make *others free*, but not at the expense of adding to their *own slavery*. (O'Brien 1833)

In the eighteenth century, and into the nineteenth, proslavery pro-
tagonists as well as radicals insisted on the fundamental similarities
in the nature of the exploitation endured by slaves and wage workers. They constructed a defence of slavery that was based on compassion for the poor and on a critique of capitalism, and in the process
they carefully crafted a place for themselves within the discourse of
humanity. Defenders of slavery in the eighteenth century 'tapped
into some of the same moral sentiments as abolitionists' (Rugemer
2004, 229) by emphasising the need for reform at home, the limits to
masters' powers over their slaves, and the favourable working conditions for slaves compared to the common labouring people of Britain
(Othello 1790). As Nigel Pleasants points out, there is a long tradition
in Britain of understanding antislavery protest as morally motivated,
and the movement as driven by what he calls 'a select band of altruis-
tic, saintly individuals' (Pleasants 2008, 206). This particular narrative
needs rewriting in all sorts of ways, but here it is important to point
out that the Quakers who led the movement had often been previously involved in slaveholding and slave trading, and were thoroughly
implicated in the economies of slave racial capitalism. Theirs was, in
many ways, an immanent critique of 'inhuman commerce', which they
needed to distinguish from other, more acceptable forms of industrialisation and commercialisation (Brace 2013b). Their key tactic was
selectivity. They were, as Pleasants argues, deeply selective about
the forms of economic oppression to which they objected, and their
opponents were quick to point out that the abolitionists were more
concerned with the distant suffering of slaves in the West Indies than
they were with the squalor and poverty on the streets of London and
other cities. Petitions against slavery from the manufacturing towns
needed to be treated with particular care, William Innes argued, since
'there is not a Tradesman in Great Britain who does not directly or
indirectly derive advantage from the African and West-India trade'.
It was scarcely credible, he went on, that they would be prepared to
diminish or endanger their earnings 'from a suffering, real or imaginary, across the Atlantic' (Innes 1792, 3).

Part of the difficulty lay in the antislavery campaigners' need to rebut
claims that they were seditious radicals who, in their support for the
repeal of the Corporation and Test Acts, aimed to remove the only bar-
riers 'we have to preserve us from the fangs of a restless and intolerant
brood' (Othello 1790, 33). William Dickson worried that certain readers

would read his letters against slavery as the product of an overheated imagination, and dismiss their author as a zealot and a rank republican, 'just as if an abhorrence of slavery implied a love of anarchy' (Dickson 1789, ix). Antislavery arguments needed to win acceptance from political and social elites who were afraid of social reform and suspected the abolitionists of pursuing a course of conduct that risked reigniting the kind of revolutionary violence and bloodshed that had been seen in Haiti. Unlike those who defended slavery, the abolitionists could not afford to allow their arguments for reform to slip into a broader critique of trade or commerce, or to address the 'problem of the poor' on the same grounds as their opposition to slavery. Instead, they worked hard to contrast the tyranny of slavery, which they saw as the negation of law and morality, with the rationality and freedom of contract.

'A LIFE OF INDOLENCE AND EASE'

The core of antislavery discourse was the assumption that slavery originated in commerce, and treated men like possessions, buying them and selling them like cattle. Like beasts, slaves were tamed 'by the stings of hunger and the lash', and their education was directed to the same end, 'to make them commodious instruments of labour for their possessors' (Clarkson 1786, 22). For the antislavery writers, this denial of command over their own labour was an injury to the slaves' self-possession, and a risk to their status as human fellow creatures. Lynn Festa argues that such 'enumerative definitions of the human' create 'a checklist of traits' and 'then reel individual cases in and out of the class of the human based on the possession of these traits or the want thereof' (Festa 2010, 4). Peckard was aware of the dangers of an approach that produced an unstable, and elastic, definition of humanity, bringing with it the possibility of 'unhumanising' individuals, and striking them out of the human race. Writing in 1788, Peckard saw that the proslavery writers had shifted their ground within the discourse of humanity to try to claim that black Africans were 'so far debased as to have lost all title to Humanity' (Peckard 1788, 2). His use of the concept of 'unhumanising' others echoed the debates about the limits of humanity in Kant and Hegel, and the abolitionist arguments about inferiority and debasement. He was clear that in arguing that the native inhabitants of Africa had no idea of civil government, no moral distinctions, no idea of religion, and no idea of a future, the defenders of slavery spread false and humiliating opinions of their natural brethren in order to justify 'the traffick in Human Blood' (Peckard 1788, 3).

This discourse of 'debasement' was highly contentious ground for the abolitionists. In delineating the effects of slavery, they wanted to argue that it risked undermining the basic humanity of those who were subjected to it, that it was of itself 'unhumanising'. Trading in men, the antislavery writers argued, caused the slaves to be treated in a low and despicable light, and their treatment created its own effects. It depressed their minds, numbed their faculties, prevented their sparks of genius from bursting forth, until 'it gave them the appearance of being endued with inferiour capacities than the rest of mankind' (Clarkson 1786, 22). Once the slaves were classed with the brutes, their consequent treatment cramped their abilities, and then the next generations mistook appearance for reality and came to believe that slaves were an inferior order of men, void of understanding (Clarkson 1786, 23). For the abolitionists, this was a gross misunderstanding. The inferiority of a particular group of people was not natural, but the result of inhuman treatment. Those who claimed a natural inferiority for the Africans (such as those we considered in Chapter 4) put far too much faith in external appearances and failed to perceive the underlying truth. This potentially radical position was undermined by the discourse of debasement which held that slavery had debased slaves almost to the level of brutes, so that immediate emancipation would lead to anarchy, bloodshed and destruction. There were many distinct threads woven into the antislavery movement, but its evangelical and its secularising aspects shared this story of debasement. As Anthony Page points out, the 'subdued abolitionism' of the Radical Dissenters meant that they were willing to support gradual over immediate abolition, to tolerate mitigated slavery until religious and political liberty had been established (Page 2011, 764). Individuals needed to be 'improved' before they were eligible for freedom.

This approach to understanding slavery and its effects was closely bound up with thinking about slavery as a system of labour, and with the ideal of wage labour emerging as normative. One of the key markers of the slaves' cramped abilities and their lack of genius was their supposed idleness. This meant that the struggle for them to come to be seen as human was tied up with their capacity for labour, and descriptions of their 'state of nature' in Africa were not only myths of barbarity and ignorance, but also myths of idleness. Part of the experience of being less-than (Farley 2004, 229) arose from ideas about labour and its intersection with property, civil society and race. The debates around fitness for freedom and dehumanisation played out not only in arguments about epidermalisation and inferiority and in the Haitian revolution, but in everyday practices and power relations in the fields and plantations.

In developing the discourse of debasement and explaining the injustice suffered by the enslaved, the opponents of slavery drew a picture of Africa as a place where the 'wretched Africans' in their own country led a 'life of indolence and ease, where the earth brings forth spontaneously the comforts of life, and spares frequently the toil and trouble of cultivation', so that 'they can hardly be expected to endure the drudgeries of servitude' (Clarkson 1786, 138–9). In the fertile country of Guinea, Peckard asserted, '[t]he earth yields all the year a fresh supply of food' (Peckard 1788, 47). This reliance on unimproved nature, their mere occupation of vacant lands, meant that the Africans 'were mostly in the savage state', with their minds limited to a few objects (Clarkson 1786, 169), unable, as we have seen, to exercise rational freedom or to be their own masters. This was a particular, mythical construction of the category of the 'African' and his relationship to labour, as the abolitionists managed and produced their own idea of Africa (B. Carey 2005, 96). In order to construct and maintain this perfect image, antislavery discourse wrote African labour and commerce out of their histories. In the eighteenth century, one of the most important sources of slave labour for the British colonies was the Gold Coast of west Africa. There, African farmers cultivated multiple crops, yams and cassava, millet, sorghum and maize, and peanuts. The women tilled the soil, prepared and planted root crops in mounds and grew complementary crops in between. Their farming techniques conserved their resources and maximised returns from the land through cultivation cycles, irrigation and soil management (Knight 2010, 43). African agricultural workers who were transported and enslaved brought with them a huge amount of skill and knowledge about how to use 'a combination of methods to produce crops on fragile soils' (Knight 2010, 64). Far from living off the spontaneous productions of nature, they were productive, improving farmers, who were also engaged in the market, and in 'pathways and "webs" of trade' through well-established commercial networks (Knight 2010, 18). In place of this industrious and enterprising society, antislavery writings told a story about the original equality of mankind, and imagined an age of dissociation and independence where people lived without government, laws or labour, 'perfectly *independent*, perfectly *free*' (Clarkson 1786, 76). For the antislavery writers, it was important to conceptualise the Africans who were captured and sold into slavery as innocent 'victims of avarice' (Clarkson 1786, 107), and to consolidate this picture they placed them outside the pathways and webs of trade, and figured their independence and freedom as separate from the market and from labour. They drew the starkest contrast possible between their life of ease, sitting under the shade of their fig trees, and the work that was expected from them on the plantations. The slaves, Clarkson argued, were 'torn from their country in a state of nature' (Clarkson 1786, 107) and conveyed to the plantations where they were considered as beasts of burden.

The proslavery writers contested this account of original freedom and independence by arguing that 'slavery was ever a condition of human life', 'the *genus* of the state of man' (Francklyn 1789, 204), with ancient and Biblical precedents, and an integral part of African commerce. Morocco, argued Gilbert Francklyn, sent thousands of camels to Guinea loaded up with salt, cowries, oil and woollen and silk manufactures which they exchanged 'with the Negroes for gold dust, ivory, ostrich feathers, and *Negro slaves*' (Francklyn 1789, 94). He acknowledged the webs of trade, but placed slavery at the heart of them. At the same time as recognising this already existing and thriving commerce, the apologists for slavery needed to argue that the white slave traders had found the Africans living in savageness and barbarity, and had gradually improved and 'reclaimed' them through their contact and intercourse with them (Othello 1790, 4). On this account, Africans were not commercial people, although their country produced commodities such as gold dust, elephants' teeth, wood and gum 'which, in a commercial light, might in time become an object' (Othello 1790, 5). Their idleness and lack of commercial ingenuity showed itself in that 'nothing but the most urgent necessity is able to incite them to any regular or consistent mode of labour . . . without which these articles cannot be procured in sufficient quantities to encourage any but a very insignificant and precarious trade' (Othello 1790, 6–7). It was well known, 'Othello' went on, that in the interior of the country, they 'eat one another rather than work for their food' (Othello 1790, 7). In the eighteenth century, the cannibal was a prime symbol of barbarism, used to establish essential difference and construct racial boundaries (Lindenbaum 2004, 493, 477). This slippage between subsistence and cannibalism reveals the potential of these imagined constructions of Africa to 'unhumanise' the other, and the central importance of labour for coming to be seen as human, and for transforming humans into moral beings. The question of the black Africans' relationship to labour, the idea that they had to be forced to work, underpinned many justifications of slavery, and opened up the question of their title to humanity. In constructing Africans as mostly in the savage state and as living a life of indolence and ease, the abolitionists conceded important ground to those whom they accused of spreading false and humiliating opinions of their natural brethren.

THE SUFFERING OF THE CARGO

Once they had been torn from their 'state of nature' and uprooted from their closest connections, the people who had been captured as slaves were subjected to the transportation to the colonies. For the abolitionists, their uprooting and their brutal treatment on board ship was about tearing the Africans away from freedom, not just about acquiring rights to their labour. In the minds of their captors, this was a crucial stage in the development of the slaves' relationship to their labour power, turning them from wild animals to domestic brutes and integrating them as commodities and labourers into the system of slave racial capitalism. The voyage, as Emma Christopher argues, was central to the process of changing 'the form of the "merchandise" as it crossed the seas' (Christopher 2006, 165). Once they reached port, the sailors prepared the slaves for market by blackening their grey hairs, polishing their skin, shaving them closely to make them look younger, and feeding them up a bit to make them look healthy. The captives were transformed into slaves, cargo into merchandise, so that once the slaves were taken off the ships they were 'unhumanised'. They were exposed to sale and picked out by the purchaser 'without any consideration whether the wife is separated from her husband, or the mother from her son' (Clarkson 1786, 132).

The kidnapped Africans left the ships and arrived on the plantations as, in Patterson's terms, socially dead, natally alienated and permanently dishonoured slaves (Patterson 1982). The slaves who worked in the fields, the vast majority of the slaves on the sugar plantations, were, according to the abolitionists, generally treated more like beasts of burden than human creatures. Slave labour undermined the distinction between humans and non-human animals by subjecting the slaves to 'uncivilised' labour. They cultivated the land with no assistance from cattle, and suffered every hardship associated with exhausting work, inadequate food, poor lodging and being treated with a degree of severity 'which border[ed] on inhumanity' (Dickson 1789, 6). Slaves tilled the ground, carried out the dung and 'must go through *all* the drudgery of husbandry, which cattle perform in every civilised country under heaven, except the West Indian Islands' (Dickson 1789, 12). Food and clothes were given to the slave to enable him to continue his daily labour, 'so that it must be considered in much the same light, as the foddering of a horse, or the expence of *fattening cattle for slaughter;* because the food is not given for any other consideration, than for the profit of the owner' (Sharp 1769, 150). Amy Dru Stanley points to the importance of time in distinguishing between slavery and wage labour (Stanley 1998, 96), and the abolitionists carefully described the slaves' working hours. They started work at five in the morning, either cultivating the fields or collecting the grass for the cattle, blade by blade. They worked without a break until nine at night (Clarkson 1786, 14). There was very little time for rest, and besides the ordinary labour of the day they were kept in mills that were never shut down, so that their sleep was reduced to about three and a half hours a night (Clarkson 1786, 142). Theirs was a life of 'unparalleled drudgery', intense and incessant (Clarkson 1786, 143). Cultivation was all manual, and the slaves dug rows of holes for the cane, up to sixty or even a hundred in a day, with each hole bordered by a ridge to help retain moisture and manure. This was recognised by contemporaries as 'severe labour', hard physical work, carried out by the strongest slaves under the driver's whip. For William Dickson, 'this circumstance alone may serve to convince the public of the state of debasement to which the negroes are reduced' (Dickson 1789, 24). It epitomised the slaves' status as commodious instruments of labour, their debasement and their brutishness, their detachment from the honourable, industrious elements of labour, and so the ways in which they had been 'unhumanised' by enslavement.

The labour they were forced to perform was not creative or improving. Abolitionists described how the nature of the slaves' servitude meant that their minds were in a continual state of depression, and they lived without any expectations in life or any hope of riches, power, honour or fame. The severity of their servitude meant that

> we cannot be surprised if a sullen gloomy stupidity should be the leading mark of their character; or if they should appear inferiour to those, who do not only enjoy the invaluable blessings of free-dom, but have every prospect before their eyes, that can allure them to exert their faculties. (Clarkson 1786, 166–7)

For Clarkson, the slaves' minds as well as their bodies had been broken by slavery. They were not encouraged to innovate or to save their labour and any attempt to do so would have been read as laziness and a desire to save their own labour at their master's expense (Dickson 1789, 25). As a result, Dickson declared, slaves were very seldom inventive and failed to seek property. The abolitionists argued that being compelled to work without pay made the slaves stubborn; their genius and inclina-tion were not consulted, and 'they have *no interest in their own labour, therefore the* [sic] *are careless of its success; no person consults their ease, therefore they consult it themselves, and are lazy'* (Dickson 1789, 56–7).

Having left the fig trees of their Lockean state of nature behind, they were taken to be incapable of exercising their property in the person through an interest in their own labour. For the defenders of slavery, the slaves lacked self-possession, but the slave 'has the advantage of the servant, in having, in his own person, a better security against excessive cruelty than the restraint of the most rigid laws, and that is, *his master's interest'* (Othello 1790, 15). Drawing on the constructions of slave own-ing as corrupt and aristocratic, Dickson asked the question 'If a regard to interest prevent not the gamester, the drunkard or the sensualist from ruining their fortunes, why is it expected to work such wonders in defence of the slave?' (Dickson 1789, 37). From both perspectives, slaves had no interest in their own labour power, and no possibility of being eligible for freedom. Once they were figured as lacking even an interest in themselves, they could more easily be struck out of the human race. It was a mark of their extreme dependence that their security relied on another person's interest in them, rather than resting on their interest in their own labour, underpinned by a property in their own person. Slaves were held in slavery, and as James Cropper put it in 1823 (Gladstone 1824, 94), 'in the language of the an old abolitionist, I will only say, if a man had stolen my horse, it would be no satisfaction to me if he proved that he fed him well and worked him easily; I want the restoration of my horse, and the Slave of his own person'.

PERPETUAL DRUDGERY AND HABITUAL INDUSTRY

This lack of an interest in their own labour not only meant that slaves were stigmatised as lazy, but that they were understood to be uncivilised by the work they were forced to do. Exhausting, hard, repetitive labour reinforced their apparent inferiority. The abolitionists described how slaves were beaten and tortured, badly clothed, and miserably fed. Women worked in the fields until late in pregnancy, and Dickson told his readers how during his time as secretary to the Governor of Barbados he was particularly astonished to see 'drivers curse both them and their squalling brats, when they were suckling them' (Dickson 1789, 12). Children were employed picking vines and insects for the chickens, then later joined little gangs for weeding and collecting grass until they were ready to join the great gang, 'a transition which compleats the hardship and misery of a field negro' (Dickson 1789, 12). Labour demands were particularly heavy in the four to six months of the sugar harvest, and each slave worked around seventy-two hours a week during crop time. The proslavery writers responded to these accounts of overwork by insisting that God had cast humans in various and different moulds, that the estates in Jamaica were well-regulated, and the work of the slaves was 'perfectly moderate, proportioned to their strengths and abilities to perform it' (Othello 1790, 16). Gilbert Francklyn, a proslavery polemicist who owned estates in Antigua and Tobago, suggested that the slave's 'severest task is not equal to the daily labour of an husbandman in England' (Francklyn 1789, 230).

While contesting this picture of comfortable and humane employment, the antislavery campaigners were aware that not all slaves performed debasing, back-breaking field work, and that some people who were not slaves carried out 'uncivilised' and unreasonable labour. This meant that the antislavery writers had to confront some of the complexities of what it meant for individuals to have an interest in their own labour. William Dickson, writing about conditions under slavery in Barbados, emphasised the hierarchies operating within slavery. Some slaves worked as porters, boatmen and fishermen in the coastal towns, and he claimed that drivers, watchmen and other mechanics and domestics lived in comparative ease and plenty. There were also skilled slaves who 'worked out', finding employment for themselves and giving their owners a weekly return out of their earnings. The custom of slaves receiving payments for their labour was quite widespread in the Americas, especially for skilled and industrial labour. Many slaves on the sugar estates in Louisiana, for example, received cash payments for woodcutting and harvest work as regular bonuses, and others received rewards for good conduct or loyalty (Bolland 1995). Slave hiring acted as an alternative to manumission in difficult economic and political circumstances and helped to keep the slave system viable. At the same time, it was a strain on social relations because the agreement between master, slave and hirer was 'intrinsically and idiosyncratically triangular', dividing ownership and control into separate spheres 'with awkward temporal boundaries' (Martin 2004, 2–3). Those who hired others' slaves regarded themselves as temporarily entitled to the full prerogatives of mastery, including force and punishment, and this could sometimes work against the owners' long-term property interests in their slaves and their future labour and earnings. Jonathan D. Martin sees this as opening up opportunities for conflict, distrust and competition between managers and hirers, giving slaves some leverage for subversion and negotiation. Managers and slaves were 'continuously enmeshed in exchanging goods for services' (Turner 1995, 5). This meant that some slaves were able to sell their labour power, and actively negotiate their own hire, and so could be understood to be exercising an interest in their own labour. They participated in decisions about where they would be hired out, and sometimes enquired into the character of their potential temporary master, exercising some influence over the course of their lives. The success of hiring arrangements rested to some extent on the slaves' co-operation and willing participation. Their owners' plans could be defeated by slaves who ran away, or burnt down the hirer's kitchen or threatened to flee, and hirers resented any attempts to restrict their mastery. Martin argues that, to an extent, slave hiring attenuated the absolute domination on which slavery rested (Martin 2004, 5) and disrupted relations of total dependence. Slave masters showed themselves to be prepared to enter contracts, and so as ready to 'give something away, including some incidents of their mastery' (Axtell 2015, 288). Slaves who were self-hired artisans and industrial workers worked alongside white workers in iron forges and furnaces, and they were relatively privileged as long as there was a shortage of their skills.

As we have seen, Dickson made clear that as carpenters, locksmiths, musicians, silversmiths and watchmakers, 'the negroes show no want of genius' (Dickson 1789, 73).

Some of these black skilled workers were regarded as having a different relationship to their labour, and to some extent escaped the pervasive and damaging stereotype of the lazy slave. Enslaved swimmers, for example, who cleared rivers of the debris that could ensnare fishing nets, and dived down to set explosives, were in the ambiguous position of 'privileged exploitation' (Dawson 2006, 1348). They earned some respite from work in the fields, some material rewards and monetary bonuses, worked largely free of direct white supervision, and were permitted to drink alcohol. The swimmers and divers exercised skills learned in Africa and so were difficult to replace, and slave owners found themselves in 'a continually negotiated relationship' with their slaves, having to concede some autonomy to the divers, and recognise their 'sterling manhood' as well as their discretion, skill and ambition (Dawson 2006, 1352–3). Hiring as a practice revealed the ways in which slaves were both labour and capital, people and property, and the tensions generated by those dualities (Martin 2004, 17). This continual negotiation of dependence and independence, security and personal liberty, masculinity and reward, meant that slaves were claiming some title over their own bodies and labour time, and slave labour was being treated as 'a bundle of property rights that could be redistributed as liquid capital assets' (Axtell 2015, 289). As Axtell argues, this opened up the possibility of slave self-purchases, and of freed people moving their survival strategies and their willingness to work into the open market, seeking their own property, using the tools of capitalism to undermine slave racial capitalism.

The negotiated relationships and enmeshed exchanges between slaves, employers and the market continued in slave provisioning grounds which generated surpluses and plugged the slaves into the cash economy. Slaves were allotted parcels of land where they could grow tree crops, vegetables, herbs and root crops, and take any surplus produce to the local markets. 'Negroes', according to Francklyn, came to market every Sunday and brought with them 'all kinds of roots, greens, herbs, and fruits, capons, fowls, pigs, pork, goats, fish, grass, wood, &c. for sale' (Francklyn 1789, 197). 'Othello' was quick to point out that in 1787, three quarters of all the circulating silver coin in Jamaica was calculated to be in possession of the slaves (Othello 1790, 17). The slave plots were a way for the owners to supply wages in kind, and to offload onto the slaves'responsibility for fuelling the labour used on the estates' (Turner 1995, 3), subjecting them to the vagaries of drought, hurricane, and variable land quality, and demonstrating the limits of the master's interest in their security. They were required to work on their own land on Sunday, so that they had no day of rest. Their plots were cultivated using slash and burn techniques that produced high yields for a few years, but required intensive weeding. The work on the plots was hard, involving cutting down heavy timber, clearing the land, and travelling long distances to market (Sheridan 1995, 58). Theft, pilfering and loose livestock caused constant problems for the slaves on their provisioning grounds, and much of the 'surplus' they managed to accumulate went on buying pickled and salt fish to try to supplement a diet that was deficient in protein and fat.

For the defenders of slavery, the provision grounds offered the slaves as much land as they were willing to work, and a reasonable amount of time for the purpose. Their vision of the slave allotments matches Peckard's picture of the African sitting under the shade of his vine and fig tree in a state of pure nature. Francklyn described how the slave lived 'in full enjoyment of his house, his family, his live stock, and his cultivated spot of ground, in safety' (Francklyn 1789, 229). The produce, the proslavery writers insisted, was sufficient for their own consumption, to sell, and to feed their stock. The slaves were permitted to raise swine, goats, poultry and all manner of livestock 'from which those who are industriously inclined lay by considerable sums of money' (Othello 1790, 17). In this context, the defenders of slavery assumed that the slaves were exercising an interest in their own labour, building up their own networks of trade, and dealing with each other in 'a commercial light'. They were able to produce their own food crops, largely unsupervised, and they organised their own subsistence production and internal marketing system. In Jamaica, slaves were allowed some time off for cultivation under the Consolidated Act of Jamaica 1792 and the Slave Act of 1816, which allocated twenty-six days in the year to cultivation, and decreed that no slave should be compelled to perform estate labour on a Sunday. Slaves paid each other wages, and by 1832, twenty-seven per cent of Jamaica's total agricultural product came from the slaves' provision grounds and was the product of wage labour. By selling food they had grown in the market, slaves became sellers engaged in market transactions, making both agreements between adults and claims to property in their moveable goods. People of colour were trading on their own account, taking an entrepreneurial approach to freedom and entering 'a hostile world as racially marked others with something to buy or sell' (Axtell 2015, 293). Slaves in Jamaica and elsewhere were 'bursting the bonds of the coerced labour economy' by participating in the capitalist economy, rather than merely serving it from the outside (Turner 1995, 46).

This economic participation meant that it was not always straightforward for the abolitionist accounts to distinguish between slavery and freedom where some slaves were paid for part of their forced labour, and some free labourers were subject to coercion and discrimination (Bolland 1995, 143). Provision grounds, trade networks and the different forms of wages paid for labour 'all contributed to generating status differentials between the slaves', with some able to exercise a degree of control over their own labour power and through their own industriousness claim the basis of self-possession. Others, the 'poorer sort of Negroes', were figured as having only what was given to them, remaining in the savage state, without the 'habitual industry' that could have made them comparatively rich (Mullin 1995, 75–8). In their debates about the slaves' and masters' interest in the labour of the enslaved, the defenders of slavery and the abolitionists reconfigured the division between the skilled and the unskilled. They hinged it on the possibility of the individual being able to exercise an interest in their own labour, and on having that interest recognised. As Axtell argues, the practices of slave hiring and of the provision grounds shifted the ground away from seeing slaves as absolute units of production towards understanding them 'as divisible bundles of marketable interests', some of which unpicked the tight stitching of the master's underlying property in his slave (Axtell 2015, 287). Slaves who could market their own goods might also be capable of selling their own labour time, and of using the rules of private property to their own advantage. For some, participating in the market could 'become a strategy of empowerment, a way to gain resources and rebuild ties to a larger social world' (Axtell 2015, 294). At the same time, as Martin reminds us, hired slaves were always slaves, and the flexibility that hiring gave to masters allowed them to convert their human property into cash crops while they 'lived comfortably off the annuities provided by the slaves they rented out' (Martin 2004, 192). The internal tensions between mastery and property generated the space for some stories of escape, but the slaveholders' 'vulgar plea of *private property in a Slave'* (Sharp 1769, 40), both as labour and as capital, continued to hold sway.

THE IDEA OF LABOUR

This mixture of labour and capital, person and property was not quite enough to distinguish a slave from a servant. The lands in Barbados were originally cleared and cultivated by white indentured servants. The labourers signed a formal legal contract, but the alternative to indentured labour was often punishment for vagrancy or vagabondage, and a kidnapping system was well organised (Miles 1987, 77). Servants were required to produce a pass in order to be allowed to leave the plantation, and they had to obtain their master's consent to marry. They could not vote, trade or make cash savings, and they were subject to corporal punishment. These elements of control were part of a wider strategy by the planters 'to demonstrate that the servant was not a free person under contractual obligations, but primarily a capital investment with property characteristics' (Beckles 1996, 576). In 1780, many of them were still retained on the estates 'where they obtain a very scanty subsistence by cultivating, *with their own hands*, little odd skirts of land which they hold as tenants' (Dickson 1789, 40). They worked the ground without using slave labour, and poor white women walked for miles loaded with their produce to towns where they exchanged it for European goods. The rest of the poor whites subsisted by fishing, mechanic employments (aligned with physical labour), and keeping retail shops, some of which bought stolen goods from the slaves 'whom they encourage to plunder their owners, of every thing that is portable' (Dickson 1789, 41). Some of them, according to Dickson, depended on robbing the slaves for their subsistence. There was in Barbados 'a redundancy of white men' and their wages as servants on the plantations or as clerks in the towns were pitifully low. Their diets were coarse, and their livings were precarious. 'Hence', Dickson argued, 'some of the book-keepers, distillers and drivers become worthless and abandoned; and in truth, as unworthy of trust as the negroes themselves' (Dickson 1789, 42). Such trust was a prerequisite for self-government, rational labour and incorporation into the social contract. Private property and market transactions might have held out some hope to the enslaved people able to trade on their own account, but for the white working poor their participation in 'masterless capitalism' (Axtell 2015, 293) and freelance hustling only served to confirm their worthlessness and redundancy. Even those who were shielded by whiteness had a worth that could be abandoned, an essential precariousness that could take them outside the parameters of trust and humanity when they lost an interest in their own labour. They had lost their inner worth and made themselves unworthy of the possession of the person entrusted to them by virtue of their racialisation. Slaves who hired themselves out and poor white workers could all be 'unhumanised' by idleness, but the fluidity of these categories is undercut by Dickson's clear assumption that the 'negroes' were inherently unworthy of trust, whatever their relationship to their own labour or to the market and however much cash they had in their pockets.

In the arguments between the abolitionists and those who defended slavery, the question of unfree labour was complicated. Being forced to labour was not in itself enough to constitute slavery. For Clarkson,

> thus then may that slavery, in which only the idea of *labour* is included, be perfectly equitable, and the delinquent will always receive his punishment as a *man*; whereas in that, which additionally includes the idea of *property*, ... the delinquent must previously change his nature, and become a *brute*. (Clarkson 1786, 106)

It was possible for those who were forced to work to maintain an interest in their labour, and not to be unhumanised. Slavery as hard labour could be a punishment that allowed individuals to keep their self-possession if not intact, then at least reclaimable. Clarkson distinguished between a proper slave 'whose actions are not *at his own disposal*' because his liberty had been bought and appropriated, and the slave condemned to the oar, to the fortifications or to other public works whose 'liberty is not *appropriated*' (Clarkson 1786, 248). These very Lockean terms of disposal and appropriation reflected the abolitionists' insistence that human liberty was beyond the possibility of either sale or purchase, and that men could bear nothing worse than the loss of liberty. It followed that 'as nature made every man's body and mind *his own*; it is evident that no man can justly be consigned to *slavery*, without his own *consent*' (Clarkson 1786, 48–9). The crux came when 'masters claim a *right* to the *perpetual service* of a man, without being able to produce an authentic written *contract*; for, without a voluntary *contract*, there cannot be ANY RIGHT' (Sharp 1769, 138).

Both slaves and servants could be required to provide perpetual service, and the proslavery writers made much of the parallels between a slave and an indentured servant who, they argued, 'is as much a slave to his master as the negro in the West-Indies is to his; and not infrequently more unmercifully treated in every other respect' (Othello 1790, 15). They pointed out that no man who was compelled by necessity to labour for his daily bread, or who 'for a scanty subsistence finds himself forced to submit to the will and caprice of another, can be said to be free' (Francklyn 1789, 13). Every man was deprived of his freedom to some degree, and '[e]very deprivation of freedom is a species of servitude *or slavery*' (Francklyn 1789, 14). After that, the question of where to draw the line between slavery and freedom was, for those in favour of slavery, merely a question of opinion and custom. The only material difference between slaves and the poor of other countries 'is that they possess somewhat less of personal liberty, and have the degrading title of slaves'. Real happiness, Innes insisted, was not affected by 'such trifling distinctions'. Slaves were compelled to submit to the commands of a master, 'but the iron hand of necessity is equally compulsory on the poor of every country' (Innes 1792, 12–13). There was little in West India slavery but the name, he went on, and this 'to the African is nothing; for he is born in slavery, and at the disposal of a merciless and barbarous tyrant, secure of neither life nor property' (Innes 1792, 13). Freedom, in the proslavery discourse, was sometimes less desirable than slavery, and unevenly distributed between Africans and Europeans, and between rich and poor, rather than being at the core of a fundamentally shared humanity. In their focus on compulsion, they drew on the opposition between those for whom slavery 'would represent a demeaning, traumatic loss and those for whom it was supposed to be natural' (Nyquist 2013, 27). Against the antislavery insistence on individual autonomy and inner worth, these proslavery thinkers used the idea of freedom from arbitrary power to position slavery as part of a continuum of subjection to force. This move blurred the line between involuntary and voluntary slavery and contested the abolitionist argument that freedom is only ever given up by force (Nyquist 2013, 351).

In the mid-eighteenth century, anyone who served another for wages was legally a servant, and could be punished by imprisonment if they left before the end of their fixed term. Servants were paid wages and served by the year, but were subject to strict legal controls. Employers were able to call on the criminal courts to enforce oral agreements. The 'compulsory labour' clause required those without visible means of support to work for whoever required their services. Apprentices were expected to live in the master's household and were not paid wages for their work. Masters were legally obliged to train their apprentices in the techniques of their craft, and in return an apprentice was legally obliged to obey his master, and was not entitled to absent himself from service. As Steinfeld argues, servants and apprentices were understood to have 'turned themselves over to their masters completely, had placed themselves in their masters' hands – both as to control over their movements and persons and as to responsibility for their well-being' (Steinfeld 1991, 40). Steinfeld characterises this as the partial juridical merger of the servant into the master. The servant's area of personal determination was severely restricted by his employment relation, and he was subject to the jurisdiction of his master (Steinfeld 1991, 59). English servants had to secure their master's permission to hire themselves out at harvest, for example, and they were forced to hand over a proportion of their outside earnings to their master. The hirer of the labourer had the right to control, use and enjoy the property of the person he hired for a specified time or purpose (Steinfeld 1991, 80). The servant leased himself out to his master. In the process, the servants, like their masters' wives, became subcontractors in the social contract, without full autonomy, because 'none of them bore full legal responsibility for him or herself' (Steinfeld 1991, 56). They inhabited the problem-space of the mobile border between subpersonhood and humanity.

This was difficult ground for the abolitionists when it came to the question of perpetual service, and the distinction between slavery and servitude. After all, as Wilberforce put it, their aim was to see 'the harshness of their present bondage being transformed into the mildness of patriarchal servitude' (Debate 1792, 10). The antislavery campaigners agreed that there was nothing in the nature of the sheer exhausting labour, even when exacted through physical coercion, that made a slave a slave. Masters had a right to perpetual service where they could produce a written, authentic, voluntary contract (Sharp 1769, 138), and trace the duty back to its source. When the proslavery lobby tried to argue that the condition of the poor in England was the same as that of the slaves in the West Indies, the abolitionists responded by arguing that they were failing to make a crucial distinction: 'they can plainly mean by the word *slave*, nothing more than what is commonly meant by the word *drudge*, or a person who toils hard, and lives on a poor diet'

(Dickson 1789, 50). For abolitionists, the distinction between slavery and drudgery hinged on consent.

The abolitionists distinguished between servant and slave on the basis of individual control over labour power. Sailors on the slave ships, peasants and indentured servants all lived lives that were close to slavery in toiling hard, living on poor diets and being subject to violence. When these groups of people resisted, they fought for wages, and for recognition of their self-possession in the form of a contract that implied they could be trusted. The British peasant, Dickson concluded, did not suffer half the miseries of slavery because he could choose and change his employer, and had the opportunity to rest on a Sunday. Unlike the slave, he had some respite from working in bad weather and on long winter evenings, and his family could not be deliberately separated from him. Richard Hillier argued that the people of England were inured to labour and did not consider it a hardship, but they were accustomed to having an interest in it, and receiving a reward for it. Hillier contrasted this hard labour to what he called the 'nakedness of slavery' (Hillier 1791, 8) and to the usurpation and tyranny of the slaveholders. It was not the labour of slavery that disturbed the abolitionists, but the lack of a written, voluntary contract between the parties, making their relationship indistinguishable from subjection to arbitrary power. In the abolitionists' selective worldview, which stressed the initial essential injury of being bought and sold over the ongoing nature of the exploitation, debt bondage was acceptable. Free-born citizens who 'from the various contingencies of fortune, had become so poor as to have recourse for their support to the service of the rich' could find themselves in a situation Clarkson defined as voluntary slavery. Where there was an express contract between the parties, the servant could demand his discharge if he was ill-used. He was treated 'with more humanity than those, whom we usually distinguish in our language by the appellation of *Slaves*' (Clarkson 1786, 4). He had the prospect of liberty, an eligibility for freedom, and a possibility of a future, which 'must have been a continual source of the most pleasing reflections, and have greatly sweetened the draught, even of the most bitter slavery' (Clarkson 1786, 20). Being poor and working hard were not enough to make someone a slave.

British miners, Hillier asserted, would not thank anyone for calling them underground slaves or for comparing them to Africans. Like the sailors defining themselves against their slave cargo, the differences between wage workers and slaves were central to abolitionists' under-standings of identity. Hillier recommended an experiment:

> The ladies in the West Indies have a happy dexterity in slipping off their shoes, and beating the heels of them about the heads of their negroes. Now, with a very little practice upon your bed post or dressing table, you will make a tolerable proficiency in the art. If ever afterwards you have an opportunity of visiting Newcastle or Kingswood, put your experiment in practice upon the head of the first collier you meet, and depend upon it, you will soon arrive at an absolute certainty about the comparative happiness of a free miner, and a slave. (Hillier 1791, 8)

For the antislavery writers, it was the legal limit on the use of the force that distinguished the slave from the servant, the miner, the peasant or the sailor. The life of the peasant was not structured by force in the same way as the slave's, because 'the peasant may defend his person against any aggressor; at the negro's peril does he lift his hand against the meanest white man, who may chuse, in the absence of whites, to attack him' (Dickson 1789, 53). This layer of outsider-ness, of lacking protection, was also about patriarchy. The persons and chastity and of the peasant's wife and daughter were effectively guarded from violence, while

> Before the negro's face, whenever his owner or manager thinks fit, his wife and daughter may be exposed naked and scourged by the ruthless hand of a driver: and will it be affirmed that their chastity is never violated with absolute impunity? (Dickson 1789, 53)

For a woman, becoming a wife who was bound to her husband as a dependant negated her slave status. Her husband became her trusted protector within the limits of the law rather than an arbitrary monarch who ruled with passion and caprice. For both husband and wife, this was the opposite of abandonment. Freedom for the 'negro's wife' meant coverture, while her husband was assured a property not only in himself but also in his wife, underpinned by freedom of contract (Stanley 1998, 59). His interest extended from his own labour to his wife's. The peasant was a drudge who worked hard and lived on a poor diet, but through his interest in his labour he was offered some protection by the social contract: 'In two *significant* words, the peasant is a FREE-MAN; the negro is a SLAVE' (Dickson 1789, 53).

For the proslavery writers, these words were much less significant. Being in a position where they must work or starve meant that the freedom of the poor was no more than nominal, an 'empty name' that would not feed, clothe or comfort them. It might, Francklyn conceded, increase the misery of a poor Englishman if he did not consider himself free, but a Negro 'who never had an idea of such a state of freedom' may be as happy as any other poor man (Francklyn 1789, 229). For these thinkers, it was poverty that created lack of freedom, and it was dependence that was racialised and associated with slavery. The defenders of slavery emphasised the ways in which the European poor labourer could not consider himself absolutely free, or equally protected by the law. He could be sent to the house of correction, whipped and sentenced to hard labour for a month for poaching. He was not allowed to leave the parish he was settled in, and he was 'compellable to work' (Francklyn 1789, 201). The labourer was not entitled to hunt, shoot or fish without being 'subject to be kept to hard labour in the workhouse, or be whipped till *his body be bloody*' (Francklyn 1789, 201). It was his poverty, his place in the social hierarchy that compromised his freedom and his interest in his labour, and the difficulty of subsisting that meant he was held in a state of servitude and bondage. If slavery was universal, the genus of the state of man, the different kinds of servitude were 'distinct species', and equally impossible to eradicate.

The defenders of slavery stressed the moderation of the slave owners and the limits to their power over their slaves, and emphasised the suffering of the poor closer to home. They challenged the moral legitimacy of the abolitionists' 'specious pretence of tender anxiety in the cause of humanity' (Francklyn 1789, 2), and argued that there was no need to 'seek abroad' for it 'as long as we can use our own humanity with propriety amongst ourselves' (Othello 1790, 39). The ways in which individuals sought to transform themselves into moral beings were contested. The proper use of our humanity was to express a tender regard for our fellow creatures by helping the sick and infirm, the poor and the aged. Their suffering, Francklyn argued, had been disregarded by all sorts of people who 'have been incited to interest themselves in the visionary distresses of the Negroes in Africa' (Francklyn 1789, 18) instead of focusing on 'the swarms of beggars, vagrants, thieves, and real objects of charity' (Othello 1790, 38) on their own streets. This proslavery discourse saw no great advantage in being free to sell your labour power, in suffering from the pain and misery of the 'extremity of cold' of Northern Europe (Francklyn 1789, 230), ending up as part of the divided and marginalised 'motley crew' of anonymous, landless, poor and mobile workers described by Linebaugh and Rediker (Rediker and Linebaugh 2002) and subject to the vagaries of 'the creative destruction of masterless democratic capitalism' (Axtell 2015, 293). The distinctions that both the apologists for slavery and the abolitionists made between the 'poorer sort of Negroes' and those who were habituated to industry or 'industriously inclined' were crucial in defining who was eligible for freedom. In abolitionist discourse, the possibilities of being worthless, abandoned and debased were in some ways brought frighteningly close by being made open to everyone, reflecting the 'democratic' elements of masterless capitalism, and made contingent on bad fortune.

CONCLUSION

The hardening racial categories that underpinned the social contract made clear that the peasant was a free man and the 'negro' was a slave. In the abolitionist imaginary, racial others were not figured as naturally incapable of ingenuity or of improvement, or as permanently condemned to the condition of nature, but they were figured as lacking in industry and an interest in their own labour (Goldberg 2002, 45). Their lack of industry in turn meant that they lacked the prerequisites to make them eligible for freedom, and for belonging to the state. Slaves, Dickson argued, could not bear any great and sudden alteration of their condition. As we have seen, to have any hope of belonging, '[t]hey must be made sensible of their value and dignity as *men* and, must be converted to Christianity, before they can be expected to act properly as *freemen*'. Otherwise, idleness, drunkenness and violence would arise from 'brutish field negroes' being suddenly raised to affluence and converted to freedom (Dickson 1789, 91). Even for the abolitionists, the slaves were figured as lacking an interest in themselves, the self-possession that grounded proper, limited, masculine and Christian freedom. Such self-proprietorship was incompatible with the 'brutishness' that they could not escape from once they had been constructed as 'negroes'. Slaves had no security, and so no real property in their labour or control over their labour power. Even the industriously inclined could only aspire to a precarious grasp on their labour, a privileged exploitation that did not translate into freedom, or into a government that would afford security to their acquisitions (Clarkson 1786, 60). As a result, an 'end to slavery often ushered in not freedom, but bondage in its various, adaptable guises' (Walvin 1996, 179), and it is this adaptability that has made slavery so difficult to define and to disentangle from other forms of exploitation.

The abolitionists' arguments about freedom, rationality and shared humanity could not help them to escape the malleability of bondage, as it resurfaced in questions about the command over labour, trustworthiness, the appearance of inferior capacities, and the division between the industrious and the idle. They continued to be haunted by the spectre of the mob. Free wage earners who were treated as if they were mere brutes, worthless and abandoned white men, debased slaves who worked like cattle and 'wretched Africans' who shed the blood of others subdued their abolitionism and tempered their notions of freedom. Their ideas about labour were inextricable from what it meant to be a man, to make your mind and body your own, and to engage with the world as someone who could defend your person against an aggressor and make contracts with others on the basis of trust. For the abolitionists, the 'nakedness of slavery' lay in the arbitrary power of the planters, the moment of unfreedom when self-proprietorship was snatched away from a person. The limits of their opposition to forced labour, their insistence that the social contract could distinguish clearly between the free man and the slave and their own distinctions between the 'poorer sort of Negroes' and the 'industriously inclined' meant that their antislavery strategies focused on rescuing those who had improved themselves, and not on imagining the continuing inequalities of what it meant to be either a 'negro' or a drudge, or a voluntary slave.

The antislavery writings of the late eighteenth century make clear that the idea of rational labour is inseparable from the state, and freedom is inextricable from self-government. In their attempts to differentiate between free and unfree labour, the ideas of contract and consent have to bear an almost unbearable weight. Not being a slave is about not being bought, transferred and sold. Non-slavery looks like a bare and formal freedom, a contract that brings only a partial incorporation into civil society and the state, a domination that is patriarchal but not arbitrary, labour that is hard and exhausting but not perpetual. The social relations of power remained virtually the same. The status of slaves would continue to inform their relationship to the state because their various freedoms and their attempts to make their own lives more tolerable were all subject to the constant threat of violation. It was based on rights 'which were readily denied, infringed or transgressed' (Walvin 1996, 156). Slaves could only ever aspire or expect to be 'freelance hustlers', migrant labourers, not fully incorporated into civil society or the state. Labour, with its connections to autonomy, morality and honour, created its own registers of difference that were riveted into the more solid, racially inflected bodies identified by Wheeler (2000). These hierarchies of labour that defined belonging and membership were also deeply gendered, and the next chapter goes on to explore how women's subjection fits into the mobile borderlands between subpersonhood, humanity and property.

Chapter 7

THE SUBJECTION OF WOMEN: LOOPHOLES OF RETREAT?

This chapter focuses on gender and slavery, and in particular on the rhetoric of thinking about wives as slaves in both the pre- and post-abolition contexts, and in the different and parallel conversations about empire that went on through the late eighteenth and nineteenth centuries. In the process of transforming humanity into moral beings, gender as a register of difference played out in complex ways that troubled the concept of personhood as a status and redrew some of the boundaries of enslavability. The place of women within the discourses of debasement and inferiority was part of both the universality and the fragmenting of humanity, pulled in both directions by ideas about nature, progress and civilisation. The borders between free and unfree labour, labour and capital, persons and property were even more undecided, and more heavily policed, for women. The distinction between honourable labour and drudgery, and questions of autonomy, morality and honour were highly gendered and mediated through marriage as well as wage contracts. The 'vision of useful men and protected wives' meant that wage and marriage agreements mutually reinforced one another (Cope 2004, 10) and enforced a particular and gendered conception of freedom. This chapter explores some of the silences and occlusions that surrounded women's experience of sexual subjection under slavery, their agency and power under conditions of 'oppressive freedom', and the spaces they inhabited and experienced as loopholes of retreat and as stifling prisons. The complications of home, the 'collapsed geography' of the plantation household, and the contested meanings of the private/public divide require us to think about the power relations within the household, between women and men, but also between women and women living in constant contact with one another (Glymph 2008).

MARRIAGE AND SLAVERY

John and Mary Hylas were slaves who were brought over to England in 1754, and were married with the consent of their respective master and mistress. In 1766, Mary was sent away to Barbados without her husband's consent, and John Hylas sued her master, John Newton (UCL, 2017a), for damages, claiming that he had kidnapped Mary and resold her into slavery in Barbados. The court found in Hylas's favour, and the defendant was bound to bring Mary back and restore her to her husband within six months, and was charged with one shilling damages (Paugh 2014, 630, Anon 1820). Mary Hylas was both enslaved and a *feme covert*, belonging to both her master and her husband. Cases involving married women were inherently problematic, and different from cases such as that of James Somerset in 1772 where Lord Mansfield ruled that a slave landing in England 'falls under the protection of the laws, and *so far* becomes a freeman, though his master's right to his service may *possibly* continue' (Anon 1820, 207). The Somerset case was a legal action against wrongful enslavement, and Lord Mansfield granted his habeas corpus petition. This ruling denied the right of Somerset's master, Charles Stewart, a Virginian planter, to exercise the rights of a slaveholder over his servant (Blackburn 2013, 134). Mansfield affirmed that being a slave elsewhere was not enough to mean that Somerset could be forcibly removed from England (Harris 2007, 447). Slave status was founded on positive law, and Mansfield's ruling confirmed that slavery 'was an institution constrained by law' (Harris 2007, 442). The case was widely interpreted as meaning that slavery was illegal in England and that slaves entering free territory were free, but slavery in the colonies was left intact and its legality was affirmed. The reception and the legacies of the Somerset case were complex, but they tended to focus on Somerset's autonomy and legal personhood asserted in the face of arbitrary power, and on the distinction between servant and slave that could be identified by contract. These questions were more complicated in the case of Mary Hylas and her 'freedom suit', which was brought by her husband, and which contained her freedom inside his. The Somerset ruling seemed to confirm the boundaries of the zones of freedom and unfreedom, but in Hylas's case the borders of contract were more mobile, and much closer to home. In arguing against Mary's forcible seizure by her slave owner and for her return to John Hylas, Granville Sharp 'relied heavily on the assertion that man and wife should be regarded as a single, indivisible and utterly harmonious legal entity' (Paugh 2014, 633).

For enslaved women without the protection of a husband and the legal status of a wife, freedom and the status of personhood were more precarious, but less circumscribed. Mary Prince was a West Indian house-hold slave originally from Bermuda who came with her owner to England in 1828, and her autobiographical *History* was published in London and Edinburgh in 1831, chronicling her enslavement to a series of abusive masters in the West Indies and her captivity in England (Wong 2001, 60). In England, Prince left her master John Wood and he returned to Antigua without her. From there he refused to manumit or sell her, so that she remained a slave elsewhere. In England, following the Somerset ruling, she was relatively free, but she could not return to Antigua as a free British subject. Returning to the Caribbean would have meant reverting to her slave status (Wong 2001, 60). The British courts did not have the power to force Wood to manumit her or to ensure her safe passage, because slavery was still legal in the plantation zone. Prince was trapped in the imperial space between freedom and slavery, but her owner kept claiming that Prince had chosen to leave his household and remain in England, 'turn-ing her agency into the very instrument of his continuing power over her' (Wong 2001, 60). She was still his property, and his right to her service continued while slavery was an institution rooted in the law.

Mary Prince emerges from her own *History*, heavily mediated by her editor Thomas Pringle and the amanuensis Elizabeth Strickland, both members of the Anti-Slavery Society, as a survivor, who was entrepreneurial, resourceful and resistant. As Wong points out, Prince was enslaved as chattel and the object of another's property, and this 'radically complicates what can be rightly identified as "agency"', but does not remove the possibility of it altogether (Wong 2001, 61). Prince described how she took in washing and sold coffee, yams and other provisions to the captains of ships, sometimes buying a cheap hog on board a ship and selling it for double the money on shore. 'I did not sit idling during the absence of my owners', the *History* records, 'for I wanted, by all honest means, to earn money to buy my freedom' (Prince 1831, 23). Prince's vision of freedom was, like Somerset's, about the difference between slave and servant. She wanted to be able to change her employer by giving notice and being hired by another one, and she demanded proper treatment and proper wages, in line with English servants (Kaplan 2006, 202). Even in slavery, she negotiated her own sale to Mr Wood: 'it was my own fault that I came under him, I was anxious to go' (Prince 1831, 20), and she asked other masters to buy her. She went to Mr Burchell and asked him to buy her with money she had saved, in the hope of purchasing her freedom. Mr Wood refused to sell her (Prince 1831, 21), or to allow her to purchase her freedom: 'if I wished to be free, I was free in England, and I might go and try what freedom would do for me, and be d_d' (Prince 1831, 27).

Mr and Mrs Wood constantly threatened to send her back to Antigua, or to turn her out of doors and let her provide for herself. Eventually, she took them at their word, 'though I thought it very hard, after I had lived with them for thirteen years, and worked for them like a horse, to be driven out in this way, like a beggar' (Prince 1831, 28). Mr and Mrs Wood rose up in a passion, opened the door and ordered Prince to leave in response to Prince's protests about doing the laundry in hot water that exacerbated her rheumatism. 'But I was a stranger, and did not know one door in the street from another, and was unwilling to go away' (Prince 1831, 27). This moment of being turned out of doors exemplifies the complications of what can be identified as agency in the context of slavery. Wong emphasises Prince's sense of dislocation and isolation in London, her dependent status as a foreigner and a stranger, and reads the Woods' action as a violent act 'that permanently severs her from Antigua and the possibility of a return home' (Wong 2001, 62). It can be made to look like a turning point and a moment of resistance, but Prince was forced to 'remain within the oppressive terms of existence dictated by the Woods' (Wong 2001, 63).

In being thrown out of doors, Prince lost her home in England, and could not go back to Antigua without being re-enslaved. She could not be forcibly returned, but if she went back voluntarily she would become a slave again. Her freedom required 'the loss of home' (Wong 2001, 64). Prince was given the illusion of choice by the Woods' violent action, but for her to exercise free will was impossible. She was driven out by her owners, and then countered this threat by 'embracing the desperate freedom on being "turned out of doors"' and publicising her story 'in the face of her continuing dislocation and dispossession in England' (Wong 2001, 69–70). 'Prince's painful sense of dependency', Wong argues, was 'fueled by her anxiety over the gendered significance of her homelessness and heightened by the possible appearance of vagrancy, poverty, and indecency' (Wong 2001, 67). Without a husband to constrain and restrain her freedom, and systematically denied the ability to return to her home, her freedom made her immediately suspect. Her agency in earning money and negotiating her own status was not enough to protect her against being considered a 'vagabond whose mobility [was] criminalized' (Wong 2001, 69).

Gillian Whitlock is interested in how Prince found 'room for manoeuvre in the text' (Whitlock 2000, 20), where the difficulty was that she could only speak by presenting herself as virtuous and domesticated, but she had to describe experiences that made virtue and domesticity impossible for her. Whitlock points to the gap between experience and telling the truth in Prince's *History*, and in particular to the problem of speaking the truth about sexual abuse and control. The challenge for the black female abolitionist 'was to be an agent without appearing to be one', 'to tell and not tell', to bring home the degradation, brutality and violence of slavery without compromising her innocence and propriety (Whitlock 2000, 21). Jenny Sharpe argues that in order to meet (or anticipate) the 'antislavery requirement' of the free and enlightened ex-slave, Prince had to exhibit the moral agency of a free individual (Sharpe 1996), and in particular of a respectable woman. She had to claim the gendered status of personhood and autonomy before they were available to her, and that meant trying to counter any appearance of vagrancy, poverty or indecency. She had to show her audience that she was not a freelance hustler, even though (or perhaps because) her enterprise and her earning were the source of her agency and power. There is clearly the possibility that Prince engaged in sexual relations with Wood to persuade him to bring her to England, and that could help to explain why he refused to manumit her once she was there, but both her engagement in transactional sex and her rape by her master were written out of the story. Sharpe focuses on Prince's efforts to earn enough money to purchase her freedom, and suggests that it is likely that she made an arrangement with Captain Abbot to serve as his housekeeper and concubine in exchange for her purchase price of $300. He lent her some cash to help her buy her freedom, 'but when I could not get free he got it back again' (Prince 1831, 23). The *History* was written to imply that the money was a loan, and it worked hard not to condone 'such negotiations as a legitimate means to manumission' (Sharpe 1996) in order to sustain its status as an abolitionist narrative. When her relationship with Abbot came to light in the text, Prince was required to recognise herself as a 'great sinner' which, as Sharpe argues, 'codes the sexual availability of slave women as their moral weakness' (Sharpe 1996).

As a slave woman, Prince existed outside the structures of domesticity but was expected to uphold its ideals (Sharpe 1996). She married Daniel James, a free black man, who became a fellow member of the Moravian Church. The *History* is careful to point out that he was industrious and comfortably off, but they could not be married in the English Church because no free man could marry a slave woman (Prince 1831, 25). Mrs Wood was angered by the marriage and stirred up her husband to flog Prince with a horsewhip. She was concerned, Prince concluded, that Prince would spend her time doing her husband's washing instead of hers. Prince wrote, 'I had not much happiness in my marriage, owing to my being a slave' (Prince 1831, 25). Her marital status offered her no protection. She was abused by Mrs Wood for being married – 'She did not lick me herself, but she got her husband to do it for her, whilst she fretted the flesh off my bones' (Prince 1831, 25) – but she always refused to sell her. Rauwerda argues that, in the end, 'Prince has no agency with which to secure her manumission, possibly even as a result of her sexual relations' (Rauwerda 2001, 402). Wood did not release her. Sharpe uses Prince's *History* and her court testimony to question 'the use of a model of self-autonomy for explaining power relations under slavery' (Sharpe 1996).

Mary Prince's story was 'explosive' because it brought slavery home, and gendered it as female. Prince, through the text, exhibited the innate longing for freedom that defined liberal personhood and was more often ascribed to male slaves (Kaplan 2006, 204).When Mrs Wood asked her angrily who had put freedom into her head, she replied, 'To be free is very sweet' (Prince 1831, 26). She had her own moment of fighting back after her old master, Mr Dowell, stripped himself naked and ordered her to wash him in a tub of water: 'This was worse to me than all the licks. Sometimes when he called me to wash him I would not come, my eyes were so full of shame.' He struck her severely when she dropped some plates and knives, and 'at last I defended myself, for I thought it was high time to do so'. She told him she would not live with him because he was spiteful and 'too indecent; with no shame for his servants, no shame for his own flesh'. She ran away to a neighbour's and stayed away all night, but then went home again, 'not knowing what else to do' (Prince 1831, 20). Throughout her *History*, Prince was presented 'as someone demanding a better life, perhaps even in Britain, not salvation through death' (Kaplan 2006, 205). She emerges from the text as a woman who was present at her own making, negotiating and reworking the constraints on her agency, and then politicising those constraints in the *History*. Her access to freedom, to wages, marriage and a home was formed and given meaning by the culture and politics of slavery and of abolitionism in which it was embedded (Featherstone and Griffin 2016). Prince's story is a reminder of how difficult it is to shoehorn enslaved women into the likeness of autonomous, enlightened individuals, and of how easy it is to render invisible the complications of just getting by (Thomas 2016). For the abolitionists who wanted to tell her story, as well as for her owners, Prince was, as Kaplan points out, an implicit threat to the social order because of the nature of the freedom she wanted to claim and the means she was prepared to use to obtain it. Kaplan reads Prince as 'doomed to oscillate between perfect victim and transgressive agent' (Kaplan 2006, 208).

Slaves were not subject to common law, and so were not protected against rape. An enslaved husband who killed the man who raped his wife was not allowed to call her as a witness. Her status as a wife was negated, her rape was displaced as adultery, and any defence of provocation was disallowed. The 'normativity of rape' established an inextricable link between racial formation and sexual subjection (Hartman 1997, 85). As Hartman argues, sexuality was deployed very differently in different contexts. For white women it was about kinship, the proprietorial relation of the patriarch to his wife, the making of legitimate heirs and the transmission of property. It was in this context that a white wife was subjected to the arbitrary power of her husband. For enslaved black women, their masters' sexuality was deployed for 'the reproduction of property, the relations of mastery and subjection, and the regularity of sexual violence' (Hartman 1997, 84). Rape was a non-existent injury for the female slave because 'the lascivious enslaved woman was a guilty accomplice and seducer' (Hartman 1997, 87). African American women lacked inviolability, and 'were judged and blamed for their own predicament' (Hunter 2016, 152). This was inextricable from their status as commodified human beings. White men 'identified rapes and slave sales as conjoined and essential parts of their very selves' (Baptist 2004, 167). As Baptist argues, the fictions of commodification were powerful enough to ensure that some people were treated as objects and men bought light-skinned fancy maids in order to rape them. Slave women were vulnerable to sexual assault because they could be sold, and they were desirable to purchase in part because they could be raped. The market gave value both to their 'sexual desirability and enforced availability' (Baptist 2004, 189). The message that African women were commodities, often raped by white men, 'added a taste of secondhand sexual power without restraint, a glimpse of the pure consumption of human beings, to the unconscious and conscious minds of many consumers' (Baptist 2004, 190).

If Baptist is right about this deep entanglement of economic and sexual desire then it makes sense of the complications of home, marriage and free labour for black women both living in and escaping slavery. The context of commodification and the power of the slave owners to separate families are crucial for understanding slave women's experience, and the ways in which their agency and their power were gendered and racialised. It is no wonder that Harriet Jacobs (1861), for example, took what Lovell has characterised as a salutary view of wage labour, where labour 'is seen as an organic expression of the self and the primary and necessary means of establishing a conception of selfhood' (Lovell 1996, 1). Like Mary Prince, her sense of self was grounded in the performance of economically valued work, and in the negotiation of contracts that showed that she could act as an agent in the market economy. In common with many nineteenth-century thinkers, Jacobs saw contract rights as a form of freedom, and self-ownership as 'the right to sell one's labor, marry freely, and engage in market exchanges in terms of equality, not as a subjugated dependent' (Cope 2004, 5). Her status as a worker underpinned her ability to 'perform her duty as a mother and a woman within a sentimental framework', and was also directly paralleled by her ability to resist Dr Flint's attempts to take her purity and to give it to Mr Sands. In doing so, 'she *takes* the power to remove this purity away from Flint and *gives* it to herself' (Larson 2006, 749). In having a deliberate affair with Mr Sands, she created a kind of contract with him based on exchange rather than subjection. As Lovell argues in his discussion of Linda Brent, the protagonist of Jacobs' *Incidents in the Life of a Slave Girl*, this partial and contingent giving of herself constituted her self-ownership: 'Only by surrendering a portion of her self-possession does [she] create a claim to herself as an agent who can act in accordance with her will' (Lovell 1996, 5). It was a conception of freedom that forced her to violate 'the most basic tenet of womanhood (virtue) to fulfil the basic requirement of contract freedom (volition)' (Cope 2004, 12). As an enslaved black woman she could not have both, and this exercise of her freedom disqualified her from the bourgeois model of self-ownership that was premised on moral self-regulation (Cope 2004, 15). Her freedom was constantly compromised by her fugitive status and her race, and by economic injustice so that her escape from slavery was a journey into capitalism, 'but not the capitalism she envisioned' (Cope 2004, 18). It could not meet her demands for a better life, or offer her protection either for her virtue or for her industriousness. It could not give her a home or an escape from the oppressive terms of her existence. The dream of her life could not be realised.

Jacobs's story and her self-presentation were taken up and interpreted by the white women of her audience in very particular ways. As Nudelman argues, Jacobs endorsed sexual purity as a shared value, but also portrayed her affair with Sands as 'an instance of her autonomy', which meant 'defining her relationship with her audience as adversarial rather than cooperative' (Nudelman 1992, 939). *Incidents in the Life of a Slave Girl* was written between 1853 and 1858 when the sexual subjugation of slave women had been widely publicised in the antislavery literature and used to emphasise the pain and suffering, and so the humanity, of the slave woman. In the process, the abolitionists created 'the canonized figure of the suffering slave' (Nudelman 1992, 941). This female body in pain was central to the process of transforming humans into moral beings. For the slave woman it brought home 'the utter availability of her humanity', her lack of inviolability and her commodification (Nudelman 1992, 941), but the same figure was mobilised to 'prompt the political agency of white middle-class northern women' (Nudelman 1992, 942). The binary of passive female slave/empowered white female liberator became a key trope of antislavery activism, underpinning a sentimental exchange in which both were humanised and moralised, universalised and differentiated. They reinforced and recreated each other through the suffering of the female slave, which authorised her victim status and her readers' sympathetic and virtuous response, suggesting a reciprocal suffering. White women were construed as sympathetic, as able to identify with the suffering of others through their readings of sentimental texts that required both an emotional response and moral action. Tracts produced by the antislavery societies called upon their women readers to imagine themselves in the place of the black female slave and to picture their own mothers on the treadmill, their innocent daughters sweeping the streets, their own children left to die. Enormous stress was placed on the experience of identification with others, on 'shared tears' and the 'congruence of feeling' between women (Sussman 2000, 150, 152), until the other's pain is only acknowledged by substituting the white body for the black body, and empathy becomes repressive and the identification an act of violence (Hartman 1997, 20). As Nudelman argues, Jacobs insisted that her white readers had never known what it was to be a slave, and she employed suffering 'to assert the irreducible difference between white women and slave women', the contrast in their experience rather than their shared tears, by articulating her own suffering and insisting on speaking as a narrator and a subject in her own story (Nudelman 1992, 957). In doing so she showed that she understood what Saidiya Hartman calls 'the precariousness of empathy and the uncertain line between witness and spectator' (Hartman 1997, 4).

In the campaigns against slavery, there was a strong focus on domesticity and the importance of maintaining separate spheres (Sussman 2000, 7; Stanley 1998). Much of the emotional power of the antislavery discourse came from their focus on 'the circumstances of the female body': 'Within the antislavery repertoire of bodily metaphors, the predominant one was the scourged body of the bondswoman, an image that symbolized the slave's utter debasement' (Stanley 1998, 25). She was 'the paradigmatic chattel' (Stanley 1998, 27), and as such a complicated contrast to the white, middle class English women negotiating coverture and their own status as subcontractors and only partial self-owners, engaged in their own struggle with despotic dominion. As Clare Midgley argues, 'the creation of an image of the modern Western woman depended from the beginning on the creation of a contrasting image of the victimised non-Western woman' (Midgley 2000, 113). As Sussman points out, white British women were able to compare themselves to slaves in ways that men could not because it was 'safe' for them to imagine themselves as interchangeable. They would never be placed in the same position as the female slave because they were guaranteed male protection (Sussman 2000, 146). Their 'bounded bodily integrity of whiteness' was 'secured by the abjection of others' (Hartman 1997, 123). In the antislavery debates in Britain, and later in the United States, the sovereignty of husbands was understood to be a fundamental dimension of freedom. Once the female slave became a free woman, and her husband a free man, she would be entitled to his protection. For the freedwoman, emancipation would mean coverture, experienced as slavery's opposite (Stanley 1998, 29). The antislavery campaigns were about helping slave women to attain what their privileged sisters already had, the real but inferior power of the subcontractor. It was a power that was understood to come from morality, not from politics, and it was balanced by the inevitable and utter powerlessness of the slave.

MARRIAGE AS SLAVERY

Campaigners for women's rights in the eighteenth and nineteenth centuries worked to complicate the binary between power and powerlessness, often obscuring their own relative privilege, bodily integrity and social protection in the process. The parallels between marriage and slavery were made by white feminists to draw attention to their legal erasure as persons, the denial of their property in the person under coverture and the ways in which their citizenship was shot through with elements of domination. In arguments which drew on Hegel's master–slave dialectic and on the ongoing conversation about empire, they argued that women were subsidising men's citizenship, and that the institution of marriage was valued above the independence of the wife as an individual. Thinking about marriage and slavery together called into question the relation of protection to obedience and the issue of the control over the body, as well as a whole set of difficulties about the contested meanings of dependence and freedom. At the heart of these arguments was the issue of contract, and its relation to the exercise of arbitrary power. Carole Pateman suggests that rather than reading marriage as a quasi-feudal institution, as a left-over from more patriarchal times, we need to understand that modern marriage is contractual, and that contract is 'the specifically modern means of creating relationships of subordination' (Pateman 1988, 118). Until the late nineteenth century the legal and civil position of a wife 'resembled that of a slave' because of her civil death, her lack of independent legal existence (Pateman 1988, 119). The law, Pateman says, rested on the assumption that 'a wife was (like) property', and her husband could sue another man for damages if his wife committed adultery (Pateman 1988, 122). She highlights the slave owner's right of sexual access to his female slaves, and to his wife. She draws attention to the laws enforcing conjugal rights which held that the husband could not be guilty of raping his wife because the wife had given herself up to her husband through their 'mutual matrimonial contract', and could not retract from it. At the end of the nineteenth century, wives could be jailed for refusing conjugal rights and husbands were legally allowed to lock their wives into their homes to obtain their rights. As Pateman puts it, the marriage contract 'is a contract of specific performance' (Pateman 1988, 123).

Wives in the late eighteenth and early nineteenth centuries lived in the problem-space between slavery and citizenship. Their legal existence was suspended under coverture, under which husband and wife were considered to be but 'one person', so that 'the very being and existence of the woman is suspended during coverture, or entirely merged and incorporated in that of the husband'. Through the marriage contract, 'women's subjection is secured in civil society' (Pateman 1988, 181) and they were subjected for life to their husbands and expected to provide perpetual service, bringing them close to the status of slaves (Pateman 1988, 145). At the same time, the space wives inhabited was not the space of slavery, but the more ambiguous gap between contract and subjection. In the end, Pateman rejects the conflation of wives with slaves because a free and equal citizen could not be an actual slave, although she could contract to be a civil slave (Pateman 1988, 124).

The idea that white wives were subjected to slavery emerged from a complex and multi-layered conversation about domination, subordination, improvement, degradation and freedom. The critique of the exercise of arbitrary power in Wollstonecraft was about the ways in which tyranny would undermine morality and attempt to crush reason. Women were slaves because they could not be citizens, because they were not ethically incorporated into the polis, and because they only imperfectly possessed themselves. For Wollstonecraft, women were created to be 'the toy of man, his rattle' (Wollstonecraft [1790] 1995, 104), made for his purposes and amusement rather than their own. Like the slaves as living tools in Aristotle's account, women in Wollstonecraft's narrative 'appear to be suspended by destiny' between heaven and earth, not quite reduced to livestock, but not enlightened by reason or given the opportunity to struggle against the world, unfold their faculties or acquire the dignity of conscious virtue. Without a clear set of morals and principles, women became passive and indolent, and bore the marks of inferiority (Wollstonecraft [1790] 1995, 105). Their sparks of genius had been prevented from bursting forth and their minds were depressed, meaning that, like slaves, they failed to exert themselves and were unable to transform themselves into moral beings. Without enlightened growth and useful work, both the powerful and the powerless were caught in a damaging and tyrannical relationship.

Wollstonecraft's language was about the supremacy of reason, of thinking and acting for ourselves as rational beings capable of autonomy. Like Kant, Wollstonecraft's focus was on independence and rightful interaction between individuals who all had the quality of being their own master. She too demanded vigilant government over the self. Like Locke, Wollstonecraft's argument was that we cannot hand over absolute power to others because we do not have it over ourselves. Women were rendered weak and luxurious by wealth, and 'made slaves to their persons, and must render them alluring that man may lend them his reason to guide their tottering steps aright' (Wollstonecraft [1790] 1995, 235). They could choose between this kind of submission and governing their tyrants by 'sinister tricks' (Wollstonecraft [1790] 1995, 235). To be virtuous and useful, a woman needed the protection of civil laws: 'she must not be dependent on her husband's bounty for her subsistence during his life or support after his death – for how can a being be generous who has nothing of his own? Or virtuous, who is not free?' (Wollstonecraft [1790] 1995, 236). Honest, independent women needed a civil existence in the state. Collective self-governance required dignity (Ober 2012) and the status of citizenship. Instead, women were domesticated through ignorance and dependence, and prepared in childhood 'for the slavery of marriage' (Wollstonecraft [1790] 1995, 248).

As a result of what Alan Coffee terms 'the stranglehold of dependence' (Coffee 2013, 121), the caprice of tyrants won out over the rational rule of law. This encouraged a culture of hidden, covert and corrupting power, both in public and in private, for both men and women. 'When, therefore, I call women slaves,' said Wollstonecraft, 'I mean in a political and civil sense; for, indirectly, they obtain too much power, and are debased by their exertions to obtain illicit sway' (Wollstonecraft [1790] 1995, 262). Her picture of women as 'literally speaking slaves to their bodies', was about women's loss of rational autonomy that undermined the possibility of rational fellowship with men. Women were slaves in the political and civil sense because they could not be citizens, because they were not ethically incorporated into the polis, and because their grasp of autonomy could only ever be precarious (Hartman 1997, 117). They were slaves not only because the power exercised over them was arbitrary, but also because the only power they were able to exercise over others was arbitrary (Coffee 2013, 123). Wollstonecraft's argument was that improvement must be mutual, 'or the injustice which one half of the human race are obliged to submit to, retorting on their oppressors, the virtue of man will be worm-eaten by the insect whom he keeps under his feet' (Wollstonecraft [1790] 1995, 272).

Wollstonecraft's analysis focused on the dangers of tyranny and domination, and their distorting effects on rational freedom and justice. Her arguments fit into the wider discourse of antityranny, where enslavement sought to dishonour and disenfranchise citizens who were meant to be free (Nyquist 2013, 1). She used slavery as a polyvalent metaphor, but her concern was to challenge the disenfranchisement of women, which she framed as political slavery that relied on women's vulnerability to force and their dependence on individuals' arbitrary power. Part of this discourse of antityranny, as Mary Nyquist argues, involved positioning selected non-European societies as existing without publicly ordered social or political relations (Nyquist 2013, 16–17). By the eighteenth century the discourse had shifted to thinking about slavery as 'an ocean away', and to a new kind of liberal imperialism that contrasted the 'pure air' of England to much more oppressive and claustrophobic social and political relations in the East. Despotism was 'that destructive blast which desolates Turkey, and renders the men, as well as the soil, unfruitful' (Wollstonecraft [1790] 1995, 116). The damaging effects of the exercise of arbitrary power were felt everywhere (but particularly in Turkey) because it denied the possibility of improvement. The displacement of despotism and patriarchal oppression onto Turkey is part of what Joyce Zonana has identified as 'feminist orientalist discourse' which figured the objectionable aspects of life in the West as Eastern (Zonana 1993, 593). Wollstonecraft uncritically associated the East with despotism and tyranny, imagining 'gendered despotism' as a defining feature of Eastern life and as a corruption of Western values (Zonana 1993, 600). In her account, women in the East 'languish[ed] like exotics' (Wollstonecraft [1790] 1995, 107), lived in harems where they were indolent, confined, under-educated and over-sexualised, and they were treated as if they were not a part of the human species. Wollstonecraft's emphasis on the sexual enslavement of women in the East added the 'erotics of suffering' to antislavery discourse (Howard 2004), giving the exercise of arbitrary power a sexual dimension.

The 'East' was a site of 'imperial irresponsibility' where Islam imposed an inferior status on women who were thought to have no souls (Howard 2004, 69). This 'problematic intersection of liberal and imperial ideas' (Botting and Kronewitter 2012, 468) continued in the writings of William Thompson and John Stuart Mill as they built on

Wollstonecraft's ideas about women's social and political enslavement under coverture. They all used anti-Muslim stereotypes to make arguments for women's rights in ways 'that treat Muslim culture as contrary to the progressive feminist values of Western Europe' (Botting and Kronewitter 2012, 472). The contrast with 'the East' rather than with Africa or America allowed the authors to highlight the barbarism of patriarchal marriage in primitive and Orientalist terms and to draw attention to the odalisque as the representative of 'the basest yet most exotic form of female subordination' (Botting and Kronewitter 2012, 472). Eastern despotism and its associations with the harem and the seraglio were used to emphasise the themes of confinement, imprisonment, brutality and sexual control. At the same time, the focus on polygamy and the otherness of Eastern subordination provided 'a reassuring substrate to their own oppression, assuring them of their relative privilege as English women in a civilized society' (Paugh 2014, 640).

The language of despotism and political tyranny was transposed into the social and brought home, so that the household became a space of terror, of fear and blood, and in particular of imprisonment. Power was reconceived in a privatised form, heightening the dangers of personal enslavement (McKeon 2005, 133). Tyrants, Wollstonecraft argued, in phrasing which captured the claustrophobia and danger of the home, '*force* all women, by denying them civil and political rights, to remain immured in their families groping in the dark' (Wollstonecraft [1790] 1995, 69). Women were 'shut up like eastern princes' (Wollstonecraft [1790] 1995, 119), confined to their cages. William Thompson, too, placed a great deal of emphasis on wives being deprived of the right of locomotion, and the ways in which they were held captive in the house: 'In his house he imprisons her or opens the doors at his option; an indulgent master is all she can look for.' She did not have the right to go in or out any more than a kitten (Thompson 1825, 85). As Pateman has pointed out, husbands had the legal right to constrain their wives to remain inside the home. The wife chained to a brutal tyrant also found that her children belonged by law to him. If she tried to leave her husband, she could take nothing with her, not even her children. He could compel her to return, either by law or by physical force. A woman, John Stuart Mill argued, 'is denied any lot in life but that of being the personal body-servant of a despot'. Everything depended on the chance of finding a husband who 'may be disposed to make a favourite of her instead of merely a drudge', and the law gave her only one chance to find a good master (Mill [1859] 1997, 149). Wollstonecraft, Thompson and Mill all used language that drew attention to the intense intimacy of men's domination over women, and to women's immobilisation within the home. In their writings we can read slavery and freedom as the founding narratives of the liberal subject, and see how they are inextricable both from each other and from the narratives of race and gender.

William Thompson's argument was that society was organised to the advantage of men in the pursuit of happiness, who paralysed and oppressed their feebler competitors, making women their slaves. Women's compensation was marriage, under which 'women are reduced to domestic slavery, without will of their own, or power of locomotion, otherwise than as permitted by their respective masters' (Thompson 1825, xi). Women were neglected in the distribution of rights, 'excluded in the true Eastern style', without consideration. James Mill in his utilitarian tract 'Article on Government' built his system of liberty on the political, civil, social and domestic slavery of women, and in doing so he 'capriciously divides the human race into two moral masses, the one of which is to be saturated with liberty and enjoyment, the other with slavery, privation, and insult' (Thompson 1825, 20). This conception of dividing the world into these two halves brought the zones of freedom and unfreedom, and the conflict between the old and the new, together under one roof, and privileged gender as the key register of difference between humans struggling to transform themselves into moral beings. The current system left women 'the most isolated and unprotected of human beings', shut out from political rights (Thompson 1825, 36), and from property.

In Thompson's view this made the marriage contract a slave contract, requiring a man to enter into a relationship based on the denial of a woman's moral status as a person. The husband, like the slave-holder, put himself in a position where he exercised all the rights over his wife that she currently exercised over herself, putting her inherent dignity and her moral worth entirely under his command. This created a moral relationship between husband and wife that involved total control by the husband, even if he never exercised it, and complete renunciation of her rights on the part of the wife (Fabre 2006). It was, Thompson declared, like the slave contracts of the West Indies, 'the law

of the stronger imposed on the weaker' (Thompson 1825, 56). He lik-
ened the contract of marriage to a slave code, no more consulting the
interests of women 'than the interests of bullocks are consulted in the
police regulations that precede and follow their slaughter' (Thompson
1825, 56–7). Men were the owners, masters and rulers of everything
while women were 'the moveable property, and ever-obedient servant'
(Thompson 1825, 57). As wives, women's civil rights disappeared and
they fell back into the state of children or idiots, 'the passive property of
their owners; protected by the law in some few respects only, like other
slaves, from the excessive abuse of despotic power' (Thompson 1825,
59). The despotism of man over woman was maintained by personal
force and established by the law. Women's dependence may have been
voluntary for a moment before the contract, but was then 'unrelentingly
forced during the whole remainder of life' (Thompson 1825, 62). She was
a victim of her owner, 'renouncing the voluntary direction of her own
actions in favour of the man who has admitted her to the high honor
of becoming his involuntary breeding machine and household slave'
(Thompson 1825, 63).

Thompson was explicit about the whiteness of the wives-as-slaves
he was talking about. Black slaves, he said, were not insulted with
the requirement to swear obedience. The 'gratuitous degradation of
swearing to be slaves, of kissing the rod of domestic despotism, and
of devoting themselves to its worship' was reserved for white women
(Thompson 1825, 65–6). For him, it was this distortion of freedom
that lay at the heart of their oppression, clearly aligning his argument
with the antityranny approach. White women were not supposed to
be enslavable, and his argument figured them as perfect victims rather
than as transgressive agents. The 'gratuitous degradation' of swearing to
be slaves was imposed upon them, and he sidestepped the complications of what can rightly be defined as agency. He termed marriage a
'white-slave code', investing one human being with all the attributes
of despotism compounded by the 'cruel mockery' of insisting on the
semblance of voluntary obedience, 'of devotedness to her degradation'.
The marriage-slave code rested on the same myth as the paternalism
of chattel slavery, the idea that the interest of wives was necessarily
involved in that of their husbands. The wife was, for Thompson, 'the
literal unequivocal *slave* of the man who may be styled her husband'
(Thompson 1825, 66). Her actions and her earnings were not under her
own control, but under the arbitrary control of someone else, putting

her inherent dignity and moral worth entirely under his command. This lack of self-government was, for Thompson, the essence of slavery. For Thompson, 'To be a woman is to be an inferior animal; an inferiority by no talents, by no virtues to be surmounted; indelible like the skin of the Black' (Thompson 1825, 164). Men looked at women as belonging to an inferior and degraded class of beings, not entitled to equal consideration. Thompson was offering a critique of a gender hierarchy that denied women's capacity for self-legislation and hardened the boundaries of human difference by connecting them to a more rigid anatomical model, and so to the idea of natural inferiority. Gender as a register of difference was undergoing the same process as racialisation in becoming indelible and hereditable, condensed into two great moral masses facing each other across an abyss.

Thompson recognised the risk that the doctrine of inferiority would undermine women's basic humanity, and relegate them to the status of subpersonhood. Like the antislavery writers, he understood that freedom was contingent on membership of civil society. Women, in Thompson's view, had been reduced to the level of automatons, 'the passive tools of the pleasures and passions of men', their actions regulated 'by the arbitrary will of masters' (Thompson 1825, 193). The system, Thompson argued, had created deep-rooted habits. Some women 'have been all their lives benumbed by the withering influence of an insolent domination' which inculcated submission to arbitrary will as a moral duty and 'encompass[ed] the slave with a superstitious horror of its own freedom' (Thompson 1825, 187). Through enforcing the marriage contract, men had surrendered the delights of equality, esteem and friendship and chosen instead to keep their slaves in 'blind unenquiring obedience', holding the whole 'motley fabric . . . together by fear and blood' (Thompson 1825, ix–x). In this sense, Thompson's approach was intersubjective, and inextricable from the choices made by European men. He used slavery as a root metaphor for explaining the subjugation of white women and the arbitrary power of white men over them. His understanding of slavery was deeply individualised, connected to notions of dishonour and the denial of autonomy. In his view, slavery was the ultimate form of arbitrary power and a grievous loss of freedom. Women subjected to marriage had lost their inner worth and become chattels, the instruments of others. This reflects a specific understanding of the social relations of slavery and liberty, designed to apply to white women who were woven into the fabric of civil society as wives and perfect victims, in a position of relative privilege inside the structures of domesticity.

It was a highly racialised understanding of gender and slavery. Thompson declared that enslaved black women were able to exercise more agency and power, to find more room for manoeuvre, than white women subjected to direct force by their husbands. They were not obliged to vow obedience to all the despotic commands of their enslaved husbands, and somehow they emerged from his account as having more freedom than the wives he described. He gave value to their transgressive agency and their position outside the structures of domesticity without accounting for the risks and dangers that it carried. They were pictured as being able to form acquaintances, friendships and attachments, and to mould their own actions according to their own views of interest, propriety and justice, 'liable to the same physical, legal, and arbitrary restraints with her male companion in slavery and no more' (Thompson 1825, 83). Slavery was an institution founded on and constrained by law and their shared legal status made the enslaved man and his companion equal in degradation and misery. The wife of a slave, on this view, was not subjected to unrelenting force, or constrained by the immoral vow of obedience. For Thompson, the state of the 'civilized wife' was worse than that of the female slave in the West Indies, and yet it was the white woman's situation which was termed a state of equality and identity of interests with those of her husband (Thompson 1825, 86). White wives were cut off from the common protection of the laws by having no property, they were made to swear obedience to domestic slavery, and they were constantly (rather than occasionally) subject to the lust and caprice of an ever-present tyrant. This coding of 'real' slavery as domestic, highly personalised and particularly degrading for white women was part of the wider process of partitioning and drawing internal distinctions within humanity. It suggested a particular binary between slavery and independence. White women were constrained by the arbitrary and unjust power of their husbands and by the institution of marriage, but it is clear that once these disabilities were removed, white women would cross the boundary into civil society and claim the status of personhood, leaving enslaved black women to fight their own battles for a better life.

For John Stuart Mill, the adoption of the system of inequality between the sexes was never the result of rational deliberation, but had its origins in a woman finding herself in bondage to men 'owing to the value attached to her by men, combined with her inferiority in muscular strength'. A mere physical fact was converted into legal right. Progress was gradual until male slavery was abolished, and female slavery was 'gradually changed into a milder form of dependence'. It was this form of dependence that Mill characterised as 'the primitive state of slavery lasting on', surviving modifications from justice and humanity, but never losing the 'taint of its brutal origin' (Mill [1859] 1997, 123). Mill's argument was that the inequality of rights between men and women had no other source than the law of the strongest. People flattered themselves that the rule of mere force had ended and that advanced civilisations could not rest on the principle of 'might is right'. Those who allowed themselves to be seduced by this narrative of progress and humanity needed to understand that the social relations that subordinated women to men had survived the rise of equality and justice, and were 'not felt to jar with modern civilisation, any more than domestic slavery among the Greeks jarred with their notion of themselves as a free people' (Mill [1859] 1997, 125). Marriage, like slavery, existed within the forwardness of modernity, and universality and rationality were used to sustain an order of gender difference that was inherited from the premodern era. Mill argued that the conditions of modern social life deformed and dehumanised both men and women as husbands and wives. He employed the rhetoric of slavery and abolition in order to suggest that the failings of marriage as an institution were historical rather than natural, and so could be subject to change. In doing so, he relied on a particular narrative of history which worked hard to relegate slavery to an unenlightened and benighted past, with no place in the new world of the modern. The rhetoric of modernity was about isolating the social subordination of women as 'a single relic of an old world of thought and practice exploded in everything else' (Mill [1859] 1997, 137). Like Wollstonecraft's insect underfoot or the worm in the bud, this for Mill was a serious question for 'the progressive movement which is the boast of the modern world' (Mill [1859] 1997, 137).

The law of servitude in marriage was 'a monstrous contradiction to all the principles of the modern world, and to all the experience through which those principles have been slowly and painfully worked out' (Mill [1859] 1997, 195–6). After the campaigns for the abolition of slavery, 'Marriage is the only actual bondage known to our law. There remain no legal slaves, except the mistress of every house' (Mill [1859] 1997, 196). Mill was drawing on slavery as the 'root metaphor' to draw attention to the power relations at the heart of marriage, and to men's exercise of absolute, arbitrary power over their wives. This most universal and pervading of all human relations ought to be regulated by justice rather than injustice. He anticipated the objection that the rule of men over women was not a rule of force, but was accepted voluntarily by women who gave their consent to marriage and made no complaint about their treatment (Mill [1859] 1997, 131). Mill pointed out first that many individual women did not accept their situation and had recorded their protests. The problem was that all social and natural causes combined against women's collective resistance. Their masters required something of them beyond actual service: 'Men do not want solely the obedience of women, they want their sentiments' (Mill [1859] 1997, 132). They wanted a willing slave, a favourite, demanding more than simple obedience out of fear. Women were not educated, expected or required to strive for self-government, agency or self-control, but for submission and yielding to the will of others. Women were taught that it was in their natures to live for others, to abnegate themselves and not to exercise their autonomy. The law of marriage was a law of despotism, and to maintain their despotic rule, men had not allowed women to learn to read and write, or to acquire any skills not required for a domestic servant.

The accepted narrative of progress was that marriage had been gradually losing its despotic edge, and civilisation and Christianity had ensured that women's rights were restored. Mill contested this consoling narrative by arguing that 'the wife is the actual bondservant of her husband: no less so, as far as legal obligation goes, than slaves commonly so called. She vows lifelong obedience to him at the altar, and is held to it all her life by law' (Mill [1859] 1997, 147). She could not act except with his permission, and all her property became his as husband and wife became one person in law. 'I am far from pretending', Mill declared, 'that wives in general are not better treated than slaves; but no slave is a slave to the same lengths, and in so full a sense of the word, as a wife is' (Mill [1859] 1997, 148). Her master could torture her and make her loathe him, and still 'he can claim from her and enforce the lowest degradation of a human being, that of being made the instrument of an animal function contrary to her own inclinations' (Mill [1859] 1997, 148). Mill contrasted this loss of bodily integrity through vulnerability to rape to the situation of enslaved women, who, according to Mill, performed fixed tasks for their masters and then withdrew into their own family lives. Like Thompson, Mill left out black women's sexual subjection to white men, and so ignored the racialised dimensions of the men's power.

Instead, Mill's vision of the power relations within marriage and of the exercise of men's dominion over women was mediated through class, which became a marker for savagery, brutality and irrationality. Violence towards women did not carry much danger of legal penalty, and Mill suggested that the'lowest classes"indulge[d] the utmost habit-ual excesses of bodily violence towards the unhappy wife'who could not resist or escape from their brutality. Her excessive dependence'inspires their mean and savage natures'not with a sense of honour and protec-tion, but with the idea that'the law has delivered her to them as their thing, to be used at their pleasure' (Mill [1859] 1997, 151). Mill was talk-ing about a vast number of men'who are little higher than brutes', and then about'ferocious savages, with occasional touches of humanity', all of whom were entrusted with absolute power over women (Mill [1859] 1997, 152). It was not possible to tell what such men's conduct would be in'the unrestraint of home' (Mill [1859] 1997, 153). Like Locke, Mill regarded the poor as unrestrained and debauched, an inferior order of men, and in this rhetoric we can see the real dangers Mary Prince was facing in being turned out of doors and treated like a beggar. As Roz-bicki argues about Locke, Mill's thoughts on the'lowest classes' should remind us that we need to think about slavery and liberty not as ideas but as specific social relations, and be alert to the deeply hierarchical understanding of society that underpinned Mill's liberal imperialism and his arguments for women's equality. Liberty'continued to be largely understood as class privilege, applicable in full only to a group entitled to it by property, reason and virtue', even as that group was expanded to include middle-class white women (Rozbicki 2001, 39). Mill readily admitted that under the present law, the great majority of the higher classes lived in the spirit of a just law of equality. On the other hand, in the'most naturally brutal and morally uneducated part of the lower classes', a man felt a sort of disrespect and contempt towards his own wife that he did not feel towards any other woman, born out of her legal slavery and her physical subjection to his will (Mill [1859] 1997, 162). In the complicated intersections of race, class and gender inside the home, working class white men emerged as mean and savage, and so as morally incompetent virtual outsiders with no place either inside the structures of domesticity or within civil society.

What happened to the enslaved black women who were blotted out of this story of slavery as despotism and tyranny, and excluded from the progressive movement that was the boast of the modern world? Kaplan argues that the radicalism and the feminism of the 1780s dissipated in the nineteenth century, until virtuous European femininity with its militant domesticity and insistence on respectability crowded out and made impossible 'a radical autonomy of mind and behaviour, whose dangerous bottom line is the will and capacity to rebel' (Kaplan 2006, 200). The emphasis shifted from Wollstonecraft's focus on women's tyranny, the possibility of agency and transgression in their 'sinister tricks', and her vision of subjects formed in complicated relations to others under oppressive terms of existence, to Thompson and Mill's more perfect and powerless victims. The capacity for autonomy and rebellion was displaced onto the figure of the black woman. Women of mixed race were regarded as even more dangerous as the visible evidence of European men's transgressive behaviour, 'so that their intrusion in to the metropolitan space [was] an unwelcome reminder of the inevitable permeability of social and moral borders between empire and "home"' (Kaplan 2006, 200). Their very existence undermined the silences and disavowals so carefully constructed by thinkers such as Thompson and Mill around the sexual subjection of enslaved black women. They refused to acknowledge the 'glimpse of pure consumption' and instead reinforced the idea of moral boundaries created by women's self-regulation inside domestic space.

THE UNRESTRAINT OF HOME

This construction of white middle-class women as domestic, respectable and subjected to unrelenting force had particular resonances in the plantation household in the Deep South in the nineteenth century. Just before the American Civil War, the plantation mistress Mary Boykin Chestnut wrote, echoing Mill, that there was no slave like a wife, and all married women, all children and girls who lived in their fathers' houses were slaves (Foster 2007). Foster discusses the popular images of the plantation mistress as the 'mother-to-all', instructing her slaves and actively managing the household. Plantation wives were presented simultaneously as closet abolitionists and as innocent victims, 'helplessly caught up in the torrent of history' (Foster 2007, 205). Foster argues that we need to think about the gendered memorialisation of slavery, and in particular the ongoing 'characterization of white women as survivors of slavery'. He considers the collective wounds and guilt over slavery to be 'too fresh to allow, willingly, a confrontation with the spectre of white female "savagery"' (Foster 2007, 317). This means that we tend to ignore the degree to which 'southern women generally seem to have worked as feverishly as their men to sustain and enhance their places in their small worlds' (Foster 2007, 318). Thavolia Glymph's work is about the plantation household as a workplace and as a field of power relations, and she explores what happens when we consider the public character of the private household (Glymph 2008). She begins by pulling apart the depiction of planter women as 'a silent abolitionist constituency' who were the potential allies of slaves, and of slave women in particular. They tended to be presented as hardworking women who were handicapped by paternalism and patriarchy, and for some historians they 'were women who found in their own subjection the basis for an alliance with slave women' (Glymph 2008, 4). As Glymph adds in her next sentence, 'slaves rarely thought this'. Historians of southern women, she argues, often gave priority to patriarchy and imagined freedom for slave women as 'the right to patriarchy and its kindred domestic norms', granting them the possibility of returning home, of finding their core identity as wives and mothers (Glymph 2008, 4). Glymph's central argument is that we need to remember that white women wielded the power of slave ownership, of life and death, and that their violence was 'integral to the making of slavery' (Glymph 2008, 5). As Foster says, the vision of the delicate southern belle was reworked by historians to be become the hard-working, self-sacrificing southern plantation mistress with responsibility for an extended household of family and slaves, suffering under the weight of patriarchal authority and somehow managing to be 'both violent and good' and endow the system with humanity (Glymph 2008, 23). In this process, which lies behind the characterisation of white women as the survivors of slavery, mistresses 'remain essentially unsullied by the violence, indecency and racism endemic to slaveholding societies' (Glymph 2008, 24). Their silence has been read as abolitionist sympathy, while their power was mistaken for powerlessness.

The plantation household was the site for the construction of south-ern white womanhood, set against the construction of the black women within the household as vessels of disorder and filth, lying, thieving, impudent, unmanageable and ignorant. White women's labour was presented by proslavery ideology as 'the central operative mechanism of the plantation household', bringing order and cleanliness to 'a world stained by black women's mere presence' (Glymph 2008, 66). In this con-text, white women were left feeling outwitted and angry as their slaves worked slowly, ran away and refused to do as they were told, rejecting the idea that their mistresses' interests were their own, even as they had to live together in close proximity and warring intimacy (Glymph 2008, 68–9). Female slaves who worked slowly and used impudent language 'impeached the ideology of white female supremacy' and, in Glymph's analysis, carved out small spaces of autonomy for themselves, and began to build an oppositional culture and a new meaning for freedom that came out of everyday struggle and resistance (Glymph 2008, 91). The resistance and agency of slave women was, Glymph argues, buried in the gendered language of domesticity as insubordination rather than rebellion, and in the collapsed geography of the household, the small-ness of the spaces in great houses and slave cabins, they were engaging in the ongoing debate about what it meant to be free or enslaved, male or female, black or white.

The general confinement of women to 'the more collapsed geog-raphy of the household' made their acts of violence seem less pur-poseful and effectual, and more savage, as Foster points out (Glymph 2008, 28). Their violence was explained as petulance, capriciousness, hysteria and ill humour, explanations that profoundly underestimated white women's agency and the 'practical reality of routine domina-tion' (Glymph 2008, 31). Glymph uses first-person testimony from plantation households to argue that in place of the sense of planta-tion mistresses being trapped by the system, we need to understand the women of the household as living in 'a kind of warring intimacy', marked by the everyday violence of dragging, biting, kicking and shak-ing and by shocking acts of cruelty, such as that described by Lucinda Hall Shaw in her account of the fatal beating and hasty burial of a slave woman and her living baby, birthed as a result of the mother's whipping (Glymph 2008, 40). Glymph argues that rather than regard-ing such incidents as exceptional cases, slaves saw them as part of a habitual pattern of inherent violence and terror. Power 'could wear a white female face', and sustaining the system of slavery required the exercise of force, as the plantation mistresses themselves recognised (Glymph 2008, 62, 64). It is significant that Mary Prince was flogged at the instigation of her mistress, calling into question the character of the English, and her status as a slave: 'In the *History* we find monstrous white women and a slave woman who has all the attributes of English middle-class domestic gentility' (Whitlock 2000, 25).

In thinking about the common ground between feminism and post-colonialism, Whitlock attributes to postcolonial criticism 'a particularly strong sense of the intimacies of identity formation, how subjects are formed and reformed in relation to others, with unpredictable inter-sections, connections and leakage between' (Whitlock 2000, 34). It is impossible to separate out the perfect victims from the transgressive agents, or to understand the meanings of freedom and slavery in isola-tion from the specific social relations in which they are entangled. The oppressive terms of existence were different for plantation mistresses, abolitionist activists, fugitive slaves and freed women. They were forced to negotiate power and powerlessness, agency and victimhood and the 'unrestraint of home' in different ways, and with very different conse-quences. Thinking about enslaved women as wives, and white wives as slaves, allows us to understand the claustrophobia of the structures of domesticity and the catastrophic boundary loss of being thrown out of doors. It brings out the gendered and racialised complications of what can be defined as agency, and shows us how those complications were connected to property, possession and exchange. The constructions and presentations of white women as closet abolitionists and perfect victims continue to play out in current debates about trafficking and modern slavery, bolstered by definitions of slavery that focus on private, intimate violence and on subjection to force. Civilised wives, or their respectable equivalents, still emerge as innocent victims as opposed to transgressive agents, and the effect is still to ignore the dangers of vagrancy, poverty and indecency for women racialised as black who continue to be judged and blamed for their own predicament. These blind spots and disavowals are part of the disjunctive history of slavery and freedom, its fits and starts and ruptures. The process of transform-ing humanity into moral beings was always an uneven process, shot through with registers of difference, but also always undertaken in close contact and in intersubjective space. The politics of 'new slavery', which we examine next in the contexts of incarceration and of trafficking, continue to be infused by the wishful thinking and consoling narrative of freedom and progress that places slavery as a legal institution firmly in a benighted past and refuses to engage with the afterlives of its warring intimacy, the fear and blood, the normativity of rape and the abjection of others.

Chapter 8

INCARCERATION AND RUPTURE: THE PAST IN THE PRESENT

This chapter focuses on the prison industrial complex in the United States to ask again about what gets remembered and how, to take us back to the question of what happens to a manumitted slave, and to revisit the figure of the slave as an uncanny object in the blind spot of modernity. Do the patterns and practices of mass incarceration suggest that the exercise of despotic power is regarded as legitimate if its objects are considered to have put themselves outside civil society? Are the processes of transforming humanity into moral beings reversible, so that prisoners can de-create themselves through civil and social death? One of the key problems with the discourse of modern slavery and its insistence on the rupture between past and present and the 'newness' of the slavery lurking in the shadows and in our nail bars is the way that it brings slavery into the present. For its core message of abolition to work, 'old' slavery has to be comfortably assigned to the past, where it was abolished by the high-minded, incorruptible and conscientious few who came to realise how fundamentally wrong it was, and the actions of like-minded consumers and activists who worked tirelessly to shine a light on the immoral activities of the slave traders and holders and to expose the inhumanity of their commerce. When slavery is brought into the present out of this story, it is often as part of a grand redemptive narrative, from the history of slavery to the future of abolition through a present in which today's slavery is invisible, a 'hidden crime', and slaves themselves are 'locked away' in obscurity. As Joel Quirk has pointed out, the literature on contemporary slavery tends either to ignore the history of slavery or to posit 'a sharp divide between past and present'. Contemporary issues such as child sexual exploitation, trafficking and servile marriage are framed as distinctively modern problems associated

169

in particular with globalisation and the disposability of labour (Quirk 2006, 566). This approach raises a whole set of questions about what slavery really means, and also about how to connect the past to the present.

Closely related to the idea of a sharp divide between past and present in modern slavery discourse is the underlying claim that race no longer matters in modern slavery. Poverty, on this account, and not racialised identity, makes people vulnerable to being enslaved. Race, Kevin Bales asserts, 'means little' in the new slavery: 'The criteria of enslavement today do not concern color, tribe, or religion; they focus on weakness, gullibility, and deprivation' (Bales 2012a, 11). In the introduction to his bestseller *Disposable People*, Bales places himself within the narrative of slavery lost and found. 'Of course', he says, 'many people think there is no such thing as slavery anymore, and I was one of those people just a few years ago.' In describing what it means to be 'one of those people', he then turns to an anecdote from his own past, to describe an encounter with segregation when he was four years old in a cafeteria in the American South:

> As we started down the serving line I saw another family standing behind a chain, waiting as others moved through with their trays. With the certainty of a four-year old, I knew that they had arrived first and should be ahead of us. The fairness of first come, first served had been drummed into me. So I unhooked the chain and said, 'You were here first, you should go ahead'. The father of this African American family looked down at me with his eyes full for feeling, just as my own father came up and put his hand on my shoulder. Suddenly the atmosphere was thick with unspoken emotion. Tension mixed with bittersweet approval as both fathers grappled with the innocent ignorance of a child who had never heard of segregation. No one spoke until finally the black father said, 'That's OK, we're waiting for someone; go ahead' (Bales 2012a, 6)

For Bales, this is a story about fairness and equal treatment, and about how 'sometimes it takes a child's simplicity to cut through the weight of custom' (Bales 2012a, 7). It fits into his story of being glad to see such blatant segregation coming to an end, while at the same time realising that emancipation was a process and not an event, and that it was a process that carried a 'residue' in bad housing, health inequalities, education and the legal system. He defines these problems which he associates with race and racism as the 'vestiges of slavery', and then goes on to distinguish these vestiges from what he describes as 'real slavery', brought to light for him not in the segregated queue for the cafeteria, but in Anti-Slavery International leaflets distributed in 1980s London (Bales 2012a, 7). He does not describe the content of these leaflets, so the reader is left to fill in the gaps between the vestiges of slavery and real slavery, but he does tell us that slavery is an obscenity, 'more closely related to the concentration camp than to questions of bad working conditions', and that there is 'nothing to debate about slavery: it must stop' (Bales 2012a, 7–8). The black family are left standing in the queue, presumably with their eyes still full of feeling and still silent, since there is nothing to debate, while they contemplate Bales's precocious humanity and their own not-actual slavery.

In his discussion of race and slavery, Bales puts ethnic and racial differences firmly in the past, where he says they were used to explain and excuse slavery and to make the slaves into others through 'tremendous investment in some very irrational ideas', and a set of contortions to explain white supremacy, and to justify their economic decisions (Bales 2012a, 10). By contrast, for Bales, today's slavery is all about the money, and modern slaveholders are 'freed of ideas that restrict the status of slaves to *others*', and they can keep their costs down by enslaving people from their own country (Bales 2012a, 11). While he recognises ethnic and religious differences between slaves and slaveholders in Pakistan, India and Thailand, Bales concludes that their caste and religion 'simply reflects their vulnerability to enslavement; it doesn't cause it' (Bales 2012a, 11). The key differences that he identifies are not racial but economic, and the common denominator is poverty, not colour. 'If all left-handed people in the world became destitute tomorrow,' he says,' there would soon be slaveholders taking advantage of them' (Bales 2012a, 11).

Tryon Woods offers a devastating critique of this kind of left-handed argument, arguing that anti-trafficking and modern slavery discourse more broadly is 'mired in an ahistoricism symptomatic of our anti-black world' in which slavery is 'evoked to cloak the movement with political saliency and emotional urgency, while obscuring the ongoing calculus of racial slavery's afterlife' (T. P. Woods 2013, 122). For Woods, Bales is summarising the mainstream perspective of white civil society and its understanding that slavery ended in 1865 and the loose ends were tied up by the 1964 Civil Rights Act. Within this narrative of legislative progress, remaining inequities, Woods argues, then attach themselves to 'the innate inadequacies of those left behind' and become the product of irrational bigotry. Any empirical evidence to the contrary is then 'unpersuasive in the face of white desire to be human, or in today's parlance, to "transcend race" and be "post-racial"' (T. P. Woods 2013, 130). This analysis does not quite reflect Bales's claim to see the vestiges of slavery in current racialised inequalities, but it does capture his story of the cafeteria queue, from which he emerges as 'post-racial' before any of those around him. His focus on skin colour and nation, and on the apparent randomness of poverty, vulnerability and economic inequality are attempts to disavow 'the facts of the ongoing relations of racial slavery' (T. P. Woods 2013, 131). Racial slavery is invoked by Bales as part of a shared past, a bittersweet struggle for both fathers as they stood in line. It emerges as something that the white family, his parents 'who were not radicals' and he, can transcend. They can leave the cafeteria behind with their notions of fairness intact and move on to tackle the 'real' slavery that happens elsewhere, particularly in the Indian subcontinent and the Far East (Bales 2012a, 22).

In taking the 'racial' out of racial slavery, and in invoking black suffering to make non-racial political demands, modern slavery discourse shows itself to be unconcerned with the black struggle or with actually existing black communities. In Woods's view, the rhetoric of modern day slavery ignores the historically specific context of the anti-black world in which the slave is paradigmatically black (T. P. Woods 2013, 126). The impulse to ignore and disavow the racial element of 'old' slavery is, for Woods and others, specifically about denying the afterlife of racial slavery, and the sense that 'blacks gained entry to the body of the nation-state as expiators of the past, as if slavery and its legacy were solely their cross to bear' (Hartman 1997, 133). For Hartman, this process of emancipation after 1865 'produced national innocence yet enhanced the degradation of the past for those still haunted by its vestiges because they became the locus of blame and the site of aberrance' (Hartman 1997, 133). In this account, slavery shaped the experience and interpretation of freedom, and antislavery and reform discourse paved the way for brutal forms of modern power. The idea of a sharp divide between past and present, and the insistence that this is not about working conditions, ignores the complicated connections between slavery and free labour, vagrancy, idleness, respectability and mobility. The race line that Bales describes in the cafeteria has very different resonances for Hartman's approach. In her account, it would be an example of how segregation enabled the perpetuation of slavery because 'the contours of the social were shaped by slavery and its vestiges and an indifference to black misery', until the spectre of black misery failed to arouse compassion and the slave was wholly overlooked (Hartman 1997, 169). The black family cannot walk away from the queue. For her, the endurance of voluntary servitude and the reinscription of racial subjection should draw our attention not to the rupture between past and present, or to the distinction between the vestiges of slavery and real slavery, but to 'the continuities of slavery and freedom as modes of domination, exploitation, and subjection' (Hartman 1997, 172).

The question then becomes one of how to understand these continuities of slavery and freedom, and how to grapple with the afterlives of slavery as domination, exploitation and subjection. For those who do not want to disavow the racial in racial slavery, this is a course that brings its own challenges and pitfalls where the alternative to Bales's 'post-racial' story is to invest in the suffering and injury of black misery so that the identity to be preserved is that of the powerless victim (Balfour 2005). Balfour is talking specifically about reparations, which are not the key concern of this chapter, but her conclusions apply to thinking about mass incarceration as well. Both involve 'a call to grapple with the ways the past is lived' (Balfour 2005, 802), compelling public witness to injuries that both endure and are constantly re-inflicted. Balfour engages with Wendy Brown's work on injury to explore how 'reckoning with the afterlife of even ancient crimes is both necessary and dangerous' (Balfour 2005, 802) and to show how the politics of reparation can disrupt both unthinking progressive narratives and the business-as-usual politics that go with them. Taking the reparations movement seriously, she argues, requires 'attending to the question of *whose* interests can and cannot stand for the common good', and so a reorientation of vantage point (Balfour 2005, 804). This reorientation means moving away from progressive narratives and a 'child's simplicity' that cuts through the weight of custom. Without asking why it is left up to the black father to make segregation socially comfortable for the white family, we cannot hope to grapple with slavery's 'complex haunting of the American present' (Balfour 2005, 805).

In the debates around mass incarceration and the prison industrial complex in the US, this idea of a 'complex haunting' carries considerable power. The racial politics of incarceration bring to the fore the question of whose interests can ground the common good, the reinscription of racial subjection, and what it means to claim what Avery Gordon calls 'the right to complex personhood' (Gordon 2008, 5). In thinking about these questions in the context of haunting, Gordon argues that we can investigate 'how that which appears absent can indeed be a seething presence' and 'learn to make contact with what is without doubt often painful, difficult and unsettling' (Gordon 2008, 17, 23). At the core of this discourse of haunting is this notion of contact and encounter and of having a particular connection with loss. It also brings with it the sense, articulated by Toni Morrison, that we can bump into a 'rememory' that belongs to somebody else, so that the past can be over, but still there waiting for you. In this sense, the ghost has a living force that feels like the return of a familiar stranger (Gordon 2008, 169, 179). For Morrison, the complex haunting is not about a return to the past, but about a reckoning with the present and its possibilities. She is calling for accountability, for the recognition that 'it is our responsibility to recognize just where we are in this story, even if we do not want to be there' (Gordon 2008, 188). A refusal to encounter the ghosts means acting as if we can erase or transcend the power relations in which we lived then and live now, as if we can just step into a post-racial world, freed from ideas that might force us to think about the making of status. Instead, by allowing ourselves to encounter 'the elusive concreteness of ghostly matter', we can pay attention to the moments 'when the over and done with comes alive', the points 'when your own or another's shadow shines brightly' (Gordon 2008, 197). The contacts and encounters between the pasts and presents of slavery are not about being able to draw straight lines from one to the other, or about being able to draw a line between them, but about these moments in the shadows, between the visible and the invisible. It is in this shadowy space that we return to the distinctions between personhood, subpersonhood and humanity.

Part of this means thinking again about race, gender and exclusion, and about how freedom, labour and belonging intersect in the 'wavering present' (Gordon 2008, 183) to construct the status of black prisoners in the afterlife of slavery. In contrast to the notions of vestige and forgetting that are implicit in the dominant discourse of modern slavery, we need to forefront the 'obligation to remember what our fellow citizens cannot reasonably be expected to forget' (McCarthy 2002, 629). Thomas McCarthy reminds his readers of DuBois's point that a segregated society required a segregated historical memory, which was created through a 'searing of the memory' by white supremacist historiography that obliterated the black experience and the meaning of emancipation. In Bales's account of his own segregated memory, he places himself in what McCarthy identifies as the American mainstream thinking about slavery, which places it in the past, relates to it as a Southern phenomenon and does not think of it as central to the American story. It becomes instead a regional aberration and a historical accident (McCarthy 2002, 634). Against this mainstream, McCarthy calls attention to the continuing volatility of race relations, where 'talk about racial injustice in the past is typically experienced by both blacks and whites, as being also about the present, and reacted to accordingly'. The passions and interests of the present, he argues, are integral to the politics of the memory of racial injustice, 'a past that is still present, that refuses to pass away' (McCarthy 2002, 635).

McCarthy argues not for drawing a direct causal line between the unjust and unremedied past and current injustices, but for a more complex narrative, 'one in which the repeated refusal to acknowledge past wrongs and the continued failure to remedy them are themselves fresh wrongs that compound the original one' (McCarthy 2004, 760). He acknowledges the risk of reinforcing essentialism through a sense of victimisation, but insists that 'it makes little political sense to maintain that a group identity forged during centuries of brutal oppression could or should be dissolved while injuries still persist' (McCarthy 2004, 768), or to try to deny what those persistent injuries are and who they belong to. In McCarthy's account, race consciousness can enhance a group's sense of effective agency and transformative power even as hierarchies of power and privilege are maintained and a history of disrespect and domination continues to structure the meanings of complex personhood and of the public good. This is fundamentally different from the rupture between past and present proposed by Bales and the rhetoric of new slavery, and it casts a very different light on how current injustices and inequalities should be understood and resisted. Within this more complex web of power relations and rememories, it is possible to get to grips with the afterlife of slavery without divorcing it from its racial past or disavowing what it means to be vulnerable.

THE PRISON IN HISTORY, THE PRISON AS HISTORY

In her ground-breaking work *Are Prisons Obsolete?*, Angela Davis talks about how we take prisons for granted, so that it is difficult to imagine life without them. In taking them for granted, she says, people are reluctant to face the realities of what goes on inside them and tend to think about imprisonment as a fate reserved for others, and in particular others who are not the objects of benevolence or the victims of avarice but who deserve their criminal status. Prisons become a simultaneous presence and absence, part of the structures of knowing and not-knowing, and of the strategic ignorance identified by Charles Mills. For Davis, prisons fill a ghostly space in the shadows 'as an abstract site into which undesirables are deposited, relieving us of the responsibility of thinking about the real issues afflicting those communities from which prisoners are drawn in such disproportionate numbers'. Davis is explicit in arguing that this acceptance of prison parallels the widespread belief in the permanence of slavery in the past, and that 'prison reveals congealed forms of antiblack racism that operate in clandestine ways' (A.Y. Davis 2003) and attach themselves to the racialised histories of Latinos, Native Americans and Asian Americans.

For the scholars and activists who are opposed to hyperincarceration and the prison industrial complex, there are clear parallels between slavery and mass incarceration and they trace its history through convict leasing, white supremacy, violence and civil death with a particular focus on the Black Codes. Moments of emancipation and reconstruction bump up against the anti-black world and the unremedied past so that after 1865 the Black Codes in the southern states imposed a system of curfews and fines and vagrancy laws that prohibited African Americans from voting, restricted their travel, denied them equal educational opportunities and subjected them to a racist legal system and to extra-legal lynching (Weatherspoon 2007, 603), reinforcing their status as subpersons and outsiders to civil society. Angela Davis argues that the ideologies governing slavery and punishment were profoundly linked in early US history through the connections between hard labour and penal labour and the central role of race in constructing presumptions of criminality. The Black Codes proscribed a range of actions such as vagrancy, absence from work, breach of job contracts, possession of firearms and insulting gestures or acts that were criminalised only when the person charged was black. The Mississippi Black Codes, for example, declared any black person who had run away, got drunk, been wanton, handled money carelessly or neglected their job or family to be a vagrant, a crime that was then punishable by incarceration and forced labour (A. Y. Davis 2003). Frederick Douglass commented in 1883 that reasonable doubt seldom had any force or effect when a black man was accused of a crime, and that 'color is a far better protection to the white criminal, than anything else' (Douglass 1883).

Critical race scholars trace a path through convict leasing to the chain gangs and peonage camps to prison plantations, from the middle passage to the plantation to the chain gang and back again. Childs characterises his work as a 'history of the present', drawing on Angela Davis's claim that pre-1865 slavery was itself a form of incarceration and insisting that what is called modern mass incarceration has been 'centuries in the making' (Karlin 2016). Prison abolitionists recognise the overt brutality of convict leasing and the ways in which the model of punishment was based on the slavery model of the South, but they also point to the importance of alternative systems of social control in the North, and the nominally colour-blind criminalisation and incarceration of black people in the North since the 1890s. Their aim is to critique a long historiographical tradition of Southern exceptionalism, and to argue that racial privilege, the protection offered by whiteness, is as important as racial discrimination in understanding the regimes of punishment in the US, and in particular what it means to be defined as a 'deserving criminal' (Muhammad 2011, 81). In doing so, they disrupt the mainstream narrative by arguing that slavery cannot be corralled either into the past or into the South and insisting instead on the importance of thinking through slavery, freedom and narratives of modernity together.

For these critical race scholars, the vestiges of slavery have persisted in the prison system in mandatory minimum sentences, harsh penalties for non-violent drug offences and the continued construction of prisons regardless of crime rates. Kim Gilmore points to the importance of recognising the role of freed blacks and slaves in nineteenth-century US abolitionism, and the ways in which their resistance and refusal challenged the labour and social systems being built on the foundations of racial slavery (K. Gilmore 2000, 197). She argues that 'mass imprisonment was employed as a means of coercing resistant freed slaves into becoming wage laborers', and that the role of the state was critical 'in mediating the brutal terms of negotiation between capitalism and the spectrum of unfree labor' (K. Gilmore 2000, 198). The capitalists used the state to recruit and discipline a convict labour force, and were able to use the penal system as a powerful sanction against rural blacks. The system, and the racism of the system, was used to achieve industrialisation in the South and take a step forward into modernity (A. Y. Davis 2003). For Gilmore, prison labour is the bridge between slavery and paid work, and the punishment system mirrored the slave order, bringing the slave system back to life. The ghosts she sees in the system are of the slaves' dreams of freedom during Reconstruction, and their resistive politics, cut short by vigilante justice, racialised violence and the state's role in criminalising ex-slaves. For her, 'The point of retracing this history is not to argue that prisons have been a direct outgrowth of slavery, but to interrogate the persistent connections between racism and the global economy' (K. Gilmore 2000, 195). Childs argues that we need to read today's 'legally perpetrated and socially accepted terror system of penal neoslavery as a continuance rather than a break from America's centuries-long history of chattelized imprisonment and white supremacist genocide' (Childs 2015).

This approach to the afterlife of slavery that uses the concept of 'neoslavery' and argues for the existence of a carceral model that can be traced from the middle passage to the plantation and the chain gang tells a very different story from that of the modern slavery narrative. For Childs, the progressive path of penal modernity has remained tightly bound up with chattel slavery in what he calls a permanent Middle Passage (Childs 2015). He uses Morrison's concept of rememory to explore how the black subaltern is caught by and in a history where the past 'is felt as an "open wound" that keeps reopening with every breath' (Childs 2015). There is no possibility of walking away, of being 'one of those people' who think there is no such thing as slavery anymore, and no need to go searching elsewhere for the 'real slavery' that others cannot see. He is talking instead about a complex history of terror, dispossession and rupture that underpins what he terms 'the predicament of liberal de jure freedom' for black people in the US. Like Gilmore, he draws attention to what happened to free and fugitive black people during the Reconstruction era, and argues that they represent a 'haunting prologue' of the collective experience of black people after the arrival of de jure freedom (Childs 2015).

While this approach to history draws clear connecting lines between past, present and future and focuses on the continuities rather than the breaks in the black experience of oppression and injustice, it is not about seeking out new slaves or about drawing bright lines between acute forms of suffering and exploitation and slavery itself. Michelle Alexander in her book *The New Jim Crow* points to the familiar stigma and shame, the system of control, political disenfranchisement, legalised discrimination and the production of racial meanings that define the current prison system. The exclusion of felons from juries, she argues, 'has put black defendants in a familiar place – in a courtroom in shackles, facing an all-white jury'. Segregating prisoners from mainstream society and taking their status for granted means that prisoners return to ghetto communities in 'a closed circuit of perpetual marginality' (Alexander 2010a, 189, 191). At the same time, she recognises the limits of the analogy between slavery and incarceration and acknowledges the way things have changed and different narratives have taken hold as racial vigilante violence has reduced, segregationist thinking has been rejected, and public discourse has shifted from racial hostility to racial indifference (Alexander 2010a, 198). This is a messier and uneven picture, and black people emerge within it not only as victims, but also as sometimes complicit in their support for 'get tough' systems of imprisonment, while white people are in some cases directly harmed by the caste system. The pattern that Alexander sees behind these tangled threads moves through slavery as exploitation, Jim Crow as subordination, and mass incarceration as marginalisation (Alexander 2010a, 207), but she does not make a claim for interchangeability or direct analogy. It is more about interrogating the persistent connections and their meanings, recognising where the past is still present and acknowledging when the shadows shine brightly.

THE PRISON ITSELF

The Californian prison population grew by nearly 500 per cent between 1982 and 2000. Of 160,000 prisoners, two thirds were African Americans and Latinos. Twenty-five per cent of them were non-citizens, and eighty per cent were represented by state-appointed lawyers for the indigent. Convicts are overwhelmingly the working or workless poor (R. Gilmore 2007, 7). Ruth Gilmore draws attention to the relationship of prison to dispossession. As a consequence of certain actions, some people lose all freedom. Historically, the poor would have been classified as vagrants and subjected to curfew, but not necessarily locked up 'because their unfreedom was guaranteed by other means' (R. Gilmore 2007, 12). Her argument is that prisons exist in order to produce social stability as 'societies decide they should lock people out by locking them in' and offer justifications for imprisonment such as retribution, deterrence, rehabilitation and what she terms 'incapacitation' (R. Gilmore 2007, 13). For Gilmore, the underlying explanation for prisons is that capital must be able to get rid of workers whose labour power is no longer desirable, and at the same time have access to new or 'previously idled labor' as the need arises. Workers without work 'must wait, migrate, or languish until – if ever – new opportunities to sell their labor power emerge' (R. Gilmore 2007, 71). In her analysis, the new state built itself in part by building prisons, and the key to understanding the growth of prisons is the goal of incapacitation and the production of prisoners. Prisons are a means of achieving dehumanisation and producing racial categories. It is this rather than the unpaid labour performed in prison that connects imprisonment to 'new slavery' for Gilmore. As it does for Davis, Alexander and Childs, the link between slavery and incarceration comes from exclusion and dispossession, and from a particular kind of rightlessness. This is not just about profit, but about the creation and maintenance of a perpetual enemy who must always be fought but can never be conquered. The connections between slavery and prison are 'more about the construction and consolidation of a certain kind of enemy status' than they are about the people who have been criminalised (Loyd 2012, 49). Both groups are treated as if they share common features that are closely related to Patterson's constituent elements of slavery of alienation, violent domination, coercive force and general dishonour until they are identifiable as 'the prison race' (Loyd 2012, 50).

It is worth exploring further what being put into this category of previously idled labour and incapacitated means for conceptions of personhood and subpersonhood. Joan Dayan proposes a 'continuum between being declared dead in law, being made a slave, and being judged a criminal' and her analysis rewrites the crossing between the state of nature and civil society not as a single act, but as a repeated ritual. She uses William Blackstone's *Commentaries on Law* to explain how natural liberty is 'the savage essence that must be ferreted out, as a stain' (J. Dayan 2001, 6–7). This killing off of natural liberty is a ritual that has to be staged over and over again, so that nature can be disguised and reproduced in law, and the stability of civilisation can be affirmed. In the process of this ritual, the law puts the criminal out of its protection and takes no further care of him. As Locke says about the person who breaks the law of nature, the criminal breaks the tie that is meant to secure him from injury and violence and puts himself outside the social contract, making himself into an outcast who may be killed like a lion or a tiger. For Blackstone, 'he is then called attaint, *attinctus*, stained or blackened' (J. Dayan 2001, 7). Dayan argues that slavery in the colonies required 'the justification of the inner depravity of those enslaved', so that blackness was equated with slavery, but at the same time the presumption of servitude and the stain of natural liberty was also inseparable from 'alternative experiments in unfreedom' such as the subjugation of the Irish, indentured servitude and the vagrancy acts that 'had already provided a template for domination' (J. Dayan 2001, 9).

Dayan moves from this discussion of legal slavery to talk about the confinement of prisoners becoming an alternative to slavery, what she calls 'another kind of receptacle for imperfect creatures whose civil disease justified containment' (J. Dayan 2001, 15). For her, this narrative offers a powerful counter-argument to the currents of Southern exceptionalism. The penitentiary in the North, she argues, 'turned humans into the living dead', especially through the mechanisms of solitary confinement and symbolic execution. A criminal punished with civil death became the slave of the state, 'so that once incarcerated, the prisoner endured the substance and visible form of disability, as if imaginatively recolored, bound, and owned' by the state in place of the slave owner (J. Dayan 2001, 15–16). The invention of criminality and the imposition of civil death reversed the process of transforming humans into moral beings. This idea of being the slave of the state is about the 'escape clause' of the Thirteenth Amendment which abolished slavery and involuntary servitude except as punishment for a crime, and for many of those who advocate for prison abolition and others who write about the reinvention of slavery as incarceration, this idea of civil death is central to their argument, and connects the treatment of legal slaves in the nineteenth century to the treatment of prisoners in the twentieth and twenty-first centuries. Rather than taking the modern slavery approach of distinguishing 'old' slavery from 'real' slavery and striving to come up with new definitions of what it means to be a slave, these ideas return in many ways to Orlando Patterson's constituent elements of slavery, and in particular to the idea of social and civil death. This has a profound effect on the focus of their analysis in its recognition of injury and subjection, its concern to explore the making of status and exclusion, and the gradual annihilation of the person through solitary confinement which 'permits the suffering of the soul before the death of the body' (J. Dayan 2001, 20). Dayan has an anonymised quotation from a prisoner she interviewed in Arizona State Prison in 1996 which summarises this sense of living death: 'If they only touch you when you're at the end of a chain, then they can't see you as anything but a dog. I've lost my skin. I can't feel my mind' (J. Dayan 2001, 20–1).

These theorists of incarceration focus on what goes on inside the prison, and especially in the restricted settings of special security units and supermaximum security prisons where inmates are spending longer and longer locked in solitary confinement, often alone in their cells for twenty-three hours a day. What was used rarely as a disciplinary tool has been redefined as normal for those held under special or secure management, and the 'conditions of confinement are manipulated in order to confirm depravity'. Dayan enumerates the savage effects of solitary confinement that takes the prisoners beyond human endurance and creates an arena for mutilation, with the inmates turning paper clips into darts and sharpening pencils into pincers in order to harm themselves. Like Gilmore, she sees this as an expression of dispossession and legal incapacitation, part of a process through which the captives endure unbearable conditions that make them feel responsible for disfiguring themselves, and for unravelling as unified moral selves. The inmates who mutilate themselves have enacted what Dayan calls the 'law's process of decreation' on their own bodies, 'making visible what the law masks' (J. Dayan 2001, 28). This notion of de-creation and of the living, disfigured dead very closely recalls Hartman's description of the slaves being overlooked because their misery failed to arouse the emotion of compassion. With individual criminals, we reach the limits of benevolence and come crashing up against questions of their agency at the margins of the state's power. As Childs argues, the temptation is to ignore the structural injuries, what he calls the 'larger social recidivism', in favour of branding individual black persons as criminals (Karlin 2016). The story of national innocence is written to leave prisoners behind, to reinscribe them as deserving of their fate, and to define them as not-slaves because their captors are the state, and not sinister modern 'slaveholders' waiting to enslave them for being destitute or left-handed. Like the slave, these prisoners have chosen to submit and live, and in this primal act of submission they are, in Patterson's terms, degraded, and their resistance overcome. They are dishonoured within an intersubjective space that is structured by the state, and not by the master's domination of the slave.

Dayan focuses on the conditions of solitary confinement in US prisons, and in particular on the indefinite confinement of gang members on the basis of their status as gang members, where evidence against them bears no logical relation to the specific deprivations they are forced to undergo. Instead of going through due process, alleged gang members are locked down in special treatment units and labelled as 'security threat groups'. She gives accounts of individuals being held in virtual isolation because of their status as purported members of these groups, where their only way out of solitary confinement is to debrief and denounce. This is not a possible route out for those who were not gang members in the first place, and those individuals who do debrief are targeted for death by gang members and sent to protective custody in another restricted segregated facility:'Anyone suspected of gang affiliation, whether he debriefs or not, is thus condemned to what amounts to solitary confinement for the rest of his life' (Dayan 2008, 500). Dayan points out that the harsh logic of supermax detention relies on arbitrary deprivations based on status, and this combination of confinement and secrecy is what Blackstone called a dangerous engine of arbitrary government that undermines the principle of habeas corpus (Dayan 2008, 501). The'residuum of liberty'that attaches to the prisoner as a legal person is no longer as important as maintaining order (Dayan 2008, 493). As we saw in the discussion of Locke, slavery and punishment have always been closely linked, and the figure of the criminal shows us the history of slavery as it coalesces around the selectivity of natural rights and the concept of enslavability.

INCARCERATION AND RACIAL CASTE

In 2010, Michelle Alexander points out, more African Americans were under correctional control (in prison, jail and on probation or parole) than were enslaved in 1850. Members of this growing undercaste are permanently relegated to second-class status, denied the right to vote, excluded from juries, and legally discriminated against in employment, housing, access to education and public benefits (Alexander 2010b, 75). In her analysis, slavery has to be understood as a legal status, endorsed by the state. It cannot be the same thing as being illegally subject to the domination of another. There has been a shift in status from slave to felon, but 'Once a person is labeled a felon, he or she is ushered into a parallel universe in which discrimination, stigma, and exclusion are perfectly legal, and privileges of citizenship such as voting and jury service are off-limits' (Alexander 2010a, 92). It is the legality of prisoners' dispossession and incapacitation that is significant, both in and out of prison. They are locked away, but not in a place where race 'means little'. In ways which recall just-war justifications of slavery and the idea of slavery as punishment, 'In the drug war, the enemy is racially defined' (Alexander 2010a, 96). As Grotius argued, men can become slaves 'by a human Fact', though agreement, crime or conquest, and criminals forfeited their own lives by some act that deserves death (Grotius [1625] 2005, 75). Slavery and the state of war, as we have seen, are mutually constitutive, and the criminalised captive is constructed as the aggressor who introduces a state of war.

People who are branded as felons are given a badge of inferiority and are caught in a cycle that sends them in and out of prison and back again and leaves them subject to constant surveillance by the police. Young black men are treated as criminals in multiple settings, in the street, at school, community centres and at home, until the entire community is seen by them as 'collaborating to form a system that degraded and dishonored them at an everyday level' (Rios 2006, 44). Rather like the indigenous peoples whose treatment was discussed in the chapter on Locke, they are mewed up within their own contracted territories, and their relationship to reason and liberty is treated as uncertain and incomplete. They end up not being integrated into the mainstream society and economy, but being constantly stopped and searched by the police and returned to prison for minor infractions. They are treated as the embodiment of risk and monitored and controlled by the state through probation officers. From his fieldwork, Victor Rios describes young men who experienced the 'overwhelming presence' of their probation officers as the forceful intervention of the state in their lives through supervision and sanctions. The youth of colour he met he describes as hypercriminalised because 'they encounter criminalization in all the settings they navigate' in a system of interconnected institutions that attempt to brand, control and contain them (Rios 2006, 52). As a social group, Alexander argues, criminals are 'deemed a characterless and purposeless people, deserving of our collective scorn and contempt' (Alexander 2010a, 138). In the US, convicted felons are not allowed to enlist in the military, possess a firearm or obtain federal security clearance. Citizens lose the right to vote and non-citizens are immediately deportable. The word 'felon' has become a label of stigmatisation, a way to signify otherness and to filter access to housing, employment and education (King 2006, 8). The prohibition on voting, Ryan King argues, is essentially a character test on the franchise, a restriction based on worthiness to vote that renders some people alien in their own country by telling them that their voices are unwelcome in the national discourse, that their interests cannot stand for the public good (King 2006, 13–15). They are incorporated into the legal and political system as felons and criminals in ways that define their status because they have ceased to belong in their own right to any legitimate social order. They live in something close to what Locke describes as the 'state of slavery', within which their lives, liberties and estates are forfeited and their rights are readily denied, infringed or transgressed. Disenfranchisement is not grounded on a legal solid principle or in considerations of the greater social good. It plays instead, King argues, to the politics of retribution and fear. They are shut out of civil society and denied the possibility and the privilege of political resistance. This, again, is about the creation of status and about where 'slavery' fits into the basic structure of politics, either as 'neoslavery' or as 'new slavery'. The anti-prison reckoning with the afterlife of slavery is in this sense both necessary and dangerous. It requires a reorientation of vantage point and a focus on the power relations that we live in now, to recognise where we are in this story, to struggle with that politics of retribution and fear rather than to insist on a post-racial world.

THE PRISON AND THE BORDER

The construction of prisoners as a characterless and purposeless people, Loïc Wacquant argues, depends on 'a vast discursive constellation of terms and theses that come from America on crime, violence, justice, inequality, and responsibility' and have been insinuated into European public debate as part of what he calls 'the redefinition of the mission of the state' (Wacquant 1999, 320). As the state withdraws from the economic arena and reduces its social role, it builds more prisons and incarcerates more people. Wacquant terms this 'the new penal common sense' that aims to apply market principles to social problems and in the process criminalises poverty and normalises precarious wage labour (Wacquant 1999, 321). This new common sense mirrors quite closely Hutcheson's justifications of the enslavement of the British poor as vagabonds and vagrants, using slavery as the proper punishment for those who ruined themselves and made themselves a public burden. Wacquant points in particular to policies of zero tolerance in public spaces, which often involve the management of 'troublesome poverty'. The rhetoric of the war on crime and of recapturing public space is, he says, 'a rhetoric that assimilates (real or imaginary) criminals, the homeless, panhandlers, and other marginal persons to *foreign* invaders' (Wacquant 1999, 327). This idea that criminals and vagabonds are foreign invaders is effective for forging a consensus around the idea that the undeserving poor ought to be brought back under control by the state, using curfews and other social sanctions as well as reimprisonment. His sense is that the few are once again enslavable for the good of the whole, and liberty has to be understood as a class privilege linked to property, reason and virtue.

By insisting that 'slavery should not be confused with anything else' (Bales 2012a, 259) and that slavery is not to do with working conditions, Bales and other antislavery activists take a highly selective approach to identifying the 'new slaves', and offer very little analysis of the background conditions that led to the creation of the vulnerability that they talk about as the basis for enslavability. As Julia O'Connell Davidson argues, this selectivity is in part explained by their attachment to a liberal narrative of advancement, which is in turn linked to these activists' vision of the state as a neutral arbiter. As she points out, slavery depended on legal, social and physical restrictions on slave movement imposed by the state. In today's world, people also find their mobility circumscribed not just by incarceration, but also by immigration laws and border enforcement. Such immigration regimes, O'Connell Davidson argues, often create vulnerability to exploitation and abuse by private individuals, empowering individuals to exercise violence over others at what Sassen characterises as 'the systemic edges' (Sassen 2016). We need to pay attention to the state-led production of political vulnerability and criminalisation that strips people of political standing and of meaningful recognition (Sheth 2016, 92). The new abolitionism, as O'Connell Davidson points out, does not challenge the right claimed by states to control and restrict freedom of movement (O'Connell Davidson 2015).

Restrictions on the right to locomotion can be read as connecting old slavery to neoslavery and the past to the present in very different ways from those proposed by the new abolitionists. Dylan Rodriguez, for example, argues that we need to understand prison as a form of violence perpetrated by the state, and recognise the capacity of the state to reform and shift its techniques of bodily coercion (Rodriguez 2008, 2–4). For Rodriguez, border militarisation, anti-terrorism and anti-gang policing are all expressions of global US imperialism, and the US prison is part of 'a *regime* of domination and strategic violence', which is global in its reach (Rodriguez 2008, 6) and encompasses not just the golden gulags of California but immigration detention prisons as well. In arguing for this model of a 'regime', Rodriguez is making the point that these are not self-contained institutions, but together form a prototype of organised punishment and social, civil and biological death through what he calls 'the kinship of captivity' (Rodriguez 2008, 7). The complex haunting of the present by the past, the elusive concreteness of the politics of slavery, is there in the state's capacity for violence that refuses to pass away.

This analysis of carceral violence builds on the arguments about mass incarceration in the US to think about prison itself as a border, and prison and border regimes as 'the culmination of many histories of struggle over colonialism, the nation-state, and what it means to be human' (Loyd, Mitchelson and Burridge 2012, 2). Contemporary penal and migration policies are tied together through a shared process of criminalisation. Citizenship, incapacitation and punishment work together 'to legally consign entire groups of people to precarious futures and premature deaths' (Loyd, Mitchelson and Burridge 2012, 4). The connection between the rise of the nation state and the rise of the prison is located, Loyd, Mitchelson and Burridge argue, in the contradiction between mobility and immobility, and in laws that 'legitimate the forcible confinement and isolation of some groups of people'. These laws, they go on, 'also draw lines of power between groups of people who will be (or expect to be) entitled to be a part of the public, share in the social wealth, and contribute to shaping the common good for present and future generations' (Loyd, Mitchelson and Burridge 2012, 7). Those who are not incorporated into this vision of the public good and complex personhood are fundamentally insecure, with a special kind of outsiderness as enemies, foreigners and strangers, but also as lazy, irresponsible and irrational. The social being of a prisoner and a migrant, like that of a slave, can be altered at any point by the will of another when they are understood to have crossed the waving line between the state of nature and civil society, or the mobile border between person and subperson.

Angela Davis argues that the globalisation of the prison industrial complex is entangled with immigration detention centres and facilities in which prisoners of war are incarcerated, the prisons in Guantanamo and Abu Ghraib and the normalisation of torture. It is, she claims, 'really easy to traffic between the various systems' (Kautzer and Mendieta 2004, 342). Guantanamo and Camp X-ray were enabled by the rapid development of new technologies within domestic prisons, and new military techniques in turn inform what happens inside supermax facilities. Angela Davis argues that the sensory deprivation, solitary confinement and lack of human contact in prison reinforces the 'everydayness of torture' elsewhere, making it possible to treat it as unexceptional and creating a situation where 'the minimum implies the supermaximum' (Kautzer and Mendieta 2004, 345). For Anne McClintock, we can trace circuits of imperial violence that are connected with 'the vast, internal shadowlands of prisons and supermaxes – the "modern slave ships on the middle passage to nowhere"' (McClintock 2009). The majority of the men held at Guantanamo were arbitrarily detained, and of the 700 held there very few could yield any information at all. Most were not picked up by the US military but by the Northern Alliance, the Pakistani military intelligence who handed them over for bounties of between five and ten thousand dollars (McClintock 2009, 65).

McClintock describes the new regime of torture to which they were subject as one in which the self was broken down through radical sensory deprivation, disorientation and extreme stress. She draws attention to the bright visibility of the outside spaces in Guantanamo, and to the invisibility of their suffering that left no traces on the body. Torture was administered 'without visible trace or touch', leaving them 'reduced to zombies, unpeopled bodies, dead men walking, bodies as imperial property' (McClintock 2009, 65). McClintock uses the language and imagery of the middle passage and of social death to conjure a vision that is at once hypermodern and saturated in the past, an open imperial wound, as the men are declared to belong to the US Marine Corps, to be the mere property of the state. The state goes to great lengths to prevent the prisoners from committing suicide, as if taking their own lives would be a unilateral declaration of war, an attempt to rob the empire of its legitimacy. The empire produces the enemy through spectacle and display, by keeping these bodies under hypersurveillance in see-through cages and cells made of mesh, but '[a]t the same time, these men are made juridically spectral, conjured into legal ghosts' (McClintock 2009, 67). Their shadows are shining so brightly that it is possible to see right through them. Lights of different colours shine on the same spot, and the light reflecting from that spot is 'an additive mixture' because it is the sum of all the light (Science Snacks 2017). Guantanamo represents another example of being made dead in law, taken outside of protection and tainted. In their orange suits that signify danger and security threats to Western viewers, the prisoners are imaginatively recoloured, as bound and owned by the state. The creation of the prisoners' status derives from America's colonial legal history and the 'law's ability to invent persons who yet remain in a negative relation to law' (Dayan 2008, 486), to bring the slave into existence. Dayan points to 'the perpetual re-creation of the rightless entity', from slave codes to prison cases to torture memos that create new classes of condemned people who have lost the right to have rights. Terrorist suspects are not told who their accusers are or how they came to make their accusations. They cannot confront the witnesses against them, and hearsay evidence is allowed to stand. The label 'illegal enemy combatant' puts them outside claims to legality and inside 'a space of incapacitation' (Dayan 2008, 489) where no law exists for them. They become, Dayan argues, 'ghost detainees' in Iraq, Afghanistan, Diego Garcia and other CIA secret prisons, who 'inhabit a spectral world that has no political boundaries' (Dayan 2008, 489).

CONCLUSION

The discourse of new abolitionism treats 'new slavery' as a hidden crime, as something that can be found only by looking behind the legal masks to find people in chains (Bales 2012a, 6). The 'disposable people' they figure as enslaved are not conjured as the enemy, but as helpless victims. In the process, the new abolitionists refuse to engage with the politics of retribution and fear, and to grapple with the dangers of the past. Their understanding of 'slavery' as illegal means that their approach cannot engage with the production of status or with the politics of slavery. The focus on individual violence by slaveholders, and on the idea of 'total control' means that the discourse allows them to glimpse 'the horror of a life captured and destroyed to feed the greed of a slaveholder' (Bales 2012a, 246), but not to understand the more complex contexts and spectral hauntings that are connected to history, the state and imperialism. The approach of theorists who focus on the afterlives of slavery in modern prisons is not about identifying alternative modern slaves, but, as O'Connell Davidson points out, the US penal system involves forcible detention, the theft of entire lives and important elements of anti-blackness (O'Connell Davidson 2015, 100). The new abolitionists make a choice not to include the prison industrial complex in their discourse of modern slavery, and for Tryon Woods (2013) that choice is part of their disavowal of the ongoing relations of racial slavery, their lack of recognition of the 'embedded reality' of rightlessness and the failure to incorporate black prisoners into the state. The same blind spots and optical illusions surface in their treatment of trafficking as a form of modern slavery.

Chapter 9

TRAFFICKING AND SLAVERY:
A PLACE OF NO RETURN?

This chapter returns us to new abolitionist attempts to define and combat modern slavery in the context of recasting trafficking as a form of modern slavery. It looks in particular at how this discourse relies on particular conceptions of property and of violence that reinscribe the individual, private character of slavery and the idea of slavery as a place of no return. Once again, freedom shows itself to have different shades, and we find ourselves inside the complex, cross-institutional, cross-discursive world of politics at the border. The new abolitionist approach to trafficking as slavery alerts us to the risks associated with regarding the body as property, and to what Anne Phillips calls 'the pervasive individualism in the claim to a property right' (Phillips 2013, 137). Understanding trafficking as a new form of slavery (or as a form of new slavery) often involves an intense focus on the narrative of the victim and on the circumstances of the female body. The woman trafficked into slavery has become the paradigmatic chattel of the new slavery. This brings us back to the discourses of 'unhumanising' and 'debasement' that haunted the antislavery writings of the eighteenth and nineteenth centuries, and reanimates the idea that slavery is a process of converting people into things (O'Connell Davidson 2016, 230). At the same time, it pushes into the background more complicated questions about labour, and about citizenship and belonging. Antislavery discourse continues to be structured around the question of who is eligible for freedom. What gives the production of a victim through a narrative of excessive dependence such traction in the current context of trafficking and migration? How is that traction related to the new abolitionism and its own investments in the role of the state, the veneer of humanitarianism and sexualised xenophobia?

THE PROPERTIES OF SLAVERY

This chapter seeks to interrogate what it means to claim that the brutally exploited and the radically excluded are the property of others. Modern slavery discourse focuses on 'the individual lived experience of enslavement' (O'Connell Davidson 2016, 248) where slavery 'at its most essential is about control'. In 2012, Kevin Bales and others in the Research Network on the Legal Parameters of Slavery produced the *Bellagio-Harvard Guidelines on the Legal Parameters of Slavery*. These guidelines use the 1926 Convention of the League of Nations as the basis for their definition, meaning that they start from the premise of ownership and the rights and powers attaining to the right of ownership. They take these powers attaching to the right of ownership to mean powers that constitute control over a person in such a way as to deprive that person of his or her individual liberty with the intention of exploiting them. The exercise of this control is usually supported by and obtained through force, deception or coercion. For Bales, this mixture of control, ownership and force sets the parameters of 'the fundamental social and economic relationship between two people that constitutes slavery' (Bales 2012b, 283). It forms, he says, a bridge between the lived reality of enslavement and the legal definition. 'Modern slaveholders', Bales argues, exercise the powers attached to the right of ownership in the absence of the rule of law and in the context of illegality. His argument is that what he calls 'the fundamental powers of ownership', control, use, management and profit, can be exercised outside a legal framework (Bales 2012b, 284). He recognises that the slipperiness of this relationship between slavery and the rule of law causes problems for prosecuting slavery, and in particular for the new slaves' would-be liberators, who have 'a clear experiential understanding of what defines slavery' that is difficult to couch in legal terms (Bales 2012b, 285). For Bales, what is required is some way of bringing together these experiential understandings that apply 'in the work of liberation and reintegration' and legal definitions, so that liberation can lead to legal action (Bales 2012b, 285).

The development of antislavery politics requires the recognition that slavery is expressed in many forms, but is, at the same time, a 'patterned activity'. Slavery has 'overarching themes of violence, possession, and exploitation', and the trafficking-as-slavery discourse works hard to identify these themes in the stories they tell about the victims of slavery, subjected to their traffickers and pimps (Bales 2012b, 285). They need to identify the two people caught up in a social and economic relationship within which one of the parties exercises ownership and control over the other without recourse to the law. Slavery, as Bales admits in a footnote, is now illegal in every country. This gives the new abolitionists some pause, but they do not allow it to disturb them too much. Instead, they reconceive slavery as a crime, a hidden activity, in which victimisation is not an event, but a process of violent exploitation that can last for decades. It is this, Bales argues, that means that the victims of slavery are 'normally unable to report that they are victims of crime' (Bales 2012b, 286). At the same time, he claims that no country is immune to this crime, 'and documented cases and victims numbering in the thousands are found in North America, Europe, Japan, and other developed countries in spite of reasonably functioning legal systems' (Bales 2012b, 287). It is not clear where these thousands of documents came from when the victims themselves are unable to report the crimes, but this re-imagining of slavery as an act of criminal violence helps to reinforce the experiential understanding of liberation and reorients slavery's relation to the law. Bales argues that in this new criminal context, '[t]o turn someone into a slave means keeping them where the law cannot protect them' (Bales 2012b, 298), but this fails to recognise the complex ways in which slavery is a relation to the law, the state and sovereign power, and that slavery is a legal, social and political status (O'Connell Davidson 2016). Telling a true crime story with slavery on one side and law on the other obscures the entangled interrelations between the two.

The exercise of ownership and control becomes a property right when it can generate duties for others. Individual property rights require recognition by others, and so a collective context in which they can be exercised and realised. Private property, in the sense of management, use and disposal, is only held by virtue of communal relations and the co-operation of others. Ownership can only be exercised in the public realm of social relations, where the owners' expectations are affirmed, legitimated and protected by law. People who are kept where the law cannot protect them cannot be the property of someone else. A definition of slavery that understands it as a relationship between two people will struggle to explain how it can be a relationship based on the fundamental powers of ownership, since the fundamental powers of ownership have to be nested within a much broader network of interactions. In his attempt to combine the legal and experiential aspects of slavery in his definition, Bales relies on the 'bundle of rights' conception of ownership, and in doing so he focuses on 'the individual, momentary owner rather than the broader position or situation of ownership'. As a result, he ignores the complicated ways in which ownership functions as social justification, within which, Dan Fuller argues, the owner is not necessarily the person with practical control over something at a given moment, but 'the normative anchor of the network of relations that attend it' (Fuller 2014, 18). To be considered an owner, with property rights in another person, an individual needs to be able to draw their authority from a framework of legal properties, liabilities and duties that persist over time, reflecting not just the momentary distribution of rights but the source of their entitlements and the social importance of their ownership rights. Property rights are good against the entire world, and impose duties on everyone else, including those who did not take part in the transaction. They cannot be narrowed down to a relationship between two people, or rest on a criminal act that cannot give the so-called slaveholder any normative authority to direct what happens to the slave. As the abolitionists of the eighteenth century worked so hard to demonstrate, the moral basis of owning a property in the person is not overridden by force. This means that it makes little sense to identify the trafficker or the pimp as holding property rights over their slaves. Instead, the new slavery argument is that, following the League of Nations definition, they exercise 'the powers attaching to the right of ownership', which does not require a legal framework because it is all about power, and not authority (Lott 2014).

The essential attribute of slavery identified by the new abolitionists is control that deprives people of their individual liberty, and is underpinned by force, threat, deception or coercion for the purposes of exploitation 'through the use, management, profit transfer or disposal of that person' (Bales 2012b, 283). These, for Bales, are the essential attributes of slavery that 'have been and are the same across geography and time' (Bales 2012b, 287). This search for the essential and timeless attributes of slavery is part of what Joseph Miller identifies as the inclination to find coherence 'even if only in the brutality of domination' (Miller 2012, 5), but it is also a highly political move, which both in the eighteenth century and the twenty-first works to project 'the social costs and amorality of growing capitalism onto slavery' (Miller 2012, 7), which is then figured as 'inhuman commerce' and criminal activity. Modern slavery is defined as a 'truly globalized criminal enterprise' (Bales 2012b, 288). It is presented as operating through globalised financial systems, criss-crossing national borders, unimpeded by the nation state. The global traffic in slaves, says Bales, 'regularly flows over and under borders', along with drugs and weapons, making clandestine use of the Internet (Bales 2012b, 289). Trafficking is presented as representing about ten per cent of global enslavement, and as highly profitable because enslaved people come from poorer countries and are then traded in richer countries. Bales goes on to point out that trafficked individuals tend to be better educated, and are tricked into slavery on the basis of their willingness to seek change and opportunity. These attributes, on this account, seem to help them to retain their value, to cross borders of geography and time, but they also turn them into abstractions, disconnected from intentions, contexts and their own agency until their exploitation is understood as 'universal within our species', because sexual use or the enjoyment of violent domination 'require few other skills or attributes other than those provided by biology' (Bales 2012b, 290). Once we are left with a definition of slavery as rooted in biology rather than history, it is clear that the definition of slavery behind the new abolitionism will always extract generalised masters and slaves from the specific situations in which they live, and present us with enslaved people who are 'already on hand and in hand, unproblematically subject to a master's compulsion to dominate' (Miller 2012, 21). Slavery, as Miller argues, can then be presented as 'an institution that is a fait accompli, accomplished, a done deal, general, and static'. This understanding of slavery as an intractable problem is at the core of the new abolitionism, allowing them to argue that 'we have left slavery as an evil lurking eternally in the hearts of men (and women)' (Miller 2012, 29), and not just in our hearts, but in our biology and in our cosmology. Slaves, says Bales, are 'something like the "dark matter" in the universe – invisible, but exerting a strong (and negative) pull on local and national economies' (Bales 2012b, 294).

As Lott points out, the focus on the powers attaching to ownership and on control allows the conception of slavery to be extended to various forms of unfree labour, whether or not a contract exists (Lott 2014). The new slavery discourse elides slavery with forced labour in a variety of industries from agriculture, mining and quarrying to brick-making, carpet-making, and domestic service. According to Bales, this 'forced labour for economic exploitation' accounts for ninety per cent of slavery in Latin America and the Caribbean, Asia, Africa and the Middle East, with the remaining ten per cent accounted for by commercial sexual exploitation. In the US and Europe, meanwhile, commercial sexual exploitation is estimated to account for fifty to seventy-five per cent of those in slavery (Bales 2012b, 287). In focusing on forced labour for economic exploitation, Bales is talking about contexts of poverty, hardship and rightlessness, where large percentages of the population are living below the international poverty line of US$1.25 a day, in the DRC (88%), Haiti (62%), India (30%) and Uzbekistan (46%). As O'Connell Davidson points out, in such contexts people's lives are constrained by debts, by harsh and unsafe working conditions for children as well as adults, and by working long hours for wages that often do not cover their subsistence (O'Connell Davidson 2015, 8). The question remains whether it is useful to characterise people living in these situations as slaves. As we have seen, to conceptualise someone as a slave often involves thinking of them as passive and inert, as swept along by the currents of history, but also as a sordid and laborious being and as an uncanny object. The attempts by slave owners, masters and the wider culture to objectify enslaved people means that they are often understood to occupy the liminal space between human and thing, where they are assigned a value and their freedom is given a price. In this strange space in between property and personhood, the slaves' story becomes one of loss, trauma and victimhood, balanced by the guilt of the witnesses and would-be rescuers who construct 'a structure of feeling' to 'occlude the role of capital and its practices' (Rupprecht 2008, 271). They do so through dramatic displays of injured humanity, and a 'generalised story of ineffable loss, passive victimhood and redemptive tragedy' that has been passed on to the new abolitionists from the antislavery movement of the eighteenth and nineteenth centuries (Rupprecht 2008, 266). It is a story that only makes sense in the context of liberal guilt, and liberal guilt, as Julie Ellison points out, is about race. At the same time, the 'signifying practice of neoliberalism . . . is a desire to avoid the subject of race altogether' (Ellison 1996, 346). As we saw in the discussion of incarceration, this is precisely the space of disavowal that the new slavery discourse occupies. The difference in the context of trafficking-as-slavery is one of spectacle and witness, in what is called forth by the 'raw, empirical, statistical experiences' of the racialised others that white Euro-American thinkers set out to theorise. Liberal guilt 'relies on visual practices of seeing pain and being seen to be afflicted by it' (Ellison 1996, 352). Rather than being locked away, in the trafficking tale of slavery lost and found, the slaves emerge from the shadows, and the new abolitionists are no longer indifferent to their misery, although they refuse to code it as black. The presence and absence of the slaves themselves play out in different ways, but the right to complex personhood is never granted to them. The suffering of the victims of trafficking-as-slavery is made highly visible, and put on display on a stage that allows for spectacular acts of charity and for the work of liberation and reintegration.

THE BORDERS OF TRAFFICKING

The difference between the incarcerated not-slaves and the trafficked slaves is about the broader disavowal of race at the heart of the new abolitionists' definition of slavery, and it is also about gender and powerlessness. The women who are the victims of trafficking are uprooted and understood apart from their troublesome poverty by the new abolitionists, in a move that they do not make for young and dangerous black men who need to be locked down. The discourse of new slavery renders these women characterless and purposeless, but does not subject them to collective scorn and contempt. However, the narrative of pain and guilt, of knowing and not-knowing, takes place against the same backdrop of the punitive ethos of the state and of carceral violence. The carceral space they inhabit is different, but their purposeless waiting on the margins of developed economies is part of what has been characterised as the 'circuitry of carcerality' that encompasses not just prisons, but also immigration detention centres and camps, and the experience of confinement 'where they are increasingly the subject of discourses and practices conceived with criminals in mind' (Gill et al. 2016, 6). The trafficked woman who has become the paradigmatic chattel of new slavery discourse is often imagined to be white, while the 'slavery' (forced labour for economic exploitation) of dull economic compulsion associated with people, particularly men in the Caribbean and Latin America, is racialised as black. For them all, once they are seen as slaves, their self-possession, property-seeking, work and voice are effaced, and they come to history 'under the heading of trauma' in ways that reinforce myths of black passivity and bolster white specta- torship (Rupprecht 2008, 19).

The current discourse around trafficking and slavery brings us back to the limits of enslavability, and questions of self-possession, labour power, race and property that structure the meanings of slavery and freedom. It also returns us to a vision of antislavery protests as morally motivated and advanced by a select band of saints who write labour and commerce out of history in their construction of 'victims of avarice'. Women who migrate for work or who sell sex are not seen as engaged in the market as market actors, but are placed outside the pathways and webs of trade unless they are deceived or coerced. Their own labour is read as bringing them no security, and their work is detached from any of the honourable or industrious elements of labour, so that they are understood to be uncivilised by the work they do. In the new abolition- ist reading of trafficking as slavery, the victim of trafficking is a slave whose actions are not at her own disposal and whose liberty has been appropriated. She turns herself over to her master completely, handing over control and responsibility to him. In this deeply disempowering narrative, the focus is on the individual trafficker and his victim, the relationship between two people that is at the heart of the new aboli- tionist conception of slavery. What get lost are the ways in which the women are continually enmeshed in exchanging goods for services and participating in masterless capitalism and its creative destruction. The new abolitionist narrative reinforces this erasure through a particular vision of rational labour that is inseparable from self-government and not available to poor women whose rights are readily denied, infringed or transgressed. Their place in the political economy of capitalism is one where their rights are not secured, but provisional and contingent, and dependent on the behaviour and disposition of other citizens.

In writing the women's labour out of the story, the trafficking-as- slavery discourse renders itself incapable of coming to grips with the women's experience of mobility, and of understanding the spaces they are forced to inhabit, between citizenship and belonging. Instead, any analysis of human trafficking needs to begin with the recognition that it occurs within a larger context in which labour migration is a reason- able pursuit. As Nandita Sharma argues, there are fundamental anti- migrant assumptions underpinning the anti-trafficking agenda and its presentation of migration as crisis-producing rather than life-saving (Sharma 2005, 89). This is turn requires recognition that people have an interest in their own labour, but make choices in constrained contexts for agency. Smuggling, as Sharma points out, is a business built by the poor for the poor and it is the state, rather than the individual trafficker, that is the locus of force and the coercion of forcible return and deportation (Sharma 2005, 95). An understanding of trafficking that focuses on the violence of the state and on coercive immobilisation, captivity and confinement reveals the new abolitionist refusal to see the afterlife of slavery in labour subordination and immobilisation, and in the state power that disciplines the mobility of labour (De Genova 2010). Immigration and refugee policies are about the denial of permanent status, wrenching open a gap between citizenship and belonging, and opening up a space that is still haunted by the figure of the slave who is denied an interest in his or her own labour, is excessively dependent on others and whose incorporation is subordinate (De Genova 2010; Anderson 2013). The trafficking-as-slavery discourse works hard to shut down the possibility of agency under oppressive conditions and its disruptive potential. The focus on the individual suffering and the body of the victim is part of the pervasive individualism of using property and slavery to frame the experience of mobility and it serves to obscure the lack of safe migration routes for women trying to exercise their freedom of movement (Sharma 2005).

People who are designated as victims of trafficking or as slaves are those whose mobilities, like Mary Prince's, are rendered suspect in a globalising world, as political elites attempt to defend and redefine 'the boundaries of production, belonging and entitlement', using 'technologies of selection, expulsion and immobilization specific to the late modern state' to leave some people on the outside and to consolidate the subordinate and degraded status of others (Weber and Bowling 2008, 356). Weber and Bowling see these processes of selection, ejection and immobilisation as leading to the emergence of masterless men, of rogues and vagabonds very much like the 'begging drones' who were eligible for slavery in Hutcheson's 1755 scheme. Their labour is treated not as their own, but as the property of others, and they are constructed as needing to be restrained from living off the labour of others and making themselves a burden on the public. These vagrants, like those in Locke's imaginary, are not only idle, but also fraudulent and dishonest, and their poverty and their mobility are constructed as symptomatic of their failure to remain in their proper place and fulfil their duties as a lower, labouring order (Rozbicki 2001, 40). In the context of globalisation, irregular border crossing has become a 'crime of arrival', and the people earmarked for control are those with perceived low economic value within global markets, who are unwanted and unwelcome (Weber and Bowling 2008). Contemporary border anxiety turns these outsiders, as Weber and Bowling argue, into 'embodiments of insecurity' (Weber and Bowling 2008, 367). In echoes of Hegel, they identify a tension between the demands of human beings to their rights to mobility and to a place on the world and 'the strategies through which states seek to constrain the mobility of those designated as unwanted' (Weber and Bowling 2008, 371). The work of perpetual boundary-setting and keeping that allows some but not others to enter into a civilised moral world of rational labour and ethical incorporation is now carried out at the state border, where the disreputable and disruptive poor are detained and deported.

Once trafficking is put into this context of border crossing and border insecurity, it becomes very difficult to ignore the 'raciological thinking' that underpins states' immigration policies. As Weber and Bowling argue, 'phenotypical and economic characteristics combine in conceptions of difference and in the practices of sorting the superior from the inferior' (Weber and Bowling 2008, 364). They identify what they call 'xeno-racism', which draws on tropes of class and skin colour, and the link between poverty and racial difference, to operate against refugees and asylum seekers irrespective of their colour (Weber and Bowling 2008, 366–7). Once again, racialisation shows itself to be a reflexive, relational process, and xeno-racism is used to place migrants outside politics and the possibility of resistance. Through the legal conventions and rules established at the border, as well as through monitoring, surveillance and brute force, the state grants certain prerogatives to itself, but denies them to migrants, allowing one side to place constraints on the other, establishing a form of political association that is objectionable in the terms Ypi applies to colonialism (Ypi 2013). This makes extracting trafficking-as-slavery from its racialised framing a difficult operation, and one that cannot be performed by using 'vulnerability' as a proxy without considering how that vulnerability is constructed, enforced and maintained and insecurity is embodied.

THE ICONIC VICTIM

The contentious politics of border control and the criminalisation of migration create another strange place that is located in the world, but not in history, and migrants and the internally excluded find themselves caught somewhere between the state of nature and civil society, where their persons are disfigured and incapacitated, and they can only come out of the shadows when they are conjured up as victims by the new abolitionists. Out of this dangerous space, fraught with the risks of deportation, labour subordination and immobilisation, the idea of the perfect or iconic victim emerges. The Trafficking Victims Protection Act of 2000 created a new 'T' visa that allowed victims of trafficking to apply to stay in the US if they suffered as a result of a severe form of trafficking in persons and complied with any reasonable request for assistance in the investigation or prosecution of acts of trafficking. This creates a situation where, as Jayashri Srikantiah points out, '[t]he same agent or prosecutor who decides whether a victim would be a good witness also decides whether the individual is a victim for the purposes of the T visa'. This means that the victim story needs to be an 'effective prosecutorial story' that fits the stereotype of a passive victim of sexual exploitation who enters the US under the complete control of the trafficker. To tell an effective prosecutorial story, the victim needs to have been forced, defrauded or coerced into commercial sex, involuntary servitude, debt bondage or slavery, and the trafficker needs to be maximally culpable (Srikantiah 2007, 160). The iconic victim has to confirm through her suffering that slavery at its most essential is about control, that she has been deprived of her individual liberty and been subjected to violence, possession and exploitation. The good, co-operative witness affirms the clear experiential definition of slavery as it is identified by new slavery discourse and by federal agencies, and she is rescued from her plight instead of escaping it (Srikantiah 2007, 187).

This focus on the girl or woman who is trafficked for sex allows her to emerge as a slave rather than an unwanted vagrant. She is not criminalised in the same way as her male counterpart who is an unskilled Mexican labourer facing civil immigration penalties and coded as an intruder, a trespasser and a lawbreaker (Srikantiah 2007, 190). In contrast, she is completely under the trafficker's control, robbed of her free will and 'blameless for any illegality surrounding immigration status' (Srikantiah 2007, 195). As long as she co-operates with law enforcement and federal agencies, her victim status offers her some kind of protection. Humanitarian assistance rests on her compliance and her difference from other illegal aliens and criminalised migrants. It is that difference in status, the insistence that others must be exercising powers attached to ownership over her, that allows her (and not them) to be defined as a slave. Her complete passivity, which, as Srikantiah points out, resonates so closely with stereotypes of foreign women and women of colour (Srikantiah 2007, 202), blots out the possibility of her consent, and encourages an understanding of slavery as the exercise of control that can exist outside a legal framework. She is treated as if she is owned, and is passive until she is rescued, when her free will is restored and she completes the passage out of slavery into a brave new world of liberation and reintegration. A human being on the move and in search of a new place in the world only becomes a slave in certain relations to others. In the case of conjuring the victim of trafficking as a slave, those others include the state, her fellow migrants and her would-be rescuers, and never just her trafficker.

The iconic, passive and blameless victim can be easily characterised as a slave, but she is remarkably difficult to identify. Her existence ignores the multiple roles that people play in the smuggling and trafficking industries, and in the markets for commercial sex. Some women trafficked to Italy from Nigeria, for example, as Eva Iacono's research has shown, become entrepreneurs in the sex markets in the destination countries by becoming madams. Iacono found that during the recruitment phase Nigerian traffickers were relatives, boyfriends, friends or husbands who offered the women assistance to travel abroad. Madams are often former trafficking victims who move on to organise trafficking networks themselves, and appear as friends rather than exploiters and are accorded respect because of their experience (Iacono 2014, 113). Iacono argues that this means that the area between victim and perpetrator is not empty, but populated by individuals who are both in the same trap. Victims are driven to become both partners in crime and independent agents over time, moving up through the trafficking hierarchy. Nigerian trafficking can be understood as a female business, with the madam embodying entrepreneurship and success because she 'has achieved a recognised social position of power and authority through her personal economic adventures' (Iacono 2014, 118). Iacono describes a phone conversation with a madam known as Aminat who told her how she was helped to arrive in Italy and paid off the money that was asked from her. 'When I finished paying', she said, 'I became a free woman, and I started to earn money for myself.' She went on to invest that money in the trafficking business to bring other women to Italy to work on the streets (Iacono 2014, 119). In doing so, she was following a career pattern that she knew was feasible. The clearing of her debts changed her status within the criminal network and gave her a new role in relation to the women she brought in. She became 'a reference point for understanding the new cultural codes in the destination country', invested with the power to protect the women, to bestow patronage on the women she trusted, and to turn them into favourites, assistants and wardens over the other women (Iacono 2014, 122). All the women are embedded in a social setting that is built around layers of trust, complicated loyalties and tangled connections. Sometimes, the madam is both victim and persecutor because she herself is being exploited by others, and forced to engage in the trafficking business by her family, who are hoping to improve their standard of living in Nigeria through their trafficked daughter in Europe. There are elements of control, of powers attached to ownership and of use, management and profit at work in Iacono's stories of Nigerian women involved in trafficking, but they do not tell the whole story of the women's agency and connections, and they do not cohere into a single narrative of slavery and the deprivation of liberty.

The prevalent constructions of human trafficking rely on gender and racial stereotypes that work together to discount women's agency, to establish an unreachable standard of victimhood, and to prioritise the trafficking of white women (Lobasz 2009, 322). Human trafficking is socially constructed on unreliable data and through academic research which is often government-funded and designed to prepare the ground for counter-trafficking interventions. It is framed through threats to national security and state borders from transnational organised crime, and haunted by the 'specter of organized crime networks and menacing mafiosi' (Lobasz 2009, 326). Transnational organised crime is figured as the dark side of globalisation, a threat to democracy, to the economic basis of society and to the rule of law. Trafficked persons embody these threats, this insecurity, these border crossings. Feminist work on human trafficking often presents victimisation in 'a sufficiently alarming way' to get the public to feel strongly and governments to act and, in doing so, their focus is on women who are not consenting, who are misled about the nature of the work they will be doing and the extent of their obligation to the traffickers. These are women who experience human rights violations including rape, assault, debt bondage and sexual exploitation, and the response to these concerns is to introduce victim protection measures, legal assistance, medical services, housing and training. This victim protection and assistance is then, as we have seen, tied to co-operation with the authorities by the UN, the EU and the US, prioritising the interests of the state (Lobasz 2009, 332) and the fight against crime and border violations.

COMBATING TRAFFICKING

Feminist engagement with this discourse is complicated and multi-layered, and for some the fight against trafficking is a fight against prostitution, a chance to affirm the ways in which women have their 'sexual victimhood in common' and how that commonality of oppression requires a transnational movement to fight sexual slavery (Lobasz 2009, 335). The victim of trafficking joins the veiled woman and the purchased bride as emblematic chattel, and they are all brought together by a narrative that insists that the criminalisation of prostitution is a necessary step towards ending human trafficking. In the US, as Lobasz points out, feminist abolitionists successfully lobbied George W. Bush's administration for a federal 'gag rule' that 'requires anti-trafficking groups who receive federal monies to explicitly reject legalized prostitution' (Lobasz 2009, 336). This abolitionist impulse, like new slavery, emphasises sexual innocence and blamelessness, and the forced deprivation of liberty through kidnapping and brutality 'in order to produce a sympathetic victim who would be politically unpalatable to criminalize' (Lobasz 2009, 340). She is a figure who has to be able to withstand 'the test of innocence and the test of pain' (Lobasz 2009, 342).

The identity of 'the prostitute' sometimes gets fixed, by language and discourse and power, as that of a victim or a slave. The way the rhetoric of slavery works in relation to prostitution is to focus intense sentiment on the deserving victims, and in the process to present those victims as incapable of making choices, of controlling their own destiny (O'Connell Davidson 2005, 25–6), as the opposite of unified moral selves who make their own choices. They are presented as figures 'so thoroughly saturated and determined by power relations' that they have no agency (M. Lloyd 2005, 10). This is in part because certain strands of feminist discourse tend to assume that the prostitute must have been forcibly deprived of her freedom to dispose over her own body, and so been subjected to the most fundamental sort of personal degradation. She has no defence mechanisms against the torture she has experienced, and 'the picture we have is of a body-self that has been so injured that it cannot recognise its true interests' (Wolkowitz 2006, 126). For those like Kathleen Barry (Barry 1995), who equate prostitution with sexual slavery, the body of the prostitute is 'de-selved'. The risk of this focus on slavery is that the women are characterised as 'so far debased to have lost all title to Humanity' (Peckard 1788, 2). In other words, women who sell sex are placed outside the process of historical change and no longer treated as subjects with their own histories who can speak for themselves. Instead, they have to be understood as 'defencelessly at the mercy of another subject' (Honneth 1995, 132–3) and as continually enmeshed in a process through which what most defines women as women is what is taken away from them by prostitution. Their security of their person is 'stolen and sold' (MacKinnon 1993) in the same way as antislavery thinkers understood slavery as man-stealing or the theft of an entire life. For Carole Pateman, mastery and subjection are renewed and affirmed through a contract that guarantees men's orderly sexual access to women, so that 'when a prostitute contracts out use of her body she is selling *herself* in a very real sense' (Pateman 1988, 207, emphasis in original). It is this notion of selling the self that supposedly gives prostitution its unique status as a form of slavery and constitutes it as a denial of humanity. Like the prisoners in Dayan's account, women who sell sex de-create themselves and experience the gradual annihilation of the person through social death (J. Dayan 2001).

It makes sense, Catharine MacKinnon argues, 'to understand prostitution as consisting in the denial of women's humanity, no matter how humanity is defined' (MacKinnon 1993, 13). Women are prostituted 'precisely in order to be degraded and subjected to cruel and brutal treatment without human limits' (MacKinnon 1993, 13). This means that, for MacKinnon and other radical feminists who would seek to abolish prostitution, sexual slavery is slavery, and radical feminist discourse denies the possibility of 'any continuities between prostitution and other kinds of (dirty, humiliating, intimate) work' (Wolkowitz 2006, 127). The sexual slavery model portrays women as owned by pimps and traffickers who act as their masters. The campaigning literature is often slightly vague about the identification of the 'master', who can be a pimp, a brothel owner or even a client (and all of these identifications are problematic). Pimps, for example, are pictured as having total physical control over the women who work for them, enforced by physical violence and extending to the idea that they can sell their 'possessions' to another pimp. Shared Hope International has a list of 'trafficking terms' on its website, where it describes 'choosing up' as 'the process by which a different pimp takes "ownership" of a victim' and the original pimp has to pay a fee to get her back (Shared Hope International 2017). Trafficking in persons, with its much-vaunted links to organised crime, is figured as part of an 'international sex slave business', an underground trade that acquires and disposes of human beings in 'a modern version of the slave trade'. In the process, the women who are trafficked across borders are understood to be sold, exchanged and traded, always without their consent and invariably for the purposes of sexual exploitation. They are defined by Kevin Bales as 'completely disposable tools for making money' (Bales 1999, 4).

This conflation of slavery, prostitution, violence and trafficking rests on a series of assumptions, frames the political debate in particular ways, and allows the 'sex slave' to stand as a condensation symbol. The first assumption it condenses is that slavery the opposite of self-ownership, reflecting the dichotomous thinking that divides the world into those who exercise full autonomy and those who are completely disposable tools like ballpoint pens. Slaves, and chattel slaves in particular, were constructed as not owning a property in the person, as not having the right not to be invaded or usurped by others. They had no right to exclude others, to resist punishment, or to protect their own physical security. The chattel slave was unable to make a will, to bring formal criminal charges against others or to appear as a witness in most civil cases. The slave had no right of petition, no property and no right of appeal. A slave's evidence was acceptable in court only if it had been extracted by torture (Williams 1998, 5). All this shows the ways in which the slave owners' property in their slaves was not just about their individual, momentary ownership, but about the broader structures within which they exercised their ownership and found their powers to be socially sanctioned and justified. The slave owners and masters were in a persistent position of authority over their slaves, reinforced by a body of law that disfigured and incapacitated their slaves. The slaves became slaves through this relation to law and to property, and not just through their relations to their master.

TRAFFICKING AS SLAVERY: PAST AND PRESENT

The conflation of trafficking with slavery relies on the idea of men generating trafficking and women in need of protection from them. In a letter to the *Daily News* on 2 January 1880, Alfred Stace Dyer described a virtuous nineteen-year-old Englishwoman courted in London by a man who promised her marriage if she would go with him to Brussels, where she was taken to a brothel. 'Intimidated from leaving the house, forced to submit her person to the last indignity that can be inflicted upon a woman, here she was a slave as was ever any negro upon Virginian soil' (Attwood 2015, 614). Dyer coordinated the repatriation of the girl, and used her experience as part of his wider campaign to portray the treatment of trafficking victims as 'infinitely more cruel and revolting than negro servitude [of old], because it is slavery not for labour but for lust; and more cowardly than negro slavery, because it falls on the young and helpless of one sex only' (Attwood 2015, 615). As Attwood argues, this was about depicting trafficking as an 'exceptional atrocity' because it entailed the sexual enslavement of innocent and vulnerable white women and girls in England (Attwood 2015, 615). Trafficking was regarded as subversive of domesticity, morally and physically corrupting the nation's future mothers and homemakers. Attwood traces a shift in this discourse at the beginning of the twentieth century as sex trafficking began to be understood in a more globalised context, and the women involved became embodiments of insecurity, and their foreign traffickers and pimps 'the male parasites of evil'. Rather than blameless victims, these women selling sex were constructed as a menace, and their foreignness was a marker of their debauchery. Trafficking, Attwood argues, was positioned as a threat to imperial power, which was in danger of being corrupted by the 'vicious foreign woman' (Attwood 2015, 617–19). The International Agreement on Trafficking of 1902 allowed for the interrogation of women travelling alone at ports and railway stations, and interventions such as buying them one-way steamer tickets to send them home. Clearly set against the unsullied innocence of young Englishwomen, these alien women were read as blighted and contaminating. Current discourses of trafficking as slavery play with both these tropes of corrupting innocent womanhood and of women as threatening others. They continue to draw on the 'sexualised xenophobia' identified by Attwood as being at the heart of the earlier discourse she analyses, helping to structure gendered constructions of what 'rescue' means for women selling sex, and reinforcing the idea that women who work in prostitution are having what defines them as women taken away from them. The understanding of trafficking as an 'exceptional atrocity', the focus on indecency, cruelty, innocence and vulnerability, continues to inform the construction of victims of trafficking, minimising the differences between them through repetition.

The shift between the late nineteenth and early twentieth centuries and today is in part about the rise of humanitarianism and the power of its appeal. As Miriam Ticktin argues, humanitarians 'engage at the level of the suffering body', a body that is positioned outside time and place, history and politics (Ticktin 2011, 254). They put cruelty first, focusing on violence, pain and suffering, where 'wounds speak louder than words' in a shared story of physical pain and human sentience (Malkki 1996, 384). 'The key to its power and its appeal', Ticktin goes on, 'is its unquestioned universality: that is, the underlying assumption is that we can recognise suffering whenever we see it, because there is a common denominator to being human, located in our bodies, particularly in our bodies in pain' (Ticktin 2011, 254). Enslavement is then understood as a form of torture, as subjection to pain and injury, to 'incessant *stripes*, *wounds* and *miseries*' (Clarkson 1786, 81). The victims of trafficking are not placed in the context of gendered regimes of property or inheritance, of structural adjustment or of imperialist policies. Instead, the context for their suffering becomes 'a certain emotional connectivity between spectator and sufferer' (Chouliaraki 2010, 109), calling forth a sympathetic response from those who interpret their unspoken suffering. Kevin Bales opens his book *Disposable People* with a description of Seba, a newly freed slave, which focuses on her body in pain, her physical symptoms and her beatings. 'Sometimes I would bleed,' she tells him. 'I still have marks on my body' (Bales 2000, 2). The slaves become broken bodies who require care and protection, designated as innocent and at the same time powerless. This kind of humanitarianism stands in for universalism. The assumption is that all kinds of difference lead back to the sameness of pain and suffering, but that assumption is built not just on similarity but on the difference between those who have the power to protect and those who need protection. We are back to the processes of universalising and particularising at the same time. It emphasises the gap between privilege and suffering, and the abolitionist belief in the universality of humanity and natural liberty always coexists with 'a panicky and contradictory need to preserve essential boundaries and distinctions' (Coleman 1994, 9). The veneer of humanitarianism, and its unquestioned universality protects similarity at the expense of not recognising the inequality and the panic, and the politics, contradictions and disavowals they bring with them (Ticktin 2011, 261).

One of the key ways of preserving boundaries and distinctions is through the identification of 'exemplary victims' (Malkki 1996, 384) who can make a legitimate claim to slave status by having endured violence intimately (Brace 2014). The process of selecting some people as victims of trafficking for the 'T' visa is a mechanism of inequality and exclusion, creating exclusionary pathways for non-victims, who are typically men and victims of labour exploitation. The trafficking-as-slavery narrative that insists on the exceptional atrocity of trafficking and the blamelessness of its victims reflects a moral panic around sex work that has framed sex trafficking as a more urgent concern than labour trafficking (Shih 2016). At the same time, as Elena Shih points out, the politics of this protection and humanitarianism open up a new space 'for American citizens to enact surveillance and patrol over what are publicly deemed as dangerous or victimized bodies' (Shih 2016, 69). They are positioned to police the essential boundaries and distinctions and to the mind the gap between privilege and suffering. In this story of slavery lost and found, their presence and absence, and their relationship to the state, comes in and out of focus. The powers that are exercised over them are not just those of their evil, parasitic traffickers, or those of a punitive state, but also the 'vigilante authority' of individual citizens 'in the light of insufficient state response to trafficking rescue and rehabilitation' (Shih 2016, 70). Like the fugitive slave patrols of the nineteenth century, these vigilante rescue efforts are where the limits to enslavability are carefully guarded and individual citizens work to try to restore a social order that promises righteous domesticity and limits the migrants' interest in their own labour.

Shih's work explores the entrepreneurialism of abolitionism, the selling of the experience of rescue through the idea of making a difference, of being a footsoldier of justice or a warrior of light (Ricky Martin Foundation 2012). Concerned citizens, styled as 'everyday abolitionists', are encouraged to find out how many slaves work for them by taking a survey, to buy slave-free goods, to take human-trafficking reality tours, to host awareness and fund-raising events, to blog, bake, accessorise, send Christmas cards and to donate to various organisations. In this everyday abolitionism, consumption is closely connected

to freedom, and to 'women's mission to women'. The moralisation of
consumption promises Western women that they can participate ethically in the market, with the power to offer opportunities and hope to
the survivors of trafficking through their own buying choices. White
women's power emerges from deep within domestic space, and positions them within the economy of liberal guilt (Brace 2014, 494). At
the same time, they are encouraged to exercise their power by raising awareness of the powerlessness of others, and of other women in
particular. The Not for Sale Backyard Abolitionist Academy teaches
people how to identify the characteristics of slavery, alert police and
identify local social services. ZOE tells people to 'know the stats, know
the signs, know the sources' and declares that 'when people are aware
of the signs of human trafficking and know where to find help, it is
easier for human trafficking victims to be identified and then given
assistance' (ZOE 2016). History, ZOE International tells visitors to
its website, is full of triumphant victories over unspeakable atrocities, specifically 'American slavery' and the Holocaust. Modern everyday abolitionists insert themselves into history at a point of their own
choosing within a very particular redemptive narrative. They reinforce
the rupture between past and present, and assign 'old' slavery to the
past in order to frame human trafficking as an unspeakable horror for
the younger generation to tackle: 'But this time we are alive. Today
we have a chance to do something about it' (ZOE 2016). Members
of the Ricky Martin Foundation can become light warriors, 'defined
by honor and bravery', whose aim is 'to do justice and find peace for
those who have been deprived of their freedom' (RMF 2012). This, as
Shih points out, is hands-on, engaged and evangelical activism that
generates a considerable amount of income through workshop fees,
donations and merchandise. It is also about taking action, in a world
where keeping silent means siding with the perpetrator, and abolitionists seek to do more than fundraising and awareness building in
order to 'make a real difference' rather than be left 'standing idle at the
sidelines' (Shih 2016).

Shih's ethnographic work focuses on the 'raid and rescue' strategy
that grows out of this rhetoric of 'making a difference'. It is an approach
that, as Govindan points out, collapses the distinctions between different forms of sexual labour, exploitative labour conditions, migration,
slavery-like working conditions, violence against women and trafficking (Govindan 2013, 516) in pursuit of emancipation and liberation

for the slaves they rescue, and the possibility of performing the role of emancipator for themselves. Shih describes a group of college-age white men bringing the enslaved into existence and making them real by going into massage parlours as potential clients and then coming back to put the sites under surveillance in the dark, hiding behind rubbish bins, taking vague notes about the clientele which they then compiled into a report to send to the police, and producing a visual map showing the location of the brothels which they posted on Facebook. The members of this group consistently maintained that they had connections to the LAPD and a rapport with law enforcement, who recognised that they were 'the real footsoldiers of justice because we are not constrained by funding or bureaucracy to pursue justice for the enslaved' (Shih 2016, 78). The underlying principles of these anti-trafficking interventions are victim relief and aftercare, and perpetrator responsibility. They work with local law enforcement and NGOs to gather information and then engineer raids on brothels, with a focus on convictions for the perpetrators and rehabilitation for the victims, often creating 'programmes that become sites of surveillance and control in and of themselves' (Govindan 2013, 517).

As Shih points out, the kind of vigilante abolitionism she is exploring is paradoxical because concerned citizens are told both that human trafficking is a growing problem and the leading atrocity for their generation to tackle, and that they cannot see it because it is by nature hidden and underground. The signs of trafficking are not always easy to spot. In response, the abolitionist groups use 'proxy markers' of poverty, recent immigration status, sexualised femininity, and racial and ethnic difference as symptoms of human trafficking. Failing to see what they set out to find in their local brothels and on the streets just confirms that they need to look deeper beneath the surface 'to uncover the realities that had been suggested through political and moral scripts about human trafficking' (Shih 2016, 83). Their efforts to combat human trafficking through this kind of surveillance training, 'knowing the signs', puts hotel employees, border control agents, postal workers, medical personnel, beauty salon workers and flight attendants in the front line 'with new forms of structural power to surveil and patrol marginalized communities' (Shih 2016, 84). The new generation of abolitionists are witnesses rather than spectators, prepared to shed a light on slavery, to speak out, and 'to continue the work of vigilance and community policing' (ZOE 2016). In the process, they enforce and extend the goals of the state, polish the veneer of humanitarianism and protection, and position themselves as agents of freedom, 'an emancipator whose efforts to rescue trafficking victims actually produce the victim as an object of intervention' (Govindan 2013, 514).

This new, active abolitionism plays to the script of punishing the few bad traffickers and setting their victims free. The appeals not to stand idle but to take a stand are aimed at members of the justice generation and are part of what Elizabeth Bernstein has identified as a culturally modernising project where the problem is the absence of law enforcement and the solution is 'a vision of social justice as criminal justice, and of punitive systems of control as the best motivational deterrents for men's bad behavior' (Bernstein 2010, 58). Through taking part, the abolitionists and rescuers define and reinforce their own autonomy as Western women and enlightened men who are civilised by the abolitionist work they do and the place in the world that it gives them. Bernstein identifies them as part of the contemporary feminist model of human-rights activism 'produced by subjects who imagine themselves more ethical and free than their "sisters" in the developing world' (Bernstein 2010, 63). They exercise this freedom as consumers of goods produced by former 'slaves' who are now employed as jewellery makers by their missionary employers, who dock their pay for missing daily prayers, being late for work and other minor infractions (Bernstein 2010, 65). This is a process of affirming the women's interest in their own labour only where it is disciplined and directed towards 'civilising' goals. The property rights of the former 'slaves' are carefully differentiated from those of their 'sisters' in the developing world, and subjected to a different set of expectations, alerting us to inequality and to what keeps us apart, rather than to reciprocity (Phillips 2013, 45). Their troublesome poverty is carefully micromanaged for them. Unlike the prisoners of the previous chapter, they are not treated with scorn and contempt, but their treatment is part of the new punitive ethos, bringing together the consumer and the carceral. The traffickers may be keeping them where the law cannot protect them, but the victims conjured into being by the abolitionists are moved into a space where the state can discipline them and the law can punish them.

Their labour is stigmatised in ways that mean that their property in the person cannot anchor them in moral and political space. Their mobility is coded as resistance and they are understood to be fugitives, hustlers and exiles (Brace 2013a, 873). They do not stay where they are supposed to be, and for women in particular, that involves leaving the domestic duties and fixed loyalties of the family. Migrating to work in domestic labour and sex work means inhabiting 'a strange in-between space, between the public and the private, the domestic and the market' (Pettman 1998) and women constructed as victims of trafficking often find themselves suspended there. The strangeness of their space contrasts with the righteous domesticity of the anti-trafficking campaigns that aim to domesticate heterosexual men and promote feminist family values. Punishing the traffickers and setting the victims free go hand in hand with a focus on ending demand, using the paradigm of feminism as crime control (Bernstein 2010). The figure of the victim of trafficking as an embodiment of insecurity is balanced by the figure of the 'security mom' as the embodiment of security, the upper-middle-class white woman who 'utilize[s] and promote[s] the carceral state in order to securitize the sexual boundaries of home' (Bernstein 2012, 247). In this context, it is the new carceral abolitionism that carves out spaces for its victims where the law cannot protect them, where they are integrated into the market as well as the state in ways that mark them as outsiders whose incorporation is subordinate, and where the family as an institution is shored up against them. Their rights remain provisional and insecure, and they remain stranded in a place of no return where their freedom is of a particular shade.

The 'raid and rescue' strategies at the heart of the new carceral abolitionism are central to a security regime that imagines women as in need of protection from violence, and the liberated slave woman as moving 'from darkness to light, from animal to human' with her rescuer as the sole agent of transformation (Govindan 2013, 514). They follow the arc of the slave narrative, but the work of 'rehumanising' is undertaken by the abolitionists who effect the transformation of the slave back into a person and pave their way to 'civilization'. In these interventions, where the victim of trafficking is understood to be a slave and under the control of another person, her work cannot be read as a form of self-realisation or coded as a form of conscious resistance, and so the process of objectification becomes irreversible (Cassuto 1996). The female figure of the migrant in the anti-trafficking campaigns is defined by the violence she has suffered, and she is positioned outside the labour market and its social connections, and outside the ethical life of the family. The underlying suggestion is that labour migration is always risky or reckless for women, and that their inviolability is always threatened by

moving abroad, so that 'the safest option is to remain home' (Andrijasevic 2007, 31). Women rescued from brothels are kept without access
to outside help or to their own money, and children are held in secure
environments to protect them from being re-trafficked and to prevent
them from returning to prostitution. Victims are constituted as 'cogni-
tively and psychically incapable of giving meaningful consent to being
rescued and therefore do not need to be asked for consent' (Govindan
2013, 527). The victim of trafficking is dependent, as Govindan argues,
on the figure of the emancipator to constitute her as both enslaved and
as liberated. Her rescuers do the work of liberation and integration,
aiming for a moment of transformation for the individual victim as they
empathise with her abject suffering, her innocence and her pain.

In Italy, undocumented migrants can have their immigration status regularised through a special residence permit granted for reasons
of social protection. People whose lives would be endangered if they
were returned home are allowed to stay in Italy and obtain a residence
and work permit on condition that they agree to leave prostitution and
participate in a social protection programme (Andrijasevic 2003, 263).
NGOs and other migrant rights groups, police and immigration officials can initiate requests for permits on behalf of victims of violence or
severe exploitation. The scheme requires the women to give up working in prostitution, and the NGO involved generally places the woman
with a family or in guest houses where they are supervised during their
'rehabilitation' and often put to work as cleaners and domestic workers
as well as in agriculture and factories. In India, the same focus is on rescue and rehabilitation. People's homes can be entered and searched by
the police and rescue officials, and women and girls can be taken from
their homes against their will and either remanded to rescue homes or
repatriated to their countries of origin. The rescue homes are privately
run and, as Svati Shah points out, they have come under scrutiny for
failing to provide adequate food, for keeping people against their will,
and for teaching the women sewing as an alternative to sex work (Shah
2004). Patrizia Testai's research in Italy found that this rescue-and-reha-
bilitation model gave enormous power to NGOs and religious groups
who run protection programmes for these women, whom they describe
as not doing anything, not engaging in anything, not really working,
sleeping – almost literally listless, characterless and purposeless – in
contrast to their own ethical standing: 'I realised then about the difference between their lifestyle and mine, their clothes and mine. Not all of
them are victims, some of them just want money' (Testai 2006).

RESCUE AND INCORPORATION

This is a tempting aspect of the sex slavery model. It offers western feminists and others the chance to 'rescue' the powerless, and to incorporate them into civil society on their own terms. Women migrant workers can be figured as outside the market economy because they are not self-owners seeking property and outside civil society because they are the victims of violence. As a result, what they need is protection, the chance to rebuild their lives as 'real' women, to give up their empty lives as prostitutes. One of Testai's interviewees, a male volunteer from a religious group, talked about his work:

> The overall aim of the programme is . . . You know what, it's easy to take a woman off the street, but it's difficult to rehabilitate her . . . she is an empty woman, deprived of her femininity, so she has to regain the ability to take care of her body, her hygiene, her sexuality . . . they are people who have lost any guideline.

And another, female, psychologist reported, 'She is a destroyed person . . . She has no point of reference, she lost her dignity' (Testai 2006). Those involved in these rescue programmes echo the language of the new abolitionists in seeing their work as liberation and reintegration, but also in understanding the women as disposable and as helpless victims who are fundamentally scarred and living lives without meaning and direction. The victims of trafficking emerge as slaves in this relation to society, in this public realm of social relations, where the expectations that others have of them are affirmed, legitimated and protected. The problem of debasement creates the same risks for the new abolitionists as it did for their eighteenth- and nineteenth-century forebears, bringing the focus to the rescuer, building on the tropes of melodrama and requiring the transformation of the individual victim. In the process, it sets up the polarities of victimhood and real choice, obscures the complex interplay of agency, poverty and restriction, and renders invisible the work of the poor and vulnerable, their interest in their own labour, and their more complicated and messy relationship to violence and to agency.

Women who sell sex are defined by the new abolitionist discourse as 'first and foremost, victims of coercion and violence' (Shah 2004, 798). The discourse constructs and then saves helpless victims, using the state as an instrument both of liberation and of punishment and control. The assumption that the most dangerous violence is perpetrated by the individual evil trafficker over his property means that certain Western feminist theorists writing on prostitution 'are able to construct an excess of vulnerability to violence *vis-à-vis* women living in the Global South' (Shah 2004, 804). In this context, as we have seen, the act of sex in the context of prostitution is represented as violence, foreclosing the women's histories and experiences of prostitution. As Shah argues, this needs to be replaced by a more expansive definition of violence that takes into account structural concerns such as class, education and infrastructure and aims for a less binary understanding of force and choice, decentring sexuality as the arena of greatest privacy and intimacy, 'and therefore greatest unqualified vulnerability' (Shah 2004, 810). This less binary understanding and the decentring of sexuality will necessarily involve giving up on the idea that trafficking ought to be understood as slavery. It also means rethinking agency by considering multiple motivations that exceed rational calculation, and by allowing agency a history, treating it as a concept that people in the past and in the present 'have defined and deployed in quite different, and sometimes disorienting, ways' (Thomas 2016, 335). Lynn Thomas's argument is that agency needs reformulating so that it is no longer used as a 'safety' argument, 'shoehorning all historical subjects into the likeness of autonomous, enlightened individuals' who can serve as characters in the rescue narrative of transformation (Thomas 2016, 326). A more complicated conception of agency is able to attend to what Thomas calls 'multiple, intersecting and shifting forces and concerns' (Thomas 2016, 330) that help to explain poor and vulnerable women's relationship to their interest in their own labour and to structural violence. Like Mary Prince and Harriet Jacobs, they are negotiating their mobility in conditions of oppressive freedom and finding their agency used as an instrument of oppression against them. They show us again the complications of what can be identified as agency, and of striving to be an agent without appearing to be one.

There are a whole range of problems with defining the concept of trafficking, closely related to the difficulties of defining slavery. It is difficult to treat as a separable, isolated phenomenon, or as a single act leading to a particular outcome. As O'Connell Davidson points out, trafficking is a process that can be organised in a variety of ways and involves a package of unfreedoms, so that it is much better understood as a continuum of experience than as a dichotomy (Anderson and O'Connell Davidson 2002). The Trafficking Protocol of

2003 assumes a neat demarcation between voluntary and involuntary migration which fails to recognise the complex variety of social relations between irregular migrants – the ways in which people can be tricked, deceived or coerced at different points in the process. Nurses brought into Britain legally by agencies from the Philippines to work in the NHS, for example, can find themselves deceived about their working conditions and their wages, and women who are aware that they may be going to work in a brothel may not understand that they are going to be debt-bonded. The new slavery rhetoric for understanding trafficking assumes that it can see the difference between 'total control' and choice, and misses the blurriness of the distinctions between voluntary and involuntary, legal and illegal migration, and the ways in which one can fade into the other. In its labelling of some as trafficked and others as smuggled the state (and the UN) assumes a neat demarcation between voluntary and involuntary migration, between wanted and unwanted migrants, and helps to create and sustain a moral framework that decides who is degraded, and who has been tricked or deceived. The state is also implicated in selecting and legitimating whose labour power counts as improving, rational and industrious – so not only who belongs, but also who owns their labour power as a form of private property, and so enjoys relative autonomy. In the process of making such distinctions the state constructs a hierarchy of acceptability and incorporation that risks naturalising people's status as outsiders and victims. Once that status is fixed, the people can only be incorporated into civil society in specific ways, through a potent mix of sentiment, coercion and exploitation that reinforces gendered and racialised norms. The assumption that women's static feminine identity has been taken from them, turned them into property and left them empty makes the focus on the new slavery a non-political analysis, as does its insistence that this more authentic identity needs to be restored to them. The coherence of antislavery and anti-trafficking campaigning comes from the focus on the brutality of domination and an analysis that places slavery outside capitalism. The campaigners work with structures of feeling and assumptions about enslavability, self-possession, labour power, race and property that deny the women designated as slaves their complex and socially recognised personhood, a place in the world and the possibility of pursuing their own projects (Mills 2015). The subjects of the trafficking-as-slavery discourse are so hollowed out that their human and labour rights cannot ground their membership of a civilised moral world. The new abolitionism, in its abstraction from the realm of social relations, from the contexts of migration and from the constrained contexts for women's agency, ignores the ways that a 'new but still male-dominant global culture may be emerging, relying on the labor of a new transnational labor force that is feminized, racialized and sexualized' (Jaggar 2005, 67). This is not about invisible 'dark matter' or about the individual compulsion to control, but about this broader political economy and the function of borders as 'an instrument of security controls, social segregation, and unequal access to the means of existence, and sometimes as an institutional distribution of survival and death' (Balibar 2001, 16).

Chapter 10

GLIMPSES OF SLAVERY

The politics of slavery have shifted their ground again, and in the twenty-first century the optics are different, and the 'additive mixture' of all the light has created a particular prism through which to view the pasts, presents and futures of slavery. The shadows have a colour. It is no longer possible to find people defending slavery or making arguments for gradual rather than immediate abolition. Slavery as an idea has become the epitome of a moral wrong, and an 'appalling anachronism' (O'Connell Davidson 2015, 9). At the same time, we live in a world saturated with inequality, violence, exploitation, oppression, brutality and indifference, and in a history full of fits and starts and repetitions, of memories and rememories. In order to understand the current politics of slavery, we need to spend some time in the discomfort of slavery as a part of our shared property-history, not as the special property of people racialised as black. The politics may be different, but the debates between the modern abolitionists and those who focus on the afterlives of racial slavery are still about the waving line between slavery and servitude, the mobile borderlands between personhood, subpersonhood and humanity, and what it means to live in those spaces and to seek to escape them. In the eighteenth century debates over slavery, Hegel located history outside Africa and inside Europe (Purtschert 2010, 1046), and set up the spatio-temporal difference between a time of development and a time of non-development. Africa, he declared, 'is no historical part of the world; it has no movement or development to exhibit'. It was, Hegel went on, still involved in the conditions of mere nature, on the threshold of the world's history. As we have seen, this sense of Africa as a state of nature is very clear in the abolitionist and anti-abolitionist writings of the late eighteenth century, where 'Africa' emerges as a space of abundance and plenty, defined by the conditions of mere nature. Conservative identity politics, of the sort that chooses to quote from William Wilberforce, is committed to defending the existing hierarchical social order and inequalities of social prestige and status. It still trades in this understanding of history, in which Africa remains in a kind of state of nature, suspended between the affective innocence of subsistence and the impossibility of progress.

This same narrative that underpinned the proslavery arguments of the eighteenth century can be compatible with what has come to be understood as antislavery discourse. There is something about 'slavery' as an idea that has no historical part in the world, and has no movement or development to exhibit. Its association with this European-constructed Africa is part of the process of taking slavery outside of history, of making slavery itself (as Purtschert says about Africa), 'a place of no return' (Purtschert 2010, 1046). The slave never becomes a protagonist of spirit, who can keep developing, but remains a 'limit-figure' (Purtschert 2010, 1047) without the possibility of an inner world. The 'slave' as constructed by the new slavery discourse exists behind a curtain, hidden in plain sight, the victim of a 'beast that lurks in the shadows' as Lisa Kristine puts it in her TED talk, and the slave is always a figure who illuminates the difference between what Purtschert calls 'a progressive modernity and its stagnating Others' (Purtschert 2010, 1049). By contemplating slavery as an abomination, and its abolition as having decisively made the world a better place, liberals can find cause for hope, 'now no less than in the nineteenth century'. Miller draws attention to the result of this approach: 'we end up lamely lamenting the fates of the enslaved, or condemning slavers as congenitally evil'. Slaves, Abraham Booth argued, are 'the proper objects of benevolence' (Booth 1792, 23). Looking back at the 'old' slavery, our retrospective judgement leaves the enslaved 'hopelessly inert' and the slavers 'hopelessly driven', undermining the possibility of thinking historically, of uncovering the meanings and motivations of those involved. We need, as Miller insists, to see them 'more fully than as victims'. When we don't, we end up seeing slavery as inherently static, a place of no return, and it becomes an intractable, moral problem, an evil that lurks within our hearts, a beast in the shadows. By taking the slavery out of history, and the history out of slavery, we end up 'airlifting the perpetrators and victims out of the deep structures of intersectional racism-sexism that ensnare all of us' (Fogg-Davis 2016, 98). This book has attempted to put slavery back into history, and into the history of political thought, and the history back into slavery, and in the process to challenge the ahis-toricism and the air-lifting of new abolitionist discourse.

Slavery, Kevin Bales insists, should not be confused with anything else, but treated as a separate and distinct type of human rights abuse. Like the eighteenth-century abolitionists, Bales focuses on the slaves'loss of control over their labour power and describes slavery as theft:'Slavery is an obscenity. It is not just stealing someone's labor; it is the theft of an entire life' (Bales 1999, 7). This is a close reflection of eighteenth-century arguments about the injustice of slavery and its relationship to owning a property in the person. It sets up slavery as a description of radical unfreedom, and then sets that unfreedom against the freedom of con-tract, as if owning a property in the person equates to freedom from ser-vitude (Shilliam 2012, 597). In her TED talk Lisa Kristine focuses on all kinds of'others'working in appalling conditions, including women and children breaking rocks. When she encountered them on her journey into modern slavery, she wanted to cry, but waited until she got home before she really felt her heart break. In the face of their suffering, she talks about how she had to rely on Free the Slaves to work within the system to help them, and how she trusted them. After Free the Slaves' intervention, the same women did the same backbreaking work, still for a scanty subsistence, but, Kristine declared, 'they do it for themselves, and they do it in freedom' (Kristine 2012). This is part of the story of abolition as rupture, as the moment that the past became the future, the happy-ever-after story of'as soon as Compact enters, slavery ceases'. Late-eighteenth-century political economists were prepared to admit that slavery was a basic relation of commercial society, but after emanci-pation the claim that'entry into the market held an immanent potential for the realisation of fuller freedom' (Shilliam 2012, 594) required the exorcising of the enslaved African from an understanding of the process of commodification. Commerce had to be distinguished from the inhu-manity of slavery, and the story of capitalist modernity had to be one of contract, consent and freedom. It is this story of consent and freedom that the new slavery discourse reinforces and reinscribes for the twenty-first century.

Modern slavery abolitionists do not ask what it is that renders black men, women and teenagers particularly exposed and unprotected, or think about how their vulnerability is politically induced (Sheth 2016, 91). At the same time, the new slavery discourse still wants to hold on to the 'thingification' of slavery, the idea that slaves are treated as inanimate objects. Women in Thailand, declares Bales, are 'things, markers in a male game of status and prestige. It is thus no surprise that some women are treated as livestock – kidnapped, abused, held like animals, bought and sold, and dumped when their usefulness is gone' (Bales 1999, 48). Tryon Woods argues that the modern slavery discourse appropriates black suffering as the model for grievance and injustice, for rightlessness and exploitation and dispossession and social death, and then uses abstract black suffering to make non-racial political demands. It emphatically has nothing to do with the black struggle or with actually existing black communities: 'their invocation of late capitalism's ills as 'slavery' demands a comprehensive disavowal of the facts of the ongoing relations of racial slavery, all the while parasitically consuming its supposed carcass to sustain the anti-trafficking movement' (T. P. Woods 2013, 131). As Joseph C. Miller argues, the abolition campaigns of the late eighteenth century were highly political, and within them 'reformers had projected the social costs and amorality of growing capitalism onto slavery in the politically safely remote West Indian colonies' (Miller 2012, 7). Bringing the figure of the 'modern slave' back in as an 'unthought category' has some interesting effects. Rather than tackling the politics of retribution and fear, modern slavery discourse refuses to engage with 'the intensity of the antagonism' by considering 'black invisibility and namelessness' (Wilderson 2010, 236–7), and the possibility that we need to question the adequacy of exploitation as a category of oppression. This means that it returns us constantly to the conundrums of defining slavery and to imagining inversions of ourselves. All we can see are their surroundings, ourselves and figments of our imagination. In the new slavery social imaginary, where working in brutally exploitative conditions for subsistence wages can be working 'in freedom' and for themselves, slaves are categorised as people denied the waged status of free labour, and the categories of consent and contract are left intact.

In order to undo the exorcism of the slave from history, we need to think carefully about race and gender domination and violence and whether they are 'constitutive to liberalism to a degree that defies redemption' (Balfour 2016, 84). Bringing the slaves back into our conversations about freedom and modernity, and giving slavery a history and a politics of its own, alters our conceptual frames much more radically than the discourse of new slavery allows. Racial and gendered domination and

violence, and the production of vulnerability, are structured and constituted through the complicated pasts, presents and futures of slavery. The
freedom and status of personhood and its roots in property, possession
and exchange can only be understood through the lens of slavery and
the uneven distribution of the category of the human. In order to understand how it is that our ideas of universal human freedom can separate
'some people whose liberties matter from others not to be included in
that favoured category' (Sen 2009, 116), we need to step into the space
between personhood, subpersonhood and humanity and confront the
ways in which the zone of freedom is rooted in property rights, and in the
codification of persons as property.

REFERENCES

Aching, Gerard (2012), 'The Slave's Work: Reading Slavery Through Hegel's Master-Slave Dialectic', *PMLA*, 127, 912–17.

Adair, James (1790), *Unanswerable Arguments against the Abolition of the Slave Trade*, London: J. P. Bateman.

Alexander, Michelle (2010a), *The New Jim Crow: Mass Incarceration in the Age of Colorblindness*, New York and London: The New Press.

Alexander, Michelle (2010b), 'The War on Drugs and the New Jim Crow', *Race, Poverty and the Environment*, 17:1, 75–7.

Allais, Lucy (2016), 'Kant's Racism', *Philosophical Papers*, 45:1–2, 1–36.

Altman, M. C. (2011), *Kant and Applied Ethics: The Use and Limits of Kant's Practical Philosophy*, London: Wiley-Blackwell.

Anderson, B. (2013), *Us and Them? The Dangerous Politics of Immigration Control*, Oxford: Oxford University Press.

Anderson, Bridget and Julia O'Connell Davidson (2002), *Trafficking: A Demand Led Problem?* Stockholm: Save the Children.

Andrijasevic, Rutvica (2003), 'The Differences Borders Make: (Il)legality, Migration and Trafficking in Italy among Eastern European Women in Prostitution', in Sara Ahmed, Claudia Castada, Anne-Marie Fortier and Mimi Sheller, *Uprootings/Regroundings: Questions of Home and Migration*, London: Berg, 251–72.

Andrijasevic, Rutvica (2007), 'Beautiful Dead Bodies: Gender, Migration and Representation in Anti-Trafficking Campaigns', *Feminist Review*, 86, 24–44.

Anon (1789), *Thoughts on Civilization*, London, n.p.

Anon (1792), *Observations on Slavery, and the Consumption of the Produce of the West India Islands*, London: T. Bossey.

Anon (1820), 'Granville Sharp and the Slave Trade', *The Weekly Entertainer and West of England Miscellany*, 11 September, 206–10.

Aristide, Jean-Bertrand (2008), *Toussaint L'Ouverture: The Haitian Revolution*, ed. Nick Nesbitt, London and New York: Verso.

Aristotle (1995), *Politics*, ed. R. F. Stalley, trans. Ernest Barker, Oxford: Oxford University Press.

Armitage, David (2004), 'John Locke, Carolina, and the Two Treatises of Government', *Political Theory*, 32:5, 602–27.

Attwood, Rachael (2015), 'Lock Up Your Daughters! Male Activists, "Patriotic Domesticity" and the Fight against Sex Trafficking in England, 1880–1912', *Gender and History*, 27:3, 611–27.

Axtell, Matthew A. (2015), 'Toward a New Legal History of Capitalism and Unfree Labor: Law, Slavery and Emancipation in the American Marketplace', *Law and Social Inquiry*, 40:1, 270–300.

Bales, Kevin (1999), *Disposable People*, Berkeley, CA: University of California Press.

Bales, Kevin (2000), *Disposable People*, Berkeley and Los Angeles, CA: University of California Press.

Bales, Kevin (2012a), *Disposable People*, Berkeley and Los Angeles, CA: University of California Press.

Bales, Kevin (2012b), 'Slavery in its Contemporary Manifestations', in Jean Allain (ed.), *The Legal Understanding of Slavery: From the Historical to the Contemporary*, Oxford: Oxford University Press, 281–303.

Balfour, Lawrie (2005), 'Reparations after Identity Politics', *Political Theory*, 33:6, 786–811.

Balfour, Lawrie (2016), 'Feminist Reconstructions, Critical Race Interventions: The Presence of the Past and the Future of Political Theories of Race and Gender', *Contemporary Political Theory*, 15:1, 80–118.

Balibar, Etienne (2001), 'Outlines of a Topography of Cruelty: Citizenship and Civility in the Era of Global Violence', *Constellations*, 8:1, 15–29.

Banner, Stuart (2005), *How the Indians Lost Their Land: Law and Power on the Frontier*, Cambridge, MA: Harvard University Press.

Baptist, Edward E. (2004), '"Cuffy", "Fancy Maids" and "One-Eyed Men": Rape, Commodification and the Domestic Slave Trade in the United States', in Walter Johnson (ed.), *The Chattel Principle: Internal Slave Trades in the Americas*, New Haven, CT and London: Yale University Press, 165–202.

Barry, Kathleen (1995), *The Prostitution of Sexuality*, New York: New York University Press.

Beatson, John (1789), *Compassion the Duty and Dignity of Man; and Cruelty the Disgrace of his Nature*, Hull: n.p.

Beckles, Hilary (1996), 'The Concept of "White Slavery" in the English Caribbean during the Seventeenth Century', in John Brewer and Susan Staves (eds), *Early Modern Conceptions of Property*, London and New York: Routledge, 572–84.

Beckmann, J. (2005), 'Mobility and Safety', in Mike Featherstone, Nigel Thrift and John Urry (eds), *Automobilities*, London: Sage, 81–100.

Belsham, William (1790), *An Essay on the African Slave Trade*, Philadelphia, PA: David Humphreys.

Bernasconi, Robert (2002), 'Kant as an Unlikely Source of Racism', in Julie K. Ward and Tommy L. Lott (eds), *Philosophers on Race: Critical Essays*, Oxford: Blackwell.

Bernstein, Elizabeth (2010), 'Militarized Humanism Meets Carceral Feminism: The Politics of Sex, Rights and Freedom in Contemporary Antitrafficking Campaigns', *Signs*, 36:1, 45–71.

Bernstein, Elizabeth (2012), 'Carceral Politics as Gender Justice? The "Traffic in Women" and Neoliberal Circuits of Crime, Sex, and Rights', *Theory and Society* 41:3, 233–59.

Binder, Guyora (1995), 'The Slavery of Emancipation', *Cardoza Law Review* 17, 2063–102.

Bird-Pollan, Stefan (2012), 'Hegel's Grounding of Intersubjectivity in the Master-Slave Dialectic', *Philosophy and Social Criticism*, 38:3, 237–56.

Blackburn, Robin (1988), 'Defining Slavery – its Special Features and Social Role', in Leonie Archer (ed.), *Slavery and Other Forms of Unfree Labour*, London: Routledge, 262–80.

Blackburn, Robin (2013), *The American Crucible: Slavery, Emancipation and Human Rights*, London and New York: Verso.

Bolland, O. Nigel (1995), 'Proto-Proletarians? Slave Wages in the Americas: Between Slave Labour and Free Labour', in Mary Turner (ed.), *From Chattel Slaves to Wage Slaves*, Bloomington and Indianapolis, IN: Indiana University Press, 123–47.

Booth, Abraham (1792), *Commerce in the Human Species, and the Enslaving of Innocent Persons*, London, n.p.

Botting, Eileen and Sean Kronewitter (2012), 'Westernization and Women's Rights: NonWestern European Responses to Mill's Subjection of Women, 1869–1908', *Political Theory*, 40:4, 466–96.

Brace, Laura (2004), *The Politics of Property*, Edinburgh: Edinburgh University Press.

Brace, Laura (2013a), 'Borders of Emptiness: Gender, Migration and Belonging', *Citizenship Studies*, 17:6, 873–85.

Brace, Laura (2013b), 'Inhuman Commerce: Antislavery and the Ownership of Freedom', *European Journal of Political Theory*, 12:4, 466–82.

Brace, Laura (2014), 'Bodies in Abolition: Broken Hearts and Open Wounds', *Citizenship Studies*, 18:5, 485–98.

Bradley, Keith (1992), '"The Regular Daily Traffic in Slaves": Roman History and Contemporary History', *The Classical Journal*, 87:2, 125–38.

Brougham, Henry (1804), *A Concise Statement of the Question Regarding the Abolition of the Slave Trade*, London, n.p.

Brown, Christopher Leslie (2006), *Moral Capital: Foundations of British Abolitionism*, Chapel Hill, NC: University of North Carolina Press.

Brown, Vincent (2009), 'Social Death and Political Life in the Study of Slavery', *The American Historical Review*, 114:5, 1231–49.

Buck-Morss, Susan (2009), *Hegel, Haiti and Universal History*, Pittsburgh, PA: University of Pittsburgh Press.

Buck-Morss, Susan (2010), 'The Gift of the Past', *Small Axe*, 14:3, 173–85.

Bull, Malcolm (1998), *Slavery and the Multiple Self*, September-October, available at http://newleftreview.org.ezproxy3lib.le.ac.uk/l/231malcom-bull-slavery-and-the-multiple-self (accessed 4 February 2015).

Burnard, Trevor (2004), 'Passengers Only: The Extent and Significance of Absenteeism in Eighteenth-Century Jamaica', *Atlantic Studies*, 1:2, 178–95.

Burnard, Trevor (2011), 'Powerless Masters: The Curious Decline of Jamaican Sugar Planters in the Foundational Period of British Abolitionism', *Slavery and Abolition*, 32:2, 185–98.

Burns, Tony (2006), 'Hegel, Identity Politics and the Problem of Slavery', *Theory and Critique*, 47:1, 87–104.

Carey, Brycchan (2005), *British Abolitionism and the Rhetoric of Sensibility: Writing, Sentiment and Slavery, 1760–1807*, London: Palgrave Macmillan.

Carey, Daniel (2006), *Locke, Shaftesbury and Hutcheson: The Defence of English Colonialism*, Cambridge: Cambridge University Press.

Cartledge, Paul (1993), '"Like a Worm i' the Bud?" A Heterology of Classical Greek Slavery', *Greece and Rome*, 40:2, 163–80.

Cassuto, Leonard (1996), 'Frederick Douglass and the Work of Freedom: Hegel's Master-Slave Dialectic in the Fugitive Slave Narrative', *Prospects*, 21, 229–59.

Childs, Dennis (2015), *Slaves of the State: Black Incarceration from the Chain Gang to the Penitentiary*, Minneapolis, MN: University of Minnesota Press.

Chouliaraki, Lila (2010), 'Post-Humanitarianism: Humanitarian Communication Beyond a Politics of Pity', *International Journal of Cultural Studies*, 13, 107–26.

Christopher, Emma (2006), *Slave Ship Sailors and Their Captive Cargoes*, Cambridge: Cambridge University Press.

Clarkson, Thomas (1786), *An Essay on the Slavery and Commerce of the Human Species*. London: J. Phillips.

Coffee, Alan (2013), 'Mary Wollstonecraft, Freedom and the Enduring Power of Social Domination', *European Journal of Political Theory*, 12:2, 116–35.

Coleman, Deirdre (1994), 'Conspicuous Consumption: White Abolitionism and English Women's Protest Writing in the 1790s', *ELH*, 61:2, 341–63.

Collins, John (1792), *The Case of the Sugar-Colonies*, London: J. Johnson.

Collins, Susan D. (2006), *Aristotle and the Rediscovery of Citizenship*, Cambridge: Cambridge University Press.

Coltman, Elizabeth (1824), *Immediate Not Gradual Abolition: or, and Inquiry into the shortest, safest and most effectual means of getting rid of West-Indian slavery*, London, n.p.

Colwill, Elizabeth (2009), 'Gendering the June Days: Race, Masculinity, and Slave Emancipation in Saint Domingue', *Journal of Haitian Studies*, 15:1–2, 103–24.

Cope, Virginia (2004), '"I Verily Believed Myself to Be a Free Woman": Harriet Jacobs's Journey into Capitalism', *African American Review*, 38:1, 5–20.

Cuguano, Ottobah (1787), *Thoughts and Sentiments on the Evil and Wicked Traffic of the Slavery and Commerce of the Human Species*, London, n.p.

Da Costa, Emilia (1994), *Crowns of Glory, Tears of Blood*, Oxford: Oxford University Press.

Davis, Angela Y. (2003), *Are Prisons Obsolete?*, New York: Seven Stories Press.

Davis, David Brion (1986), *Slavery and Human Progress*, Oxford: Oxford University Press.

Davis, David Brion (2006), *Inhuman Bondage*, Oxford: Oxford University Press.

Dawson, Kevin (2006), 'Enslaved Swimmers and Divers in the Atlantic World', *Journal of American History*, 92:4, 1327–55.

Dayan, Colin (2008), 'Due Process and Lethal Confinement', *South Atlantic Quarterly*, 17:3, 485–507.

Dayan, Joan (2001), 'Legal Slaves and Civil Bodies', *Nepantla: Views from the South*, 2:1, 3–39.

De Genova, Nicholas (2010a), 'The Deportation Regime: Sovereignty, Space, and the Freedom of Movement', in Nicholas De Genova and Nathalie Peutz (eds), *The Deportation Regime: Sovereignty, Space, and the Freedom of Movement*, Durham, NC: Duke University Press, 33–69.

De Groot, Joanna (2006), 'Metropolitan Desires and Colonial Connections', in Catherine Hall and Sonya O. Rose (eds), *At Home with the Empire: Metropolitan Culture and the Imperial World*, Cambridge: Cambridge University Press, 166–90.

Deslauriers, Marguerite (2006), 'The Argument of Aristotle's Politics I', *Phoenix*, 60:1–2, 48–69.

Dickson, William (1789), *Letters on Slavery*, London: J. Phillips.

Dobbs, Darrell (1994), 'Natural Right and the Problem of Aristotle's Defence of Slavery', *The Journal of Politics*, 56:1, 69–94.

Douglass, Frederick [1845] (2015), *Narrative of the Life of Frederick Douglass*, Irvine, CA: Xist Classics.

Douglass, Frederick (1883), 'Address by the Hon Frederick Douglass on the Twenty-First Anniversary of Emancipation', 16 April 1883, available at http://antislavery.eserver.org/legacies/the-lessons-of-the-hour/the-lessons-of-the-hour.pdf (accessed 8 June 2017).

Drake, Kimberly (1997), 'Rewriting the American Self: Race, Gender, and Identity in the Autobiographies of Frederick Douglass and Harriet Jacobs', *MELUS*, 22:4, 91–108.

Draper, Nicholas (2010), *The Price of Emancipation: Slave-Ownership, Compensation and British Society at the End of Slavery*, Cambridge: Cambridge University Press.

Drescher, Seymour (2002), *The Mighty Experiment: Free Labor versus Slavery in British Emancipation*, Oxford: Oxford Univesity Press.

Dubois, Laurent (2006), 'An Enslaved Enlightenment: Rethinking the Intellectual History of the French Atlantic', *Social History*, 31:1, 1–14.

DuBois, Page (2008), *Slaves and Other Objects*, Chicago, IL and London: University of Chicago Press.

Ellison, Julie (1996), 'A Short History of Liberal Guilt', *Critical Inquiry*, 22:2, 344–71.

Engels, Friedrich (1892), *The Condiiton of the Working Class in England*, available at www.marxists.org/archive/marx/works/ download/pdf/condition-working-class-england.pdf (accessed 4 June 2017).

Epstein, James (2006), 'Taking Class Notes on Empire', in Catherine Hall and Sonya O. Rose (eds), *At Home with the Empire: Metropolitan Culture and the Imperial World*, Cambridge: Cambridge University Press, 251–74.

Fabre, Cecile (2006), *Whose Body is it Anyway?*, Oxford: Oxford University Press.

Farley, Anthony Paul (2004), 'Perfecting Slavery', *Loyola University Chicago Law Journal*, 36, 225–55.

Farr, James (1986), '"So Vile and Miserable an Estate": The Problem of Slavery in Locke's Political Thought', *Political Theory*, 14:2, 263–89.

Farr, James (2008), 'Locke, Natural Law and New World Slavery', *Political Theory*, 36:4, 495–522.

Featherstone, David and Paul Griffin (2016), 'Spatial Relations, Histories from Below and the Makings of Agency: Reflections on the Making of the English Working Class at 50', *Progress in Human Geography*, 40:3, 375–93.

Femenias, Maria Luisa (1994), 'Women and Natual Hierarchy in Aristotle', *Hypatia*, 9:1, 164–73.

Festa, Lynn (2010), 'Humanity without Feathers', *Humanity*, 1:1, 3–27.

Fick, Carolyn E. (1998), 'Dilemmas of Emancipation: from the Saint Domingue Insurrections of 1791 to the Emerging Haitian State', *History Workshop Journal*, 46, 1–16.

Fischer, Sibylle (2010), 'History and Catastrophe', *Small Axe*, 14:3, 163–72.

Fischer, Sibylle (2004), *Modernity Disavowed: Haiti and the Cultures of Slavery in the Age of Revolution*, Durham, NC and London: Duke University Press.

Fisher, N. R. E. (1993), *Slavery in Classical Greece*, London: Bristol Classical Press.

Fogg-Davis, Heath (2016), 'An Argument for Reviving the Pragmatism of Early Critical Race Feminist Theory', *Contemporary Political Theory*, 15:1, 80–118.

Foster, W. H. (2007), 'Women Slave Owners Face Their Historians: Versions of Maternalism in Atlantic World Slavery', *Patterns of Prejudice*, 41:3–4, 303–20.

Fox, William (1791), *An Address to the People of Great Britain, on the Propriety of Abstaining from West India Sugar and Rum* (6th edn), London: James Phillips. ·

Francklyn, Gilbert (1789), *An Answer to the Rev Mr Clarkson's Essay on Slavery and Commerce of the Human Species*, London: Logographic Press.

Frank, Jill (2004), 'Citizens, Slaves and Foreigners: Aristotle on Human Nature', *The American Political Science Review*, 98:1, 91–104.

Fuller, Dan (2014), 'Ownership as Authority', *The King's Student Law Review*, 5:1, 16–29.

Garner, Steve (2007a), 'Atlantic Crossing', *Atlantic Studies: Global Currents*, 4:1, 117–32.

Garner, Steve (2007b), *Whiteness: An Introduction*, London: Routledge.

Garrigus, John D. (2007), '"To establish a community of property": Marriage and race before and during the Haitian Revolution', *The History of the Family*, 12:2, 142–52.

Geggus, David Patrick (2002), *Haitian Revolutionary Studies*, Bloomington, IN: Indiana University Press.

Gill, Nick, Deirdre Conlan, Dominique Moran and Andrew Burridge (2016), 'Carceral Circuitry: New Directions in Carceral Geography', *Progress in Human Geography*, 1–22, https://doi-org.ezproxy3.lib.le.ac.uk/10.1177/0309132516671823

Gilmore, Kim (2000), 'Slavery and Prison – Understanding the Connections', *Social Justice*, 27:3, 195–205.

Gilmore, Ruth (2007), *Golden Gulag: Prisons, Surplus, Crisis, and Opposition in Globalizing California*, Berkeley, CA: University of California Press.

Gilroy, Paul (1993), *The Black Atlantic: Modernity and Double Consciousness*, London and New York: Verso.

Gisborne, Thomas (1792), *On Slavery and the Slave Trade*, London: sold by J. Stockdale, J. Debrett and J. Phillips.

Gladstone, John and James Cropper (1824), *The Correspondence between John Gladstone Esq, M.P., and James Cropper, Esq., on the Present State of Slavery in the British West Indies and in the United States of America*, Liverpool: Thomas Kaye.

Glymph, Thavolia (2008), *Out of the House of Bondage: The Transformation of the Plantation Household*, Cambridge: Cambridge University Press.

Goldberg, David Theo (2002), *The Racial State*, Oxford: Blackwell.

Gordon, Avery (2008), *Ghostly Matters: Haunting and the Sociological Imagination*, Minneapolis, MN: University of Minnesota Press.

Govindan, Padma (2013), 'Rethinking Emancipation: The Rhetorics of Slavery and the Politics of Freedom in Anti-Trafficking Work in India', *Interventions*, 15:4, 511–29.

Green, Cecilia A. (2006), 'Hierarchies of Whiteness in the Geographies of Empire: Thomas Thistlewood and the Barretts of Jamaica', *New West Indian Guide*, 80:1–2, 5–43.

Grotius, Hugo (2005), *The Right of War and Peace*, ed. Richard Tuck, vol. 1, Indianapolis, IN: Liberty Fund.

Guasco, Michael (2007), 'To "Doe Some Good Upon Their Countrymen": The Paradox of Indian Slavery in Early Anglo-America', *Journal of Social History*, 41:2, 389–411.

Hall, Catherine (2014), 'Gendering Property, Racing Capital', *History Workshop Journal*, 87, 22–38.

Hall, Edith (1989), *Inventing the Barbarians: Greek Self-Definition through Tragedy*, Oxford: Clarendon Press.

Hall, Stuart (1998), 'Breaking bread with History: CLR James and the Black Jacobins', *History Workshop Journal*, 46, 17–32.

Harper, William (1838), *Memoir on Slavery, Read Before the Society for the Advancement of Learning of South Carolina*, Charleston, SC: James S. Burges.

Harris, Cheryl I. (2007), '"Too Pure an Air": Somerset's Legacy from Antislavery to Colorblindness', *Texas Wesleyan Law Review*, 13, 439–58.

Hartman, Saidiya (1997), *Scenes of Subjection*, Oxford: Oxford University Press.

Heath, Malcolm (2008), 'Aristotle on Natural Slavery', *Phronesis*, 53:3, 243–70.

Hegel, G. W. F. [1807] (1976), *Phenomenology of Spirit*, trans. A. V. Miller, Oxford: Oxford University Press.

Hillier, Richard (1791), *A Vindication of the Address to the People of Great Britain, on the Use of West India Produce*, London.

Hinshelwood, Brad (2013), 'The Carolinian Context of John Locke's Theory of Slavery', *Political Theory*, 41:4, 562–90.

Hirschmann, Nancy (2002), 'Liberal Conservatism, Once and Again: Locke's "Essay on the Poor Law" and Contemporary US Welfare Reform', *Constellations*, 9:3, 335–55.

Hirschmann, Nancy (2008), *Gender, Class and Freedom in Modern Political Theory*, Princeton, NJ and Oxford: Princeton University Press.

Honneth, Axel (1995), *The Struggle for Recognition*, Cambridge, MA: MIT Press.

Hoogeveen, Dawn (2015), 'Sub-Surface Property, Free-entry Mineral Staking and Settler Colonialism in Canada', *Antipode*, 47:1, 121–38.

Hopgood, Stephen (1999), 'New Economy, New Slavery', *Times Higher Education*, 12 November.

Howard, Carole (2004), 'Wollstonecraft's Thoughts on Slavery and Corruption', *The Eighteenth Century*, 45:1, 61–96.

Hundert, Edward (1972), 'The Making of Homo Faber: John Locke Between Ideology and History', *Journal of the History of Ideas*, 33:1, 3–22.

Hunter, Tera W. (2016), 'Writing of Labor and Love: Gender and African American History's Challenge to Present Day Assumptions and Misinterpretations', *Souls: A Critical Journal of Black Politics, Culture, and Society*, 18:1, 150–4.

Hutcheson, Francis (1755), *A System of Moral Philosophy*, London: A. Millar.

Hutchings, Kimberly (2003), *Hegel and Feminist Philosophy*, Cambridge: Polity.

Iacono, Eva Lo (2014), 'Victims, Sex Workers and Perpetrators: Gray Areas in the Trafficking of Nigerian Women', *Trends in Organized Crime*, 17, 110–28.

Innes, William (1792), *A Letter to the Members of Parliament Who Have Presented Petitions to the Honourable House of Commons for the Abolition of the Slave Trade*, London: J. Sewell, J. Murray and J. Debrett.

Jaggar, Alison (2005), '"Saving Amina": Global Justice for Women and Intercultural Dialogue', *Ethics and International Affairs*, 19:3, 55–75.

James, C. L. R. (1980), *The Black Jacobins*, London: Penguin.

Jean-Marie, Vivaldi (2013), 'Kant and Trouillot on the Unthinkability of the Haitian Revolution', *Souls*, 15:3, 241–57.

Jensen, Derrick (2001), *The New Slavery: an Interview with Kevin Bales*, 1 October, available at www.derrickjensen.org/2001/10/new-slavery-interview-kevin-bales (accessed 19 April 2017).

Johnson, Walter (2016), 'To Remake the World: Slavery, Racial Capitalism and Justice', available at http://bostonreview.net/race/walter-johnson-slavery-human-rights-racial-capitalism (accessed 21 April 2017).

Kant, Immanuel [1920] (1997), *Lectures on Ethics*, Cambridge: Cambridge University Press.

Kaplan, Cora (1998), 'Black Heroes/White Writers: Toussaint L'Ouverture and the Literary Imagination', *History Workshop Journal*, 46, 32–62.

Kaplan, Cora (2006), 'Imagining Empire: History, Fantasy and Literature', in Catherine Hall and Sonya O. Rose (eds), *At Home with the Empire: Metropolitan Culture and the Imperial World*, Cambridge: Cambridge University Press, 191–211.

Karlin, Mark (2016), *The Inseparability of Capitalism, Racism, and Imprisonment: An Interview with Dennis Childs*. 17 March, available at www.opendemocracy.net/beyondslavery/mark-karlin/inseparability-of-capitalism-racism-and-imprisonment-interview-with-dennis (accessed 11 May 2017).

Kautzer, Chad and Eduardo Mendieta (2004), 'Law and Resistance in the Prisons of Empire: An Interview with Angela Y. Davis', *Peace Review*, 16:3, 339–47.

King, Ryan (2006), 'Jim Crow is Alive and Well in the 21st Century: Felon Disenfranchisement and the Continuing Struggle to Silence the African-American Voice', *Souls*, 8:2, 7–21.

Klein, Lawrence (1994), *Shaftesbury and the Culture of Politeness: Moral Discourse and Cultural Politics in Early Eighteenth-Century England*, Cambridge: Cambridge University Press.

Kleingeld, Pauline (2007), 'Kant's Second Thoughts on Race', *The Philosophical Quarterly*, 57:229, 573–92.

Knight, Frank C. (2010), *Working the Diaspora: The Impact of African Labor on the Anglo-American World, 1650–1850*, New York and London: New York University Press.

Kohn, Margaret (2005), 'Frederick Douglass's Master-Slave Dialectic', *The Journal of Politics*, 67:2, 497–514.

Konrad, Victor (2015), 'Toward a Theory of Borders in Motion', *Journal of Borderlands Studies*, 30:1, 1–17.

Kristine, Lisa (2012), *Photos that Bear Witness to Modern Slavery*, January, available at www.ted.com/talks/lisa_kristine_glimpses_of_modern_day_slavery (accessed 27 March 2014).

Larson, Jennifer (2006), 'Converting Passive Womanhood to Active Sisterhood: Agency, Power, and Subversion in Harriet Jacobs's Incidents in the Life of a Slave Girl', *Women's Studies*, 35:8, 739–56.

Lindenbaum, Shirley (2004), 'Thinking about Cannibalism', *Annual Review of Anthropology*, 33, 475–98.

Little, Allan (2004), 'Nigeria's "Respectable" Slave Trade', 17 April, available at http://news.bbc.co.uk/1/hi/programmes/from_our_own_correspondent/3632203.stm (accessed 16 March 2014).

Lloyd, Genevieve (1984), *The Man of Reason*, London: Routledge.

Lloyd, Moya (2005), *Beyond Identity Politics*, London: Sage.

Lobasz, Jennifer K. (2009), 'Beyond Border Security: Feminist Approaches to Human Trafficking', *Security Studies*, 18:2, 319–44.

Locke, John [1689] (1991), *Two Treatises of Government*, ed. Peter Laslett, Cambridge: Cambridge University Press.

Locke, John [1697] (1997), *An Essay on the Poor Law*, ed. Mark Goldie, New York and Cambridge: Cambridge University Press.

Lott, Tommy L. (2014), 'Contextualizing Slavery's Wrongness', *Slaveries Old and New: British Academy*, London, 30–31 March.

Lovell, Thomas B. (1996), 'By Dint of Labor and Economy: Harriet Jacobs, Harriet Wilson, and the Salutary View of Wage Labor', *Arizona Quarterly: A Journal of American Literature, Culture, and Theory*, 52:3, 1–32.

Loyd, Jenna (2012), 'Race, Capitalist Crisis, and Abolitionist Organizing: An Interview with Ruth Wilson Gilmore', in Jenna Loyd, Matt Mitchelson and Andrew Burridge (eds), *Beyond Walls and Cages: Prisons, Borders, and Global Crisis*, Athens, GA and London: University of Georgia Press, 42–54.

Loyd, Jenna, Matt Mitchelson and Andrew Burridge (2012), 'Introduction: Borders, Prisons, and Abolitionist Visions', in Jenna Loyd, Matt Mitchelson and Andrew Burridge (eds), *Beyond Walls and Cages: Prisons, Borders, and Global Crisis*, Athens, GA and London: University of Georgia Press, 1–15.

MacKinnon, Catharine (1993), 'Prostitution and Civil Rights', *Michigan Journal of Gender and Law*, 1:1, 13–31.

Malkki, Lisa H. (1996), 'Speechless Emissaries: Refugees, Humanitarianism, and Dehistoricization', *Cultural Anthropology*, 11:3, 377–404.

Marden, Ronald (2006), '"That all men are created equal": Rights Talk and Exclusion in North America', in Gurminder K. Bhambra and Robbie Shilliam (eds),

Silencing Human Rights: Critical Engagements with a Contested Project, Basing-stoke and New York: Palgrave Macmillan, 85–102.

Martin, Jonathan D. (2004), *Divided Mastery: Slave Hiring in the American South*, London: Harvard University Press.

May, Theresa (2013), 'Slaves May Work in Your Nail Bar Too', *The Telegraph*, 24 November, available at www.telegraph.co.uk/comment/10470717/Theresa-May-Slaves-may-work-in-your-nail-bar-too.html (accessed 16 March 2014).

McCarthy, Thomas (2002), 'Vergangenheitsbewaltigung in the USA: On the Politics of the Memory of Slavery', *Political Theory*, 30:5, 623–48.

McCarthy, Thomas (2004), 'Coming to Terms with Our Past, Part II: On the Morality and Politics of Reparations for Slavery', *Political Theory*, 32:6, 750–72.

McClintock, Anne (2009), 'Paranoid Empire: Specters from Guantanamo and Abu Ghraib', *Small Axe*, 13:1, 50–74.

McKeon, Michael (2005), *The Secret History of Domesticity*, Baltimore, MD: Johns Hopkins University Press.

Midgley, Clare (2000), *Women Against Slavery: The British Campaigns, 1780–1870*, London: Routledge.

Miles, Robert (1987), *Capitalism and Unfree Labour*, London: Tavistock.

Mill, J. S. [1859] (1997), *On Liberty and Other Writings*, ed. Stefan Collini, Cambridge: Cambridge University Press.

Miller, Joseph C. (2012), *The Problem of Slavery as History: A Global Approach*, New Haven, CT and London: Yale University Press.

Millett, Paul (2007), 'Aristotle and Slavery in Athens', *Greece and Rome*, 54:2, 178–209.

Mills, Charles (1997), *The Racial Contract*, Ithaca, NY: Cornell University Press.

Mills, Charles (2002), 'Kant's Untermenschen', in Andrew Valls (ed.), *Race and Racism in Modern Philosophy*, Ithaca, NY: Cornell University Press, 169–93. UNC Colloquium 2002, available at *www.decolonialitylondon.org/wp-content/uploads/2015/08/Kants-Untermenschen.pdf* (accessed 20 February 2017).

Mills, Charles (2007), 'White Ignorance', in Shannon Sullivans and Nancy Tuana (eds), *Race and Epistemologies of Ignorance*, Albany, NY: State University of New York Press, 13–38.

Mills, Charles (2014), 'Kant and Race, Redux', *Graduate Faculty Philosophy Journal*, 35:1–2, 125–57.

Mills, Charles (2015), 'The Political Economy of Personhood', 16 June 2015, available at www.opendemocracy.net/beyondslavery/charles-w-mills/political-economy-of-personhood (accessed 23 January 2017).

Muhammad, Khalil Gibran (2011), 'Where did all the White Criminals Go?: Reconfiguring Race and Crime on the Road to Mass Incarceration', *Souls*, 13:1, 72–90.

Mullin, Michael (1995), 'Slave Economic Strategies: Food, Markets and Property', in Mary Turner (ed.), *From Chattel Slaves to Wage Slaves*, Bloomington and Indianapolis, IN: Indiana University Press, 68–78.

Muthu, Sankar (2003), *Enlightenment Against Empire*, Princeton, NJ and Oxford: Princeton University Press.

Nisbet, Richard (1773), *Slavery Not Forbidden by Scripture: A Defence of the West-India Planters*. Philadelphia, PA, n.p.

Nudelman, Franny (1992), 'Harriet Jacobs and the Sentimental Politics of Female Suffering', *English Literary History*, 59:4, 939–64.

Nyquist, Mary (2013), *Arbitrary Rule: Slavery, Tyranny and the Power of Life and Death*, Chicago, IL: University of Chicago Press.

Ober, Josiah (2012), 'Democracy's Dignity', *American Political Science Review*, 106:4, 827–46.

O'Brien, J. (1833), 'Negro Emancipation', *Poor Man's Guardian*, 15 June, 189–90.

O'Connell Davidson, Julia (2005), *Children in the Global Sex Trade*, Cambridge: Polity.

O'Connell Davidson, Julia (2015), *Modern Slavery: The Margins of Freedom*, London: Palgrave Macmillan.

O'Connell Davidson, Julia (2016), '"Things" Are Not What They Seem: On Persons, Things, Slaves, and the New Abolitionist Movement', *Current Legal Problems*, 69:1, 227–57.

Othello (1790), *Strictures on the Slave Trade, and Their Manner of Treatment in the West-India Islands in a Letter to the Right Hon. William Pitt*, London: W. Richardson.

Page, Anthony (2011), 'Rational Dissent, Enlightenment and Abolition of the British Slave Trade', *The Historical Journal*, 54:3, 741–72.

Pateman, Carole (1988), *The Sexual Contract*, Cambridge: Polity.

Paton, Diana (2001), 'Punishment, Crime, and the Bodies of Slaves in Eighteenth-Century Jamaica', *Journal of Social History* 34:4, 923–54.

Patterson, Orlando (1982), *Slavery and Social Death*, Cambridge, MA and London: Harvard University Press.

Patterson, Orlando (1991a), 'Slavery, Alienation, and the Female Discovery of Personal Freedom', *Social Research*, 58:1, 159–87.

Patterson, Orlando (1991b), *Freedom: Volume 1*, New York: Basic Books.

Patterson, Orlando (2012). 'Trafficking, Gender and Slavery: Past and Present', in Jean Allain (ed.), *The Legal Understanding of Slavery: From the Historical to the Contemporary*, Oxford: Oxford University Press, 322–59.

Paugh, Katherine (2014), 'The Curious Case of Mary Hylas: Wives, Slaves and the Limits of British Abolitionism', *Slavery and Abolition*, 35:4, 629–51.

Peckard, Peter (1788), *Am I Not a Man and a Brother? With all Humility Addressed to the British Legislatur*, Oxford: T. Payne and Son.

Pettman, Jan Jindy (1998), 'Women on the Move: Globalisation and Labour Migration from South and Southeast Asian States', *Global Society*, 12:3, 389–403.

Phillips, Anne (2013), *Our Bodies, Whose Property?* Princeton, NJ and Oxford: Princeton University Press.

Pleasants, Nigel (2008), 'Structure and Agency in the Antislavery and Animal Liberation Movments', in David Grumett and Rachel Muers (eds), *Eating is Believing: Interdisciplinary Perspectives on Vegetarianism and Theology*, London: T and T Clark, 198–216.

Plumer, Thomas (Sir) (1807), *The Speech of Mr. Plumer, at the Bar of the House of Lords, on the Second Reading of the Bill for the Abolition of the Slave-Trade*, London, n.p.

Pocock, J. G. A. (1975), *The Machiavellian Moment*, Princeton, NJ: Princeton University Press.

Prince, Mary (1831), *The History of Mary Prince, a West Indian Slave*, Kindle edition.

Purtschert, Patricia (2010), 'On the Limit of Spirit: Hegel's Racism Revisited', *Philosophy and Social Criticism*, 36:9, 1039–51.

Quirk, Joel (2006), 'The Anti-Slavery Project: Linking the Historical and the Contemporary', *Human Rights Quarterly*, 28:3, 565–98.

Ramsay, James (1787), *A Letter to James Tobin, Esq. Late Member of His Majesty's Council in the Island of Nevis*, London: J. Phillips.

Rauwerda, A. M. (2001), 'Naming, Agency, and "A Tissue of Falsehoods" in The History of Mary Prince', *Victorian Literature and Culture*, 29:2, 397–411.

Rediker, Marcus and Peter Linebaugh (2002), *The Many-Headed Hydra: The Hidden History of the Revolutionary Atlantic*, London: Verso.

Rios, Victor M. (2006), 'The Hyper-Criminalization of Black and Latino Male Youth in the Era of Mass Incarceration', *Souls*, 8:2, 40–54.

Ripstein, Arthur (2009), *Force and Freedom: Kant's Legal and Political Philosophy*, Cambridge, MA and London: Harvard University Press.

RMF (2012), available at https://people4children.wordpress.com/2012/11/29/light-warriors-a-rmf-membership-program-to-end-human-trafficking (accessed 20 January 2017).

Roberts, Neil (2015), 'Rousseau, Flight and the Fall into Slavery', in Jane Anna Gordon and Neil Roberts (eds), *Creolizing Rousseau*, London and New York: Rowman and Littlefield, 193–224.

Rodriguez, Dylan (2008), '"I Would Wish Death on You . . ." Race, Gender, and Immigration in the Globality of the U.S. Prison Regime', *The Scholar and Feminist Online*, 6:3, 1–9.

Rosivach, Vincent J. (1999), 'Enslaving "Barboroi" and the Athenian Ideology of Slavery', *Historia: Zeitschrift für Alte Geschichte*, 48:2, 129–57.

Rozbicki, Michael (2001), 'To Save Them from Themselves: Proposals to Enslave the British Poor, 1698–1755', *Slavery and Abolition*, 22:2, 29–50.

Rugemer, Eric (2004), 'The Southern Response to British Abolitionism: The Maturation of Proslavery Apologetics', *The Journal of Southern History*, 70:2, 221–48.

Rupprecht, Anita (2008), '"A Limited Sort of Property": History, Memory and the Slave Ship Zong', *Slavery and Abolition*, 29:2, 265–77.

Sack, James A. (1993), *From Jacobite to Conservative*, Cambridge: Cambridge University Press.

Sassen, Saskia (2016), 'At the Systemic Edge: Expulsions', *European Review*, 24:1, 89–104.

Schofield, Malcolm (1999), *Saving the City: Philosopher Kings and Other Classical Paradigms*, London: Routledge.

Science Snacks (2017), *Colored Shadows: Not All Shadows are Black*, available at www.exploratorium.edu/snacks/colored-shadows (accessed 29 May 2017).

Scott, David (2004), *Conscripts of Modernity*, Durham, NC and London: Duke University Press.

Seliger, Martin (1968), *The Liberal Politics of John Locke*, Melbourne: Allen & Unwin.

Sen, Amartya (2009), *The Idea of Justice*, London: Penguin Books.

Sexton, Jared (2014), 'The Vel of Slavery: Tracking the Figure of the Unsovereign', *Critical Sociology*, 1–15.

Shah, Svati P. (2004), 'Prostitution, Sex Work and Violence: Discursive and Political Contexts for Five Texts on paid Sex, 1987–2001', *Gender and History*, 16:3, 794–812.

Shared Hope International (2017), available at http://sharedhope.org/the-problem/trafficking-terms/ (accessed 12 January 2017).

Sharma, Nandita (2005), 'Anti-Trafficking Rhetoric and the Making of Global Apartheid', *NWSA Journal*, 17:3, 88–111.

Sharp, Granville (1769), *A Representation of the Injustice and Dangerous Tendency of Tolerating Slavery*, London: Benjamin White.

Sharp, Granville (1776), *The Just Limitation of Slavery in the Laws of God*. London: Benjamin White.

Sharpe, Jenny (1996), '"Something Akin to Freedom": The Case of Mary Prince', *differences: A Journal of Feminist Cultural Studies*, 8:1, 31–57.

Sheridan, R. B. (1995), 'Strategies of Slave Subsistence: The Jamaican Case Reconsidered', in Mary Turner (ed.), *From Chattel Slaves to Wage Slaves*, Indianapolis and Bloomington, IN: Indiana University Press, 48–67.

Sheth, Falguni A. (2016), 'If the Present Looks Like the Past, What Does the Future Look Like? Feminist and Critical Race Scholarship in Political Theory', *Contemporary Political Theory*, 15:1, 80–118.

Shih, Elena (2016), 'Not in My "Backyard Abolitionism": Vigilante Rescue against American Sex Trafficking', *Sociological Perspectives*, 59:1, 66–90.

Shilliam, Robbie (2012), 'Forget English Freedom, Remember Atlantic Slavery: Common Law, Commercial Law and the Significance of Slavery for Classical Political Economy', *New Political Economy*, 17:5, 591–609.

Smallwood, Stephanie (2004), 'Commodified Freedom: Interrogating the Limits of Anti-Slavery Ideology in the Early Republic', *Journal of the Early Republic*, 24:2, 289–98.

Spencer, Vicki A. (2015), 'Kant and Herder on Colonialism, Indigenous Peoples, and Minority Nations', *International Theory*, 7:2, 360–92.

Srikantiah, Jayashri (2007), 'Perfect Victims and Real Survivors: The Iconic Victim in Domestic Human Trafficking Law', *Boston University Law Review*, 87, 157–211.

Stanley, Amy Dru (1998), *From Bondage to Contract*, Cambridge: Cambridge University Press.

Ste Croix, G. E. M. (1988), 'Slavery and Other Forms of Unfree Labour', in Leonie Archer (ed.), *Slavery and Other Forms of Unfree Labour*, London: Routledge, 19–32.

Steinfeld, Robert J. (1991), *The Invention of Free Labor*, Chapel Hill, NC and London: University of North Carolina Press.

Sussman, Charlotte (2000), *Consuming Anxieties: Consumer Protest, Gender and British Slavery, 1713–1833*, New York: Stanford University Press.

Swaminathan, Srividhya (2009), *Debating the Slave Trade: Rhetoric of British National Identity, 1759–1815*, Farnham and Burlington, VT: Ashgate.

Sweeney, Carole (2007), 'The Unmaking of the World', *Atlantic Studies*, 4:1, 51–66.

Sweet, James H. (2013), 'Defying Social Death: The Multiple Configurations of African Slave Family in the Atlantic World', *William and Mary Quarterly*, 70:2, 251–72.

Talisse, Robert B. (2016), *Engaging Political Philosophy: An Introduction*, New York and London: Routledge.

Testai, Patrizia (2006), 'Trafficking and Modern Slavery', *The Market and its Discontents*, University of Nottingham: ESRC Seminar Series.

'The Debate on a Motion for the Abolition of the Slave Trade in the House of Commons' (1792), London, Monday 2 April.

Thomas, Lynn M. (2016), 'Historicising Agency', *Gender and History*, 28:2, 324–39.

Thompson, William (1825), *Appeal of one Half of the Human Race, Women, Against the Prestensions of the Other Half, Men*, London: Longman, Hurst, Rees.

Ticktin, Miriam (2011), 'The Gendered Human of Humanitarianism: Medicalising and Politicising Sexual Violence', *Gender and History*, 23:2, 250–65.

Turley, David (2000), *Slavery*, Oxford: Blackwell.

Turner, Mary (1995), *From Chattel Slaves to Wage Slaves*, Bloomington and Indianapolis, IN: Indiana University Press.

UCL (2017a), *John Newton: Profile and Legacies Summary*, available at www.ucl.ac.uk/lbs/person/view/2146643091 (accessed 27 May 2017).

UCL (2017b), *William Innes*, available at www.ucl.ac.uk/lbs/person/view/8223 (accessed 10 May 2017).

Uzgalis, William (2002), 'An Inconsistency Not to be Excused: On Locke and Racism', in Tommy L. Lott and Julie Ward (eds), *Philosophers on Race*, Oxford: Blackwell, 81–100.

Wacquant, Loïc (1999), 'How Penal Sense Comes to the Europeans', *European Societies*, 1:3, 319–52.

Walsh, Moira M. (1997), 'Aristotle's Conception of Freedom', *Journal of the History of Philosophy*, 35:4, 495–507.

Walvin, James (1996), *Questioning Slavery*, London: Routledge.

Weatherspoon, Floyd D. (2007), 'The Mass Incarceration of African-American Males: A Return to Institutionalized Slavery, Oppression, and Disenfranchisement of Constitutional Rights', *Texas Wesleyan Law Review*, 13, 599–617.

Weber, Leanne and Benjamin Bowling (2008), 'Valiant Beggars and Global Vagabonds: Select, Eject, Immobilize', *Theoretical Criminology*, 12:3, 355–75.

Weheliye, Alexander G. (2014), *Habeus Viscus: Racializing Assemblages, Biopolitics, and Black Feminist Theories of the Human*, Durham, NC and London: Duke University Press.

Wheeler, Roxann (2000), *The Complexion of Race: Categories of Difference in Eighteenth-Century British Culture*, Philadelphia, PA: University of Pennsylvania Press.

Whitlock, Gillian (2000), *The Intimate Empire: Reading Women's Autobiography*, London: Continuum.

Wilderson, Frank B. (2010), *Red, White and Black: Cinema and the Structure of U.S. Antagonisms*, Durham, NC: Duke University Press.

Williams, Bernard (1998), 'Necessary Identities', in Tommy L. Lott (ed.), *Subjugation and Bondage: Critical Essays on Slavery and Social Philosophy*, Boulder, CO and Oxford: Rowman and Littlefield.

Wilson, Jamie Diane (2016), 'Transatlantic Encounters and the Origins of James Henley Thornwell's Proslavery Ideology', *Slavery and Abolition*, 37:1, 117–38.

Wolkowitz, Carol (2006), *Bodies at Work*, London: Sage.

Wollstonecraft, Mary (1995), *A Vindication of the Rights of Men and a Vindication of the Rights of Woman*, ed. Sylvia Tomaselli, Cambridge: Cambridge University Press.

Wong, Edlie L. (2001), '"Turned out of Doors:" Voluntary Return and Captive Agency in the Case of Mary Prince', *Prose Studies*, 24:3, 59–72.

Woods, Joseph (1784), *Thoughts on the Slavery of the Negroes*, London: James Phillips.

Woods, Tryon P. (2013), 'Surrogate Selves: Notes on Anti-Trafficking and Anti-Blackness', *Social Identities*, 19:1, 120–34.

Ypi, Lea (2013), 'What's Wrong with Colonialism?', *Philosophy and Public Affairs*, 31:2, 158–91.

Zelnick-Ambramowitz, Rachel (2005), *Not Wholly Free: The Concept of Manumission and the State of Manumitted Slaves in the Ancient Greek World*, Leiden and Boston, MA: Brill.

ZOE (2016), available at www.gozoe.org/what-is-human-trafficking (accessed 13 January 2017).

Zonana, Joyce (1993), 'The Sultan and the Slave: Feminist Orientalism and the Structure of "Jane Eyre"', *Signs*, 18:3, 592–617.

INDEX

241

EU representative:
Easy Access System Europe
Mustamäe tee 50, 10621 Tallinn, Estonia
Gpsr.requests@easproject.com

www.ingramcontent.com/pod-product-compliance
Lightning Source LLC
Chambersburg PA
CBHW050348270326
41926CB00016B/3647